Life
After
Death

- by Charlie Hayes

A Former Racing Driver's
Story Of Spiritual Awakening

Coming Home To The Eternal Dance Of Being

Loving To Be

Copyright © 05 December 2006
Charles David Hayes
All rights reserved.

ISBN-13 978-0-9766619-8-6
ISBN 0-9766619-8-5

US $27.95

Cover Photo: "25"
The 1968 Cro-Sal McKee Oldsmobile - driven by Charlie Hayes
Also used by Paul Newman in the film "Winning"
Copyright © 2006 Don Markle
donmarkle@hotmail.com

"Charlie's journey to understanding was a wild ride, and his story makes for very interesting reading. I'm so happy to see this generous expression of sharing coming so clearly and enthusiastically from someone who was a self-admitted 'tough nut to crack.'"

- Annette Nibley, www.whatneverchanges.com

For The Eternal Presence - Appearing as Nothing - And Everything - A Thank You Is Softly Uttered - In Humble Gratitude - With Infinite Respect And Love - By No One For No One - Just Being - In Love With Love

Thank You to

Werner Erhard

Gurumayi Chidvilasananda

Sri Sri Ravi Shankar

Wayne Liquorman

Kali Ishaya

John Wheeler

"Sailor" Bob Adamson

John Greven

Annette Nibley

Byron Katie

Burt Jurgens

Nathan Gill

Leo Hartong

and

Tony Parsons

Thank you all For Loving
Always- In All Ways

Oneness IS

Oneness knows no boundaries

Oneness is Loving Being Accepting

Empty like a Clear Sky

                   Full Like a Sacred Moon

Oneness Opens Its Arms and Embraces All

Saints and Thieves are All Simply Being Loving

Being as-it-is - One-Not-Two -

Oneness IS - Loving *YOU.*

Ultimately

This book is a description of that which cannot be described. It is pointing to something more Real than what we call life. It is NOT a prescription - although parts of it will appear to be prescriptions of methods. Be with the paradox of this. In actual fact there is no method and no teaching - no path no goal. But That Is The End. The book must start where we ARE – in the middle. Read through it from beginning to end – and see what you see. Perhaps there will be awakening. - And perhaps not. We shall see when the end is the end.

Seeker Of Truth
Follow No Path
All Paths Lead Where
The Truth Is Here

— e.e.cummings

The Dimension
of man
is Infinite

— Formula One Driver and Can-Am
Racing Champion Bruce McLaren

"Seeking is the most effective
way to avoid awakening."
— Tony Parsons

This book is pointing

to something that

you don't know

that you don't know.

What could that be?

This Is It.

When The Two Become One

There is Paradise

As It ever was will be IS

Now

There is Only Being

In Love With You

In Love with You

In Love with You

When the I dies

Paradise is Found

In Its Absence

You Are

The Way

The Truth

The Life

I Am You
You Are Life Itself

Table of Contents

BEGINNING AT THE END OF THE SEARCH..................14
FOREWORD: IT IS SAID..................15
INTRODUCTION 17
POSSIBILITIES IN ONENESS..................23
GLIMPSES BEYOND THE MIND: BEING THE RACING..................27

PART ONE: BEGINNING THE JOURNEY FROM SUFFERING TO FREEDOM

1. WHAT IS A "ME?"..................30
2. THE AMAZING DREAM..................31
3. AN OLD MARRIED MAN AT EIGHTEEN..................34
4. RACING: BEING AWAKE AND ALIVE..................35
5. FROM ZERO TO HERO..................37
6. SCARED TO DEATH IN A SHELBY COBRA RACE CAR..................39
7. MAKING AN INTERNATIONAL NAME - FOR "ME"..................40
8. FIVE HUNDRED MILES TO HEARTBREAK..................42
9. BEING – AWAKE AND ALIVE..................45
10. SUDDEN DEATH..................47
11. COMING BACK TO "REAL LIFE"..................49
12. DREAMS TURN TO NIGHTMARES..................50
13. SCARED TO DEATH? GET DRUNK - AGAIN!..................52
14. LIFE OF A SALESMAN..................53
15. LIVIN' HIGH ON THE HOG IN TINSEL TOWN..................55
16. DEATH OF A SALESMAN..................57

PART TWO WAKING UP FROM THE NIGHTMARE OF MY LIFE

17. AWAKENINGS..................60
18. PRAYING TO DIE..................62

19. MY HEAD GOES INTO THE TIGER'S MOUTH 64
20. GO DIRECTLY TO JAIL. DO NOT PASS GO........................65
21. I ESCAPE FROM HELL - FOR A WHILE................................68
22. GATE GATE – GONE BEYOND!...69
23. BACK IN A MATERIAL WORLD...70
24. WERNER ERHARD, 'EST,' AND INTEGRITY.......................72
25. MUKTANANDA REDUX..74
26. RATIONALITY IS GONE. THERE IS ONLY TERROR. 77
27. DOWN AND OUT IN BEVERLY HILLS................................80
28. BACK ON TOP? WHAT A ROLLER-COASTER!....................82
29. THE NEVER-ENDING SEEKING...83

PART THREE
TRUE AWAKENING

30. ARROGANT IGNORANCE..85
31. PARADISE FOUND, PARADISE LOST 88
32. NO WAY..90
33. I AM THAT..92
34. GETTING KICKED OUT OF SATSANG................................94
35. ENDLESS FRUITLESS SEEKING - THEN HERE CAME TONY.....96
36. DEPRESSION AND AWAKENING 97
37. CONTROL..100
38. THE FINAL TRUTH?..102
39. FINAL UNDERSTANDING - NOT.....................................103
40. IT HAPPENS..107
41. NIGHT DREAMS, WAKING DREAMS, REALITY 109
42. AWAKENING TO THE ORIGINAL STATE...........................112
43. THE ETERNAL IS..115
44. THE UNBORN..116
45. I THINK THEREFORE I AM. REALLY?..............................117
46. WHO IS THINKING?...119
47. HOS: HUMAN OPERATING SYSTEM...............................121

48. A FAKE SEEKER AND A FAKE SAGE..................122
49. NOTHING MATTERS – EVERYTHING MATTERS...................124
50. STAY WITH THAT LOVINGNESS OF BEING......................125
51. YOU ARE HERE, BE-ING..................................126
52. ONE FINE DAY - I MET BYRON KATIE........................127
53. INQUIRE WITHIN - HERE, NOW............................129

PART FOUR
POINTERS FROM THE SAGES

54. THE ABSOLUTE TRUTH OF ALL TIMELESS TIME..................133
55. POINTERS FROM THE AVADHUT GITA........................134
56. THE AVADHUT SAYS, LEARN FROM ALL......................139
57: NOT THIS NOT THAT....................................141
58. SELF-LIBERATION - POINTERS FROM BUDDHISM 144
59. SEE FOR YOURSELF....................................148
60. THE ORIGINAL STATE..................................149
61. A PRIORI..150
62. NOTHING I SAY OR WRITE IS "THE TRUTH"..................151
63. TO BELIEVE OR NOT TO BELIEVE.........................152
64. THE ADVAITA DIET...................................154
65. THE TRUTH THAT SETS US FREE 157

PART FIVE
DIALOGUES WITH SEEKERS

66. IT'S ONENESS RINGING THE BELL TO ONENESS 160
67. FINISHED 163
68. IT'S NOT LUCK - IT'S COMMITMENT........................164
69. DECISIONS DECISIONS - WHO MAKES THEM?..................166
70. DO NOT BELIEVE THIS - OR ANYTHING ELSE 168
71. WHY ACCEPT THE FALSE AS TRUE? 169
72. THIS IS SEEN - BUT 174
73. CLARITY & NON-CLARITY BOTH ARISE IN BEING 175

74. PARADISE IS HERE - NOW 177
75. STILL A PERCEIVED 'I' 178
76. THERE IS NO 'TIME' - IT'S A MENTAL CONSTRUCT 179
77. THE IDEA 'I AM THIS BODY' IS FALSE 181
78. THIS IS THE GOOD NEWS 183
79. THE I THAT GETS IT - OR NOT - IS A FALSE ENTITY 185
80. THIS IS IT 187
81. WHY DO YOU RAVE ABOUT TONY? 189
82. REIKI - A POINTER TO ONENESS 190
83. 'PERFECT PEACE' WIPED OUT THE "ME" 192
84. PRESENCING-BEINGNESS IS ALWAYS 'ON' 193
85. WHAT IS IT THAT I DON'T KNOW THAT I DON'T KNOW? 195
86. THE SELF WAS NEVER LOST 197
87. NO THING HAPPENED 198
88. INVESTIGATE THE FALSE AND SEE IT AS FALSE 201
89. NOT KNOWING IS THE DEATH OF THE FALSE 203
90. A NOTE ON DISCUSSIONS OF TEACHERS & TEACHINGS 205
91. NEW AGE BABBLE WILL NOT ERASE A SUFFERING 'ME' 206
92. WHY THE APOLOGIES TO TONY AND WAYNE? 208
93. DOESN'T SELF-INQUIRY REINFORCE SEPARATENESS? 211
94. FASCINATED BY IMAGINATION 213
95. THE HABIT OF IDENTIFICATION 215
96. WHAT IS THE "I" THAT SAYS, "I SEE?" 216
97. ALL THAT IS, JUST IS, AS IT IS 218
98. IT'S ALL SO SIMPLE 221
99. BODHI SVAHA 223
100. STAY WITH THE BASICS AND ASK "WHO AM I?" 224
101. WHAT A PARADOX! 226
102. AFTER THE QUESTIONING 227
103. BURN AWAY THE FALSE CAUSE OF SUFFERING 228
104. 'WHO BELIEVES THIS?' IS MY NEW "KOAN!" 230

105. CONTINUING TO IDENTIFY AS A BODY-MIND 232
106. WHO ANSWERS THE 'UNANSWERABLE QUESTION?' 234
107. WHO AM I? WHO ARE YOU? DON'T KNOW!.....................235
108. THE LITTLE PERSON INSIDE INSISTING 'I'M ME'.............236
109. INVESTIGATION CRITICAL FOR ENDING SUFFERING 238
110. I WOKE UP AT HOME AS A NEW SELF.........................241
111. THE ESSENCE OF FREEDOM.....................................242
112. THAT NON-PERSONAL SELF OF ALL............................250
113. STUCK IN THE BELIEF THAT I'M SEPARATE 253
114. WHERE'S THE BLISS?..256
115. SEEKING & PSYCHOLOGICAL SUFFERING HAVE ENDED.....262
116. THE DEEP YEARNING FOR TRUTH.............................264
117. THE WORK..267
118. A PERFECT STORM...269
119. A PERFECT STORM SUBSIDES..................................273

PART SIX
WHO IS THERE TO INQUIRE?

120. ASK YOU..275
121. PARADIGM-ING..277
122. NOW THERE IS MORNING..279
123. "ADVAITA-SPEAK"..281
124. RESIDUE..283
125. WHAT IS LOVE?...284
126. WHAT IS THE MIND?..285
127. WHAT IS WORRY?..286
128. I LIVE IN LANGUAGE..287
129. "BRAIN" OR "MIND?" TOO MANY THINKERS..................288
130. WHAT IS THE REAL AUTHENTIC ME MYSELF AND I?........290
131. THE BIG BANG IS NOW AND NOT NOW......................291
132. BEING NOT-KNOWING..292
133. NOT BEING NOT-KNOWING.....................................295

134. LIFE IT-SELF..301
135. CODA TO THE RIFF...302
136. R.I.P. LISTENING TO LOVE.......................................303
THE END: THE LAST OF ME. THIS AS-IT-IS REALLY IS IT..........307
A FEW BOOKS & WEBSITES TO PONDER................................308
CONTACT - "ONE ON ONE"..309
KEEP IT SIMPLE, SEEKER!..311

Even a good thing

is not as good

as no thing.

- A Zen Koan

At The End Of The Search

"Charlie tells it like it is and delivers the timeless message of Advaita in the tradition of Sri Nisargadatta and Bob Adamson. From the very first pages you are given the tools to know who you are and to investigate that until there are no doubts left. I am so grateful to Charlie for creating this guidebook and sharing his time and energy without which knowing that "I Am" would have been mere words. Through the efforts of people like Charlie, there is a growing movement in Advaita today that was first sprouted in India, cultivated in Australia and has now taken root here in America. If you are finally finished wondering when "you" will get it, read this book and end the search. Good on ya Charlie!"

- Amazon Review by Gregory LeBlanc of
Charlie's previous book, "From I Am To I Am, With Love"

Darkness within Darkness

The Gateway to Mystery

- Lao Tzu

Foreword: It Is Said

It is said that there are many paths to home - many ways to attain Enlightenment - Awakening and Liberation.

It is said that if one finds a Guru and follows his path one will attain what the Guru attained.

I have bad news and good news.

The bad news is - that is a story of cause and effect without a single shred of truth in it. There is NO cause of Awakening and Liberation. Furthermore, there is no such thing as a seeker to attain that or a Guru to teach that. Therefore - what actually - but only apparently - happens, is that the seeking and following of various paths keeps the desired Liberation - the escape from the prison of the bound-up thinking egoic mind - from happening.

Because Liberation is NOT a happening - and not a "product" of some "action" by a "seeker."

What does this signify? Just this:

When Liberation happens - it happens to no one. And when there is no one - it is seen (by no one) that it never even happened at all.

What apparently happens is that a dreamed character evaporates - through no agency - no action - no process - no path - no pathless path. When IT happens - the whole paradigm of an it to happen and a someone it happens to simply evaporates. Like ripples in space - we were never here.

Now: *The ULTIMATE Bad News is* - There Ain't No Such Thing As Awakening Or Liberation!

The good news is - there is no enlightenment, no liberation, no path, and no goal - there is no one! *What could no one do to gain its own release in freedom?* Relax. Have a cookie.

Do or undo - and if awakening happens - laugh and cry until you die. No-Liberation is of no person from any bondage - for no one by no one. Being no one - no one loves being. Being. Loving. Be. Have another cookie.

The whole thing is a tale told by an idiot - a "me."

When the me dissolves in the Love that is all there is, then that world and me reappear - but there is no longer any belief in separation.

Life is living itself through all the body-minds and plants and animals and stars and - universes - And It Is All Totally This - Ordinary Everyday Awareness. (NOT Awareness OF - Just - Awareness.)

That separateness that seemed to plague us becomes a matter of great profound insignificance - and now all that is, is Being - arising presently - as every blessed and every damned thing and non thing that was is will be ever and never - now.

For quite a while after an initial awakening in 2002, there was a "flip-flop" - seemingly coming into Being and then the "me" reappearing to claim its own absence - ego-me and no-ego Me - in and out of Being. This was, in a sense, the little ego coming back in from the rear - to claim its own absence! How droll!

And then there came a "time" that this me-ing and be-ing was realized - by no one so to say - that all this "flip-flopping" me-ing and be-ing was not apart from Oneness - dancing with itSelf in the Play of Living.

Now. Just Now.

ONLY Now.

The Beloved Dances with passion, aliveness, joy. There is simply no exclusion - anything and everything is seen as *That*. Life ItSelf. This is the Eternal No State State of Being - Just Loving Being.

The Sanskrit word *Advaita* points to this elegantly:

The translation is -

Not Two.

I Am - as You Are - Life Itself. We are Not Two.

Stormy Rage and Loving Peace

Never Touch The Empty Sky Of Awareness.

~ ~ ~

Introduction

Beginning At The End Of The Pathless Path

What Is Spiritual Enlightenment?

Awakening - and Liberation. Absolute Freedom - Living *As* Unconditional Love.

Liberation Already Is.

Liberation is Everything - And Nothing.

IT is Being - Being appearing as the story with feeling and thinking of great expectations, dashed hopes, marriage and kids, divorce and child support, broken homes and unbroken elation, the story of anger, rage, joy, freedom, bondage, happiness, grief, depression, elation, mania, glee, despair, hopelessness, and Bliss.

Filled with Sound and Fury - Signifying . . . Nothing.

And . . . Everything.

The story is Being - Storying.

THIS Is Love - Being All That Is.

THIS - Ordinary Life As It Is - is IT.

That's All Folks.

Note - some bits of material in this book are repetitions of concepts that appeared in "From I Am To I Am, With Love."

This is intentional.

Welcome.

Are you a "seeker?"
Looking for that Peace That Surpasses Understanding?
Stop searching for a few moments.
Rest Here and Now in the Silent, Brilliant Stillness That Pervades All Of Creation - and Realize - This Stillness IS What You Really Are.
THIS is The Return To loving Life - AS IT IS.
Being Like a little child again -
playing in the garden called life.
Those Who Are Absolutely Free Of Suffering
Point Out - Repeatedly - One Simple Truth:
Ultimately all suffering is based
upon just ONE CORE BELIEF.
This belief is usually stated - or sensed - as
"I am a person." Or simply,

"I'm ME."

We claim to "know" this.

But - is it true?

We don't see that this is ONLY a belief - because of the habit of identifying ourselves as that "person."

This has been believed to be the "experiencer and knower" of all that happens to "it" - from a very early age - and that belief has never been examined.

Here is a simple investigatory question:
Who IS this "ME" - that I am SOooo sure IS who I am?
Who:
What Am I?

"Who Am I?"

When we believe - or when there is a deep background sense, unthought yet "known" - that we are a person - suffering becomes inevitable. When this belief is dismantled - by our own true Self, NOT through any effort on our part - our nearly constant suffering comes to an end. This happens all by itself. We cannot wake ourselves up. How can a hypnotized character dehypnotize itself? Impossible.

Who is the hypnotist? Not the subject. Who is the dreamer? Not the dream-figure chasing its tail in the dream.

Seeing that it is hopeless is a sort of non-volitional surrender. The Beloved ItSelf shows us this - and then time ends and all is seen to be a loving all-embracing nothing.

This is Enlightenment. This is Love.

This "ending" is simply the dissolution of the false - which occurs as the absence of a personal "me" - and in this Presence there is no one left to resist or avoid what simply IS - Life As It Is.

Whatever is happening in Consciousness, it is only when it is "happening to me" that there is suffering. Asking that one believed to be the "me" in your body-mind organism, "Who Are You?" or "Who is thinking 'I'm Me'?" *may* seem to produce the result of the dissolution of the belief in a separate person - but ultimately, this is the Self Waking ItSelf to ItSelf.

This is incomprehensible to the hypnotized character.

In the final event what will naturally be revealed is what you already always are and could never NOT be - The True Self of ALL beings.

But "you" obviously cannot do it - because there ain't no you apart from You. Paradoxes abound. Confusion may happen.

These two - paradox and confusion - are wisely said to be the twin guardians at the gateless gate to your True Natural Peace.

So - love them. And they may let you through.

BUT! ONLY So to speak. Actually - we are inside Paradise - knocking on the gate from the inside.

A Story Of "Me"

This book begins with a story - the tale of a former professional racing driver's sometimes accomplished - but more often nightmarish - life, in the world of the twentieth and twenty-first centuries.

Ultimately, this story can be nicely summed up by the words of William Shakespeare: "A tale told by an idiot, filled with sound and fury, signifying ... nothing."

I am not my story - and you are not your story.

What is shared herein is a report of Spiritual Awakening - "Self-Realization" - which occurs as the end of false identification of oneself as what – in Charlie's case - had been a fairly rotten character, according to others who knew him early on - in this grand opera we call Life.

There is a profound possibility shared herein - a simple and yet longed-for possibility.

What is it? LOVING TO BE.

BEING- Absolute Freedom - abiding AS Eternal Unconditional Love.

Prelude To A Dream

A Ferrari Formula One racing driver, Alfonso DePortago, once said, *"If a man is awake and alive he can live ten years, in two hours on Sunday."*

That one is right on.

It reminds me of the high wire artist who said, "Life is on the wire. Everything else is just ... waiting."

Yeah. Like the Samuel Becket play, "Waiting For Godot." It's horrible; Godot never comes! That can create suicidal despair. I know. I was there. Until my auto racing career started.

And after my auto racing career ended.

But understand this: It's *Just* A Story. It's like a dream or a movie.

Anyway - herein there *is* the story. A story of a tiny body that appeared (as the substory 'time' would have us believe) in December of 1936, destined to become first a jazz musician, a reckless drug and alcohol user, and a dangerous driver.

Then that unruly thing was tamed somewhat into a world class professional racer - but then again it devolved into a drug and alcohol addict, a thief and con man.

Ultimately, it became a "Spiritual Seeker" - one looking for what he was missing that had his life be a miserable mess!

Before the search began in real earnest, and some messes were cleaned up, this was not a nice person at all!

You'll find some disturbing things in this book - tales of cruel indifference to other people, even family, and what it was like to be really, really crazy. Mental hospital crazy!

You'll also find steps that this crazy man was led to take - so to speak - that helped to free him from the idea of being a bad guy, a rotten father, a terrible insult to others, and a madman.

And ultimately to the natural dropping of all stories and the welcome re-discovery that our story is NOT what we are.

So the crazy man was led home.

Led by what - or whom?

Perhaps these four ways to say it will make sense:

- Intense Suffering

- Divine Grace

- The True Self Of All

- No one. It simply - happened.

Ultimately, the real You - the Real Self - are the True Teacher - your own Divine Beingness is the Teacher - and That teaches you from within you.

THAT True Teacher-Self leads the confused person to Home in Being. And then - as always - wherever you go, whatever time it is, you ARE.

Always Here Always Now.

And In the Here and Now there is NO suffering. It's all over.

Now there is a resting in the arms of the Beloved.

Loving to Be.

Unpredictable? Yes. Possible for anyone? Yes.

If it could happen to that jerk, it can happen for anyone!

This ending of all beginnings - and this resting in the arms of the beloved - begins right here, right now. Exactly where you are and no matter whether you are new to spirituality or a "seasoned seeker."

> *The journey of a thousand miles begins with a single step* - Lao Tzu

Look at it this way: whenever "I *think*" I know what is real, that very thinking is making me suffer. Therefore I must somehow be led by Oneness to an inner examination to uncover the false to know what is REALLY REAL.

Discovering what you don't know that you don't know *begins with not knowing.* Be willing to know nothing at all. Your bringing that not-knowing to this book might make a real difference in the ending - by Oneness - of your own suffering.

Take on reading this book from a space we can call Not Knowing and see what is revealed. Give up all knowing and believing - and believe nothing. Let Oneness take you by the hand and lead you to see for yourself. Let Her use the ways of looking described in this book to prompt you to look and discover who you really are - beyond beliefs, beyond concepts, beyond history, beyond imagination, beyond words, beyond language, beyond emotions, beyond sensations, beyond feelings, beyond love and hate, beyond good and evil, beyond all - and then beyond the beyond.

What can happen then?

Anything?

Everything? Nothing?

I don't know.

Possibilities In Oneness

This Book Is About YOU And For YOU.

A Friend - a young man with whom the author talked in the ways described in this book - wrote this e-mail. He beautifully expresses - from his own understanding and experience - how the possibility of authentic freedom from suffering unfolded for him. His words are reprinted here with his kind permission. The Friend Writes,

Swimming in the sea of this "hereness," nowness," and "aliveness" - "awareness" - "consciousness". And down to the essence of it all, that is all there is!!! Anything else is concept and not IT.

I found out that these teaching pointers that are offered by nonduality sites and teachers are just descriptions of what you and I ARE, and what you are seeking, you ALREADY ARE. You are, in essence, by seeking, chasing your tail – like I did.

And the belief that by figuring the teachings out (like the mind has been trained to do) will lead to final enlightenment, IS FALSE. It's just another one of the many false beliefs in a "you" – a "person" who can "learn" and be enlightenment.

That story kept me going around in endless tail-chasing circles - until it was exposed/pointed out by my best freakin' friend Charlie (who in essence is no one, who is oneness, which is who you are in essence too) and then the search officially ended and the belief in a "me" that could ever figure this out just dropped!

And In One Instant of Now It Is DONE.

I found out that this is about SEEING what is real/not real, through moment by moment by moment by moment by moment investigating. It can be seen right here, right now.

It is always "accessible" - because you're already IT! I've always been IT. You've always been IT. All there is, is IT.

How I missed it I'll never understand.

My sharing - like the sharing on Charlie's site and in his books - is just descriptive terms – pointers, pointing to what you are seeking - which is total freedom from all the suffering about "me" and "my life". The mind is a machine, in essence, and it is conditioned to do what it does, and there's no YOU responsible for thinking these thoughts that arise like bubbles in the space.

Now - It is my absolute complete final understanding – that there's no me and no you that is responsible for anger, sadness, bad thoughts, evil thoughts, etc. Thoughts, as you can see for yourself right now, just arise and subside on their own, in awareness, and there is absolutely no "person" inside doing that thinking - or anything else!

You can easily see this for yourself!!! See thoughts arise like clouds in awareness. You have NO control over any of it. It's a machine at work on its own, functioning as it does. It's conditioning.

I wanted so much to control it, to understand it, to stop thinking thoughts that cause suffering and that seem to make my life, my story and my existence sheer hell. It can be seen right now that you are what is being pointed to. I saw it finally. You can too. Then you will wonder – like I did – how you missed the obvious presence of Being for so long.

I am sharing this to point out nothing to no one.

All these words are just energy playing, to communicate this one simple thing: <u>That you are already done!</u>

Drop the story of how your life may change after you may get enlightened like all these apparent others. I once held many expectations of how my life will be after I "figure all of this shit out and get enlightened."

Not that "you" can really DO that - but it CAN happen.

It seemed – ONLY seemed! – that the more I listened to, and read, the pointers offered by all of these apparent 'other' teachers, the closer I was moving along in the process towards the end of it all, that penny-dropping moment of getting over all of my shit, just like they have!!!!

But once I saw that ALL expectations are bullshit, that they're just imagined, future stories of a 'me' getting enlightened, to see all there is is this sea of consciousness, always here, always now.

You and I are swimming in it. I want to shout from the rooftops -YOU ARE IT ALREADY, HERE NOW!!!!!

Here, the search is over, as it's seen that there's no "person" in the machine.

The last bondage – a last belief - was that "I'm not yet enlightened because" – because . . . there is still anger, frustration, regret, sadness, pain that arises – so the mind says this means that "something is wrong and I've veered off path." That belief was a major source of keeping the "me" believed to be real. Then, also, within my imagined story - What that belief also says - is I AM enlightened!! Both claims are just bullshit!

In actuality, seen in each fresh moment, EVERYTHING arises in this aware, conscious, presence on its own and there's no one inside this machine doing ANYTHING!

THIS Is Liberation.

All there is, all there EVER is, is this, here, now, presence. Close your eyes. That presence is what is being talked about. YOU CAN'T GRASP THIS AS AN EXPERIENCE, but it is there, always because you ARE IT.

IT is the sea of Consciousness. You are in the ocean - and you ARE the ocean. It is what gives everything life, and everything appears in this sea of consciousness.

YOU ARE THAT NOW, JUST THAT. Everything is an appearance in this sea, EVERYTHING; with no independent existence, ability or volition. It's oneness, happening NOW. NOW. NOW. NOW.

Analyzing these teachings, pointers, and words was a source of frustration for me - and another form of suffering.

Don't go there.

It is also possible, when you understand you are already what is being pointed to, then you may see that YOU ARE THE POINTERS!!!!!!! It is nothing you will ever imagine!

You are in the sea; you ARE the sea – and, just another wave with no independent existence. It's all a show.

All there is is THIS. Aliveness.

If there's confusion, you may want to give Charlie a ring. He's been there for me since I met him. Again, don't try to figure this out on your own.

~ ~ ~ ~ ~

Beautifully and passionately expressed, my dear friend.
Thanks very, very much.
A note regarding the paradox of all this - it is a kind of Final Truth that YOU - your own true Self - IS the Only Teacher. The True One-Self does all the work.
Until that is seen clearly, however, as my friend here has said, an outer teacher-friend may seem to be needed. There were several for me - over 32 years. Finally there was Gurumayi, Sri Sri, The Ishayas, John Wheeler, "Sailor" Bob Adamson, Annette Nibley, Byron Katie, and Tony Parsons – and then - no one. The Self Is The Only Thing That Is.

Test them in the Heart

Please don't settle for fakes - there is an abundance of "false prophets" with half-baked "teachings" appearing presently on the Internet and in books. Find that One who lights the Light of Aware Consciousness for you. You will FEEL it when you do. Don't settle for the paltry dust of understanding - seek the final Loving Being that resonates within the Heart- and points the Way to Freedom, in Absolute Bliss.

There is NO cause of Awakening and Liberation. When the search is over - there is absolutely NO idea left that there was any cause, any will, any volition that brought about the end of the seeking and the arising of liberation. Liberation is uncaused and eternal. It Is. No One Gets That. There IS No One. This is the great open secret - the Mystery of Life.

Glimpses Beyond The Mind: *Being The Racing*

A half hour or so before the race is to start I find myself unwilling to be with people ... I cannot engage in idle chatter ... I must sit quietly and alone in my road car, windows up, doors locked, engine humming softly, air conditioning creating coolness and white sound. I sit. I Am. There is nothing. I am that nothing. At Peace for now ... but I later come to see this is only a temporary experience of peace. Never mind, at the 'time' it is - just Being. I come out and hear sounds, the announcer talking, engines being started and vroom vroom as the mechanics clear the engine's throats then mostly silence as the racecars are wheeled out to the starting line for the standing start of the Los Angeles Grand Prix. (It is late 1965.)

There is stillness, perfect silence. I Am that.

Then it is time to go.

I rub my face, stretch, grab my helmet and stroll out to the grid. So many people. Brightly painted racecars decorated with myriad sponsor's messages. The crowd a blur, humming, murmuring, anticipating wild excitement... eager. I step into the car. The crew helps me strap in. Everything is calm and yet there is anticipation. So soon there will be frenetic action, sound and fury. I put in earplugs, work my head into the helmet, and sit.

Waiting.

The grid is cleared of all except the cars and the drivers. An official announces, "Gentlemen, start you engines." (No ladies in this race, today...)

I flip off the safety cover and flick a switch up. The system is armed. Another safety cover up, and a spring-loaded toggle is nudged up and the start whirs, the engine coughs, sputs, fires. Rummm Rummm Rumm BLAT. Brraap. Braap.

Plugs cleared, the right foot relaxes and sets at a steady fast idle, 1500 RPM. I wait and watch. Not Knowing. The inner trembling begins, like a precursor to orgasm. Energy roams the body and tries to trigger the mind to label the experiencing as fear and add, "I am afraid" - but it cannot.

The mind is in abeyance. It rests in ... the instant. There is No time. Just Now. The green flag drops. Rear wheels spinning furiously grabbing the tarmac, the car-driver complex launches itself toward turn one. In the lead. Everything becomes nothing, and nothing becomes everything.

There Is Just - The Racing.

There Is Nothing.

There Is Everything.

Melted In - And AS - One Essence.

This is Home - there is no one -

Now Awake Alive flying free from

Nowhere to nowhere.

But ONLY when there is the racing.

Then it's back to the suffering "me."

Part One

Life After Death

Beginning The Journey
From Suffering To Freedom

1. What Is A "Me?"

Parts of this story originally appeared in earlier discussions with fellow seekers who wanted who wanted to know what led to my search for Self ... and many wrote that they were struck by what they felt to be an honest, no holds barred expressions of "my story" - and said that "they saw themselves in me."

That seemed to awaken a seeing that if this unfolding of true-nature could occur for Charlie it could occur for them.

For those who still believe in a separate "me" these anecdotes are included here. Just don't believe a word of it. Don't believe anything! Find when the believer got born, and who he or she is ... if you can.

As always there must be the paradoxical disclaimer: Investigate who you are, all the while realizing that there is no one to do any investigation!

Remember! The entire text is just a story or a string of stories arising presently. What is a story? Sort of a legend - Charlie is a legend in the mind! As you will discover in this book, so is what you consider to be "you" ... and that discovery is the beginning of Absolute Freedom.

Just allow for a knowingness that all stories are JUST stories. Nothing ever actually happened! All that is appearing here and now is simply words, pictures, concepts, *stuff* ... *Source, the Uncaused Unmanifest Energy of Aliveness*, manifesting its Self and appearing as ALL that IS, including all these "words" arising right now where you are ... which is ... here.

No Thing ... arising as not knowing.

I can hear it in the space: "I don't care a damn about your "personal story," Charlie! Get ON with it!"

Ten-four.

If you prefer to cut to the chase feel free to skip the Back Story. Just jump ahead to Part Three, Page 84.

The story is just shared here as a demonstration that True Seeing is possible even for the most idiotic ego-bound seeker!

2. The Amazing Dream

My own suffering led me to search for answers to life's mystery. Here is how that all started:

From the age of about four I was a miserable little clod of ailments and grievances, griping about everything, and complaining that the world could bloody well care less whether Me, Myself or I was happy, or not. And the search for some kind of life that would be satisfying began. I became a master at self-pity. Seemed like a good idea at the time. It got me a lot of attention.

My dad was an attorney who enlisted and became a Commander in the U.S. Navy in World War Two, and got killed on a ship, The Indianapolis. So there was no father to whip me into shape. My poor mother was terrified of me ... by this time I had realized that I could get about anything I wanted, by scaring the poop out of her. I became a world-class thrower of tantrums.

I had two sisters, one of whom used to refer to our adult relationship as an armed truce. The other (younger) one - a really sweet girl - made the mistake of first loaning me money, and then later investing in my business. She lost a bundle. So a sense of guilt got added along the way, of course.

Since I "knew" that it WAS this (unexamined, assumed) "me" that was "doing all the doing, creating its own destiny, climbing up in life by stepping on the other, weaker people," of COURSE there was regret, remorse, guilt and self-loathing!

Imagine a Six Foot Three Inch 250 pound scary looking giant two-year-old and you'll get the idea! MY "terrible Twos" lasted till I was over 68 years old!

When I was six I started getting VERY good at lying and conning.

New face on the puppet: Pinocchio! And I felt alone, a misfit, my family's "Black Sheep."

So, of course, later in life, I became a master salesman. But not really a master ... a master would have been ethical! I was a con.

And then there was the stealing.

To try to stifle the despair I would do dangerous stuff even then. Like stealing from the men's wallets at the country club in the locker room - then getting rid of the loot because I felt so damn guilty.

But I couldn't stop.

When I was about eight, late at night I would sneak out of the house and streak the neighborhood naked. So much for the dignity of this staid neighborhood (Chevy Chase, Md.) But man, I loved it. The thrill was electric! Somehow I never got caught at streaking - OR stealing (at that time - but later? Say tuned!) - Though there were a few close calls.

Variations on this happened for years ... I felt like an outcast. I didn't fit in anywhere and I had no friends except for a couple of other aliens with whom I would fly model airplanes and learn great new words like fuck, my personal favorite!

"I've arranged for you to be a Senate Page, Charles"

I grew up across the street from one Carl Vinson, who now has an aircraft carrier named for him; he was chairman of the Armed Services committee in the fifties. When I was around fifteen Representative Vinson invited me over to his porch one summer day and over iced tea told me he had made arrangements for me to become a Senate page.

There was a LOT of respect for my father in D.C. and this was but one expression of that.

I had NO clue what kind of opportunity that was. I said no, thanks anyway; I would rather shoot pool and build model airplanes.

Duh.

See, I was born with a silver spoon in my mouth but I spit the damn thing out. The reactive mind is a very stupid mechanism.

Essentially, I was angry, depressed, lonely, and totally defiant of anyone who tried to talk to me about what I was becoming.

By the age of fifteen I had quit school in the eighth grade. I was already drinking and doing drugs by then. And hanging with my black musician friends in the D.C ghettos. Playing a mediocre be-bop Jazz on Saxophone. And driving before I had a license, drunk and high, sailing off the road at 5 AM in a friend's taxicab.

Because at that time I had no clue about cornering speeds I demolished an innocent mailbox in that little process!

A man out walking his dog (at 5 AM!) saw this and took down the license number. When the cops came knocking on the taxi driver's door he gave me up in a heartbeat. I would have done the same.

So the police arrived at my mother's house and took me in - poor mom - she was beginning to sadly realize that through NO fault of her own, she had somehow given birth to a terrorist.

At the police station, I'm mug-shot, fingerprinted and lectured - but no record was kept. Since I was not yet old enough to drive and still considered a juvenile, I got off with a slap on the wrist.

I was becoming more and more of a total jerk, a know-it-all, and an outcast, a loner, "arrested in adolescence" - both literally and figuratively.

But I got really good at pretending to be nice, polite, happy, and socially adept. It was all an act, pasted on top of a "Me" that was lonely, sad, and scared beyond belief.

3. An Old Married Man At Eighteen

In 1955, at the ripe old age of 18, I got married to a beautiful 21-year-old woman. I had fallen deeply into lust with this girl, which I thought was love. She later admitted in a moment of candor that a large part of her attraction to me was that she thought I had a lot of money. I did have some. But never "enough."

I remember sitting on the edge of the bed on my wedding night thinking, "What have I gotten myself INTO?" Something was wrong; I was all alone despite my very pretty bride's presence next to me in the bed. I did not fit in anywhere.

By 1958 I have some money, I am married, and a father to a kid we named Charles David Hayes III- Dave - who later turned out to be a really fine man. That was Grace.

I am, however, NOT happy. Since I quit school about all I could be was a salesman, and somehow I got damn good at it! But to face the pretenses I lived AS, I was seeking escape from the drudgery and boredom of "day by day in this petty pace," as Shakespeare put it.

Then there was my "best friend" - with whom my wife ended up falling in love. And that was the end of *that* family affair.

But while I moaned about the loss of love and the betrayal by a best friend, I secretly breathed a great sigh of relief! Marriage was another form of bondage for me - essentially, I did not - deep down like other people at all. Even my wife! Because deep down I was seething in self-loathing. My self-esteem was not bad - it was nonexistent.

I would be a "lone wolf" for much of my life.

Perhaps something in me craved solitude and contemplation of the meaning of this crazy life in this maddening world, wherein there was never-ending frustration.

YES.

4. Racing: Being Awake And Alive

By now I owned a Jaguar XK140 Roadster, thanks to a small inheritance received at age 21. This led to spectating at nearby sports car races and as I was watching the Jaguars race around, I found myself thinking, Jeez, I can do that - and I can do it a helluva a lot better than THOSE guys!

I started driving the Jaguar in sports car races, in June of '58 - for which I at least had to stay sober - and through no creation of my own, the genes and conditioning for some reason had "me" get damn good at that.

In spite of a very shaky start!

To get the car ready to race, I had given the Jag to a great mechanic/race driver named Steve Spitler. Steve and I became friends as he went through the car to make sure it was as safe and as fast as he could make it. Steve was also preparing a rocket-fast Jaguar D-Type - the model that had won the famous 24 hour race at LeMans, France - for another friend, and would be testing it at the same racetrack in Marlboro, Maryland on the weekend of my debut.

On Friday, after a rudimentary "driver's school" put on by the Sports Car Club Of America, I was quick right out of the box and in no time was running faster than the other cars in my class, so all was happiness. I LOVED racing. It was in my blood from the git-go.

Then the unthinkable happened.

It was an open practice on Saturday. I was hustling the Jag around, happy as a pig in you know what, when Steve came alongside in the D-Type and with a little wave squirted away toward a fast right hander in a burst of acceleration that would make a funny car driver blush. Sheesh, that thing was quick!

The D-type disappeared around the corner and as I approached a couple hundred yards back, I saw a great cloud of dust appear and nearly simultaneously a flag marshal jumped out and began waving a yellow flag - caution, slow down.

I came down to a 30 MPH pace and made my way around the corner, where I saw to my utter dismay a crumpled upside-down D-Type Jaguar, the beautiful British Racing Green bodywork twisted and bent.

And there was Steve, lying in the middle of the road, unconscious. He had not been wearing a seat belt - remember this was 1958! There were not a lot of rules in those early days of U.S. Sports Car racing.

Back in the pits, I quickly shed my helmet and went to inquire - but then I saw an ambulance leaving the racetrack. So I jumped back in my (still street legal) Jaguar and followed - I just had to make sure Steve was okay.

At the hospital I somehow go past everyone and into the emergency room. The ER doctors were working on Steve, who was thrashing his head back and forth. I was relieved - he was alive! He was moving! I knew he'd be okay then, so I went back to the track and finished practicing for next day's race - I felt that I needed to "get back on the horse" straight away

After practice was over I noticed Steve had not returned to the track so I sought out my instructor and asked him if he had heard anything about how Steve was recovering.

The guy, a cold fish Air Force Colonel who fancied himself to be a racer but who was just another also-ran, casually said, "Steve Died." The shock was immense! The grief was unmanageable. The rage was violent within my soul.

I went home and threw my helmet across the living room, scaring hell out of the wife, and swore, "That's IT. I am never driving in another frigging race again ever. Steve got killed today."

She didn't know what to say - so she wisely said nothing.

I went to bed - still in shock.

But - at seven the next morning I awoke, said, "I gotta get going, I can't be late!" And grabbed my helmet bag and off to the race I went. I could not NOT race. I was already addicted - despite what I had seen.

Racing had already become a drug I had to have at any cost. And man, would it COST - as time went on.

But that day I easily won my first race. And kick-started a career that would take me all the way to being named one of the top ten racing drivers in the world, in 1966.

Such is the nature of *any* addiction:

Despite terrible side effects, the fix must be had.

5. From Zero To Hero

From 1958 until 1968 I raced all over the United States, in Canada, England, Japan, and the Bahamas - and met many great drivers and wonderful people – champions all – like Luigi Chinetti, Carl Haas, Lorenzo Bandini, Roger Penske, Mark Donahue, Masten Gregory, Nino Vacarella, Stirling Moss, Jimmy Clark, Jackie Stewart, Bobby Unser, Peter Revson, A.J. Foyt, Parnelli Jones, Dan Gurney, Bob Bondurant, Mario Andretti – the list is too long to include here. But you get the idea.

I understand that these names may mean nothing to you, if you are not familiar with the world of Professional Motorsports. Suffice it to say, these are the Michael Jordans and the Arnold Palmers and the Wayne Gretzkys and the Dan Marinos of that domain.

Stirling Moss was in particular "my hero" and a kind of mentor as we raced identical Ferraris at Nassau in 1961 and played the game of tag for a few laps in the race, until Stirling got bored with the game and drove off in an incredible display of transcendental talent.

The man did not cast a shadow.

Stirling was perhaps the greatest of the great – until a crash ended his career in Formula One in 1962.

Remaining active in racing despite not having the same abilities he once had in a Formula One car, Stirling has been a great spokesman and representative of this great sport.

He is now SIR Stirling Moss.

There were several wins in Amateur Racing and a few championships. I turned pro in 1962 and accepted an offer to drive for Ferrari's American branch, "North American Racing Team.

I ran second in the world championship race at Bridgehampton with the GTO. Then at Nassau I finished fifth overall and first in the GT category in the main event. I shared that car with the great Formula One Ferrari driver Lorenzo Bandini - Lorenzo drove the car in the "Tourist Trophy" race on Friday. I was happy to be able to equal Bandini's times on the Nassau circuit in the same race car.

But even happier was my friendship with Bandini - a wonderful guy, filled with the joy of being alive.

Lorenzo and I visited the Playboy Club in Miami before catching the boat to Nassau - and the "Bunnies" were agog over this marvelous, charismatic, charming Milanese. I loved him deeply - he was like a brother.

I was devastated for weeks when he died at Monaco in flames. Horrible sight, and the bloody television people played the footage of my great friend burning to death in the overturned fuel soaked Formula One car over and over. I was outraged. But as all racers must, I got over it - or so at least I pretended. Though the thought of the possibility that I could also burn to death in a race car remained as a huge fear.

Onward I go - stuffing down my fears of the very real dangers. In those days the cars had little or no safety engineered in, as do the racecars of today. But I was blind to that. I preferred to believe I was indestructible even though I had seen several good friends get bumped off in race cars - I figured "It'll never happen to ME." *Stupid is as stupid does?*

Anyway, I continued pretty well unabashed, and in 1964 I got the opportunity to drive a Porsche quasi-factory car in the U.S. Road Racing Championship. I attracted a lot of attention as the car was a small one – under two liters, an Elva-Porsche – and I consistently outran bigger cars that had two or three times the horsepower. "Cobra" creator and racer Carroll Shelby noticed this - and recommended me for the job of driving the "Lang Cooper" in 1965. This was a Chevrolet powered 180-MPH monster owned by Olympia Brewery heir Craig Lang.

That car almost killed me as stuff kept breaking and sending the car careening out of control. After three close brushes with death all agreed that that car should go. Craig generously gave me the engines to use and I spent my last few zillion bucks to purchase a McLaren Group Seven Sports Racing car – and with that car I really "made my bones." I had a mixed season in the McLaren but I was fast - really fast.

And at the biggest race of the year - The Times Grand Prix at Riverside, California, I came in fourth behind Formula One World Champion Jim Clark and other world class superstars. My career seemed to finally be on firm ground.

6. Scared To Death In A Shelby Cobra Race Car

As luck would have it, Carroll Shelby invited me to drive a factory Cobra in a world championship race at Bridgehampton, New York. He had entered something like six cars and I was to be on a team that included such stars as Dan Gurney, Ken Miles (later killed testing at Riverside Raceway, a sad moment!) and many others - so I thought, '*I must be hot stuff to get on a team like this.*'

Those delusions of grandeur were shattered as I took my first laps around the demanding, dusty, hilly, rough tempered Bridgehampton circuit.

I was accustomed to the factory Ferrari I had driven there in 1962 - and was quite unprepared for the rough and ready hot rod the Cobra was. I rode high in the cockpit, and felt like I was half out of the damn car - which was like a buckboard with a million horsepower. The thing was a bear to drive - at least, to me - all raw power and scary heart-stopping handling.

It was all I could do to keep the thing pointed straight, never mind make a decent lap time.

Talk about a wakey-wakey, as Miles used to put it! I found myself in absolute awe of guys like Bondurant, Gurney and Miles who seemed to hardly break a sweat as they smashed lap record after lap record! Brave as Batman, AND enormously skilled, these guys. If course I would never admit I felt that way - not publicly. Not then. Now - who cares?

Anyway, I soldiered on, but early in the race something broke. The gods were smiling on me that day! I hightailed it the hell outta there in great relief and headed back to the relative sanity of my 180 MPH McLaren Can-Am car.

Somehow I escaped without being accosted by Shelby's people or the press after the car broke down. What a relief that was!

Not my finest hour . . .

Carroll Shelby never called me again.

7. Making An International Name - For "Me"

After a thrilling 1965 season in the McLaren Mark One, peaking in that solid fourth place at Riverside Raceway behind such greats as World Champion Jim Clark, I formed a team of my own in 1966 and bought a Mark II McLaren Can-Am car, with the help of Carl Haas, at that time the McLaren Importer and distributor for America, and sponsors Goodyear, the giant car dealership Nickey Chevrolet of Chicago, Valvoline, Aeroquip, Wiggins Aerospace, and K&B Model Cars.

The car was beautifully prepared by Ed Schafer and was featured on the cover of Road & Track - the premier car book - and suddenly I was really famous. At least in the world of cars.

It was wonderful - while it lasted...

We were off to a wild start at the season opener - at Stardust Raceway in Las Vegas - in which the radiator was destroyed while I was running second - by a shower of gravel thrown up in an off-road excursion by the leader, Lola driver Jerry Grant.

Next we were at Riverside Raceway with a repaired and updated racer - and arriving with only a few moments left in qualifying, we set the fastest time, bumping Grant off pole and enjoying a kind of vindication of the disaster at Vegas.

The race was easy - I led from the start and built a large gap out front. Grant blew the engine in his Gurney-Weslake Lola trying to catch up! I was cruelly happy about that!

Then I began to get woozy from the enormous desert heat - it must have been 150 degrees in the cockpit and we didn't have "cool suits" or water bottles in those days. I was fighting like crazy to stay conscious! I never told anyone about that. Until now.

But I was damned if I was gonna stop and get a drink while I was leading the freakin' race! Foolish? Yeah. But as Coach Lombardi said, winning wasn't everything - it was the only thing.

Divine intervention happened though.

The ring and pinion gear in the transaxle wore itself out from excess heat and the car stopped - before I could stupidly kill someone - me or others - and that was that.

Finally, The Thrill Of Victory!

Then, it was on to the third race of '66 at Laguna Seca Raceway near Monterey, California, a favorite up-an-downhill twisty circuit. I set the fastest time, and won the race easily. Wow. Finally! My first nationally reported major win!

Around this time the car and racing weekly journal AutoWeek published a column from Motorsports writer Dennis Cipnic, wherein he rated racing drivers from all types of Motorsports all around the globe - World Champions in Formula One, NASCAR winners, Indy 500 winners, US Road Racing winners - he covered ALL types of auto racing in his assessment.

And there was my name - I was said to be one of the Top Ten racers in the world.

This bunch included such luminaries as Parnelli Jones, Dan Gurney, A.J. Foyt, John Surtees, Mario Andretti and others of that ilk - all of them real champions with a helluva lot better resume than mine.

But I was happy as a pig in mud - and even started believing my own press. That gave me a new and louder arrogance!

Deep down though - I "knew" that I wasn't really good enough to be named a top world class driver - I was just covering that up by looking good to myself.

And Then - The Agony Of Defeat!

And then the ego got bit in the butt - hard!

The win - and the top ten rating - was marred by two subsequent transporter road accidents on the way back to the East Coast for the next race - these badly damaged the car, injured one of my crew such that he retired from the sport, and killed our hopes for a U.S. Road Racing Championship. I went from Hero to Zero in a split second.

Yep - shit happens!

8. Five Hundred Miles To Heartbreak

The rest of the season was a mixed bag - and at the very last US Road Racing Championship event, a 500 mile race at Elkhart Lake's Road America in Wisconsin, we finally seemed to have gotten it all gathered up again and I easily set fastest time and won the pole.

I had enlisted a co-driver for this event - which turned out to be a mistake. But who knew?

As the race progressed I built a huge lead over the second place McLaren of Chuck Parsons, and then the fates struck.

Pitting in the lead, I turned the car over to my co-driver, Earl Jones, who soldiered on in good position, while Parsons pitted for his only stop - he would drive the race solo. Chuck was a great driver, and a very smart cookie. He figured that since I had appointed a co-driver he could gain a real advantage by going the distance himself and thereby only making one stop. By way of explanation, these cars were NOT designed for pit stops - there were no Formula One or Indy style fuel rigs. We filled the tanks with five-gallon cans and a funnel! A pit stop for fuel took like a minute and a half! Contrast that with the eight SECOND stop for fuel and tires of a modern Formula One car.

So Chuck had outsmarted us. Despite the fact we were quicker, he had the double advantage of saving the second stop, plus being able to run an easier pace thereby conserving his tires, engine and stamina.

It seemed that his strategy would fail, however, as at the 400-mile mark I was back in the car leading by about half a (four mile) lap - and it looked like we had the race in the bag.

It Was The Biggest Race Of The Season - And I Was Winning!

But Then . . .

At around the 420 mile mark, the engine oil temperature started climbing - and I tried not to look at the gauges as the water temp also began climbing.

I could sense the engine losing power little by little, as the thing was using itself up - I had had to run hard to regain the lead after taking the car back from the co-driver at the second pit stop.

These engines didn't mind being run hard for the normal race distance of most events - 200 miles. But now we were at 420 miles.

So now I was having to conserve the failing engine - and was additionally slowed by losing power - and Chuck was creeping ever closer.

Then we had to make a fast stop two throw three or so quarts of oil at the engine in a last ditch effort to save the thing long enough for the win. Chuck gained a bunch then, but I went out still leading, and figuring that what the hell, there is nothing left to do, I pushed as hard as I could to keep out front.

But little by little steady old Chuck Parsons gained - and on the last lap he was all over the back of me trying to find a way around my sick car.

That Last Lap Broke My Heart.

As we came out of the last corner the exhausted engine dropped a cylinder and Parsons pulled alongside for the run up the hill to the finish line. I desperately wound the engine way past the red line to avoid the time it takes to shift - but it was not enough - Parsons nosed ahead and took the flag FOUR ONE HUNDREDTHS OF A SECOND in front.

An incredibly close second is still First LOSER.

I didn't know whether to cry or kill myself or kill someone else. I had NEVER know a human being could endure such raging anger and utter despair.

It was the darkest moment of my racing career - and strangely, the grief and despair was identical to that which welled up when I attended my mother's funeral years later.

These were moments over which I never really got - Until 2006.

1967

There are many stories to be told about my 1967 season, which began with a disaster - I had ordered a car from McKee Engineering to contest the season, but I didn't get sponsorship.

So the car was sold to Ralph Salyer, whose crew chief was Gene Crowe (later to become Paul Newman's Chief.)

The team fitted an Oldsmobile racing engine provided by the factory and modified with the wizardry of Gene, and Ralph started racing it in amateur events.

Another McKee owner, Tod O'Seid, offered me a drive at a couple of races in his car, but it wasn't really competitive - so after two events I was back in Limbo.

Then one late summer day Ralph called and asked me if I would like to drive the car that was originally built for me in upcoming pro races - starting with a Mid-Ohio U.S. Road Racing Championship race, where future Indy winner Mark Donahue, my old nemesis Chuck Parsons, and many other great and lesser stars, would be appearing.

I quickly (and gratefully) agreed!

This one-off - called the Cro-Sal McKee Oldsmobile, was an odd looking rocket on four wheels. The bodywork was bulbous and as aerodynamic as a barn door. But this "Motorized Bull Fiddle," as the witty motor racing writer Henry Manney called it, was already FAST and with a few demon tweaks I qualified up front - and was able to run in a solid second behind Donahue until we ran out of gas a quarter mile from the finish! Another heartbreak. But I shrugged it off - I was just happy to have proved to myself that I still had the stuff to run up front given a good race car.

But I hesitate to add any more to this for the moment, as it would only distract from the core message of what is truly possible for YOU – the reader. So let's leave it with a final racers tale – the day the racer died – and how that led to eternal freedom being revealed as the only Reality.

9. Being – Awake And Alive

Over the winter Gene Crowe and I redesigned the bodywork and created an aerodynamic "wedge shape" - to make downforce and hopefully make the car stick better in the corners.

The season started with a huge thrill - we were invited to participate in the filming of a major motion picture - "*Winning*" - starring Paul Newman, Joanne Woodward (Paul's wife) and Robert Wagner. NEAT people! - Newman and I hit it off right away and he elected to drive my racecar for the road racing parts of the movie. And he arranged a bit part for me - which made me some money and was great fun.

Paul is a very real, very warm and friendly guy - very easy to be with. No star-like ego at all - which was very refreshing. And as it turned out he was a natural - he later became a fine driver and won many races.

Then we began our actual racing season - and had our ups and downs - but we were feeling good about our chances for a few wins as we tweaked the car and got faster bit-by-bit.

But Then . . .

It was qualifying for the 1968 "Can-Am," the Canadian American Challenge Cup. This round was at Mosport Park, near Toronto. My all time favorite racetrack.

Up hill and down, fast sweeping off camber bends. A racer's Paradise.

We're being timed, for the best one lap of balls to the wall racing against the clock- trying to set a single hot lap that the others guys can't match.

The racecar is working better than it ever has and I am stoked.

This was the happiest moment of my life.

Superstar Peter Revson was there that day driving a factory McLaren, as was Bruce McLaren himself.

And a lot of other great drivers.

Legendary Formula One and Indy 500 Stars are here racing today! I am a legend among legends - a star among stars.

Which all turned out to be . . .

The Great Dream Of An Ego!

We knew we had no chance for the pole. I was a good racer, but if I were to make a truthful assessment, I was not all *that* great against Formula One stars like Bruce McLaren, F1 Champ John Surtees, Bob Bondurant, Graham Hill - also an F1 Champ - and great Sports Car Aces like Jim Hall, and all that lot.

Not only that, but our small team with its lone race car, committed though we were, and fast and nimble though our car was, certainly was NO match for the highly sponsored factory McLarens, Lolas and Chaparrals. We were realistic about that.

So I was not altogether displeased to be running around sixth at this stage - and hoping to move up to maybe fourth of fifth.

So I was standing on it.

Right out on the very edge – 110%!

Then ...

I was turning into a downhill left-hander at about 140 MPH. The car was stable as I bent the thing into the turn, all four wheels loose in a controlled drift. As the apex comes up in this corner, the hilltop crests and starts to sharply slope down toward the hairpin turn at the bottom, "Moss' Corner." It's a little bit off camber, and the car gets very, very light at this point.

Drifting, flat out, I was in heaven. There were no limits. I was 'Home' (so I thought, because I "knew" this "experience of Oneness" was 'home'.)

I was flying, supremely free.

Man, was I ever Awake and Alive.

There was no mind, no thought, just ... a total experience of BEING. Being ... Fully Awake and Fully Alive.

It was Bliss. Total Joy. Total Freedom. Flying all alone at the speed of light. There was nobody in the car. It was all oneness ... Being ... free and unbounded. I was no longer Charlie. I was EVERYTHING. The Car. The Road. The Sunny Cloudless Sky.

Then in one Instant outside of Time - It was all over.

10. Sudden Death

I died that day at Mosport.

I was flying through that very fast section of road, dancing through that sweeping off-camber downhill left hand bend. The road was not level, it tilted to the right; moreover it crested a hill and swooped down like a roller coaster with no tracks, making the issue of grip very dicey.

Suddenly -Bang!

There is a loud cracking sound.
Then there is nothing.
Not Blackness. Not even that!
I and world are gone.
Everything - is gone.
Deep sleep death.

Much later I am told that a hub carrier, an alloy casting that holds the wheel to the suspension, had broken, and the right rear wheel had immediately come off, which sent the car out of control and careening toward God Only Knew What.

The "what" was Charlie's temporary death.

Later I heard that everyone who saw the crash was aghast, as they saw a 'lifeless' form slumped in the cockpit and they 'knew' that 'Charlie is Dead!' There was much shaking of heads, and "Wow, how terrible," uttered, as the medics gathered up the lifeless organism and bundled it sadly into the meat wagon.

For about an hour, as time measured the instant, the Charlie entity was totally gone. Then Charlie came back, but who Charlie was for himself and others as a racer had died forever, when the car hit an earth bank at Moss' Corner backwards, still going probably 120 MPH.

Much later, at a very long meditation retreat, there arose - during a session of sitting - a vision.

It was though a memory-movie was playing, and I saw the wheel fly off, the car careen out of control, the car hit the embankment - fortunately read end first so the engine, behind the driver in these race cars, takes the brunt of the impact.

I watch the body die instantly!

Then I am above watching as the dead body gets unbelted by the paramedics, laid out on a gurney, and trundled into an ambulance, and all the while something, a space-like seer - bodiless timeless eternally alive - looks down from a couple hundred feet above and watches. Then there is a deep sadness, and grief. Then - total blackout.

Next thing I know, I am in an emergency medical facility at the race track.

From Hero to Zero

As a friend, Frank Gardner, once said, *"That nasty business of going from 120 MPH to ZERO is just a bit hard on the old nervous system."*

Tell me about it. This body had backaches and headaches - and a lot of suffering thoughts about all that - for over 37 years.

11. Coming Back To "Real Life"

I awake to see the kind and concerned face of my Crew Chief, Gene Crowe, gazing at me. As he sees my eyes open he grins in relief.

The first thing I say is, "How bad is the car? Can we run tomorrow?"

Gene and everyone else laughed a little nervously at that. The car would take THREE MONTHS to rebuild; it was as close to a total loss as a car can get without *being* a total.

Then I try to get up.

My head swims, my legs feel like water. I learn later I had gotten quite a serious concussion.

When the car hit, my head was thrown back hard against the roll bar. The helmet evidently saved my physical life - but that was questionable, as it turned out - from my perspective now, I cannot know WHAT saved the life of that body!

But nothing could have saved my Racing Life.

That helmet was sent off for testing - required in all serious crashes - and the report came back, "*The guy in that busted crash helmet could not possibly have lived through that crash.*"

Indeed.

Upright and Dead

To paraphrase that famous quote, "*Life was in the Race Car. Everything else was just waiting.*"

Little did I know that the next three decades would be all about waiting. Waiting for physical death to claim my body, because there was no longer any LIFE for me.

But I didn't know that yet. I would not know that till the team arrived with the rebuilt car at the Laguna Seca Road Course near Monterey, California, in October. Then it hit me full force. But I am ahead of the story.

12. Dreams Turn To Nightmares

I flew home to California on Sunday - and with the cooperation of the flight attendants, who seemed to love my hero-racer stories, got half sloshed on Scotch, trying to dull all the physical and emotional pain of the happenings at Mosport.

My gorgeous second wife, Evey, picked me up at the airport. She had no idea what had happened other than I had broken my big-boy's toy. And she was more than a bit pissed that I was half drunk still despite a long nap and coffee before landing.

On the way home I insisted we stop for "just one drink." Two hours later she poured a now wiped out dead racer into the car and took it the rest of the way home. This was not a good thing - she knew better than anyone what a lush I could be when there was no race car to drive. And she suspected it would be a while before I would be doing any more racing.

She thought I was hurt. She did NOT know I was DEAD. Poor girl. That was the beginning of the end of a great marriage. Who wants to live with someone who is upright and dead?

Anyway, she was right about the racing. The car, a near total, was back in Illinois being reconstructed.

There was not all that much they could save and besides they wanted to do some re-design of things like hub carriers!

For the next three months I ran the racing parts business I had started in 1967 and which was, at this point, doing very well. I was selling parts, gearboxes, and engines to racers all over the country, as well as in England, Japan, and South America.

But the drinking had started again and it would effect everything - marriage, business, racing.

I was pretty sure that I could still race, though I did have some real niggling doubts.

But I figured, HOPED, that once I got back in the car I would have that same freedom and be able to do as well as I had done till then.

That was a dream.

The Truth was a Nightmare!

Failing the Test: Confirming I AM DEAD ... Upright but Dead

Finally the car was done, in time for the Can-Am round at Laguna Seca, another favorite circuit. My biggest win had come at Laguna in 1966. So I was very, very excited and hopeful.

But the nightmare was about to begin in earnest.

At Laguna the car wouldn't turn. There apparently was a glitch in the suspension. It was quickly repaired but this did nothing to instill confidence in a car that had damn near killed me already. But I soldiered on.

Then in qualifying I drove it off the road! I froze up at the wheel, and was unable to work the controls. I slid off at about 100 MPH and fortunately there was plenty of room so I didn't hit anything.

Limping back into the pits, I was met by the concerned car owner and crew chief. In answer to their questioning looks, I said, "I drove it off the road. My fault." This was a rare bit of honesty from me that surprised everyone, especially me!

We ran in the race the next day but I remember nothing of that day whatsoever. After going off on Saturday, and telling Gene and Ralph what happened, all the rest is a blank. Must have been really scary!

Then we went to Riverside and I managed to get through that weekend without any major incidents. I don't remember anything about that race either, except for one VIVID recollection. I was driving down the back straight at about 180 MPH, and as I braked for Turn Nine I had the thought, "I wonder what will happen if a wheel falls off HERE?" That was a scary thing. Because there is no time for thinking about survival in a race car. If you are doing that you are no longer racing, and you are WAY over your head.

I really knew then that it was over but I would deny that with all my ego could muster for another two years.

Denial got me to what turned out to be my final race - at Stardust Raceway in Las Vegas.

13. Scared To Death? Get Drunk - Again!

At that last 1968 Can-Am round in Las Vegas, I got roaring drunk the night before the race. This just does NOT work. The car owner, Ralph Salyer, had to come drag me out of bed when I didn't show up at the track - then in the race, I froze up and drove off the road at great speed in Turn One. Shaken to the core though I was, I still believed that I could get it back - that no-brainer talent that had gone when my head hit the roll bar.

But the car owner, and the sponsors, all knew I was DONE. I was just the last to realize it.

I was utterly terrified. I had tried to stuff it deep. And failed

So I opted out for a while, at least that's what I believed. Avoiding the harsh reality. Actually, nobody wanted to hire me to drive or sponsor me any more. Then when one of my inspirational role models got killed testing a Can-Am car the shock was electric!

I still remember getting the word before the press got the story, in a Telex from Carl Haas: "Terrible news - Bruce McLaren just got killed testing his new Can-Am car in England!"

If Bruce McLaren, one of the most careful and prudent of the really fast lot of current champions, could get killed doing this, so could I, and in fact almost did - then I had to face the fact that I was scared shitless that my body would be killed off.

Believing in an imaginary future, my career was done.

I had gone from Here to Zero.

And I was miserable - without racing, I couldn't see how I could live - yet I HAD to.

I had a son. Charles Edward Hayes had been born on March 10th, 1968. He became a good reason to keep on keeping on ... as I realized, *"My God, I love that boy!"*

So - as Sinatra sang it - "I pick myself up and get back in the race". That's my life - a rat race of survival without real freedom and joy, until 38 years later.

14. Life Of A Salesman

I had opened a parts and race car sales business in 1967, "Hayes Racing Equipment," to keep the wolf away when the racing wasn't paying. By 1970 we had expanded and were the premier supplier for many race teams. We were selling Lola Race Cars and Hewland Racing Gearboxes as a distributor for Importer Carl Haas, plus racing engines and all manner of other exotic stuff, doing a big worldwide business.

But the addiction to race, even if I couldn't drive any more, having lost my nerve in 1968 after the crash, continued to assert itself. So I started a couple of race teams. I ran two cars in the Questor Grand Prix for Formula One and Formula 5000 cars at Ontario Motor Speedway in California, for Bobby Unser and Ron Grable (Bobby retired with mechanical problems but Ron came seventh overall and first in F-5000 in the race.)

We had a ton of sponsorship money to work with. But we spent three tons of money trying to win - all borrowed, of course.

I kept borrowing more and more to feed the addiction. Driver Mike Hiss was working for me so I put him into first, a Lola Formula Ford, then a Lola Formula B (now called Formula Atlantic) and set out to rule the world.

That team broke us. Anything that could go wrong did go wrong, so it seemed.

Hiss later became a Rookie Of The Year at the Indy 500. But not on my team. According to racing scuttlebutt, his sponsor had come to see me about supporting my racing team - but Mike did what most racers would do - rather than bring the guy to me - he split from our sinking ship to run his own show. Smart move - but when I found out I was NOT happy.

Later I realized that had the roles been reversed I would have absolutely done the same thing. In that seeing there is forgiveness. But in any case I don't know if it *actually happened* that way - that was just the rumor.

I also ran Mike Brockman in a Lola F-5000 car at Laguna Seca. And spent even more money, which I was generating by falsifying invoices and factoring them, getting paid for stuff I never sold. God, that was so stupid as I look back on it.

But the addiction to racing was in complete charge. I was simply not up to being responsible. Still the spoiled brat!

I can thankfully, laugh now at how stupid that behavior was. And it is so clear now that there never was a "person" in this bag of meat and bones that could "take responsibility" that the story is even more laughable.

That said, I don't laugh about people who lost money with me. The truth doesn't justify anything.

How To Make A Small Fortune In Racing

Hey - as anyone who knows racing will tell you, it is actually very easy to make a small fortune in racing. All you need to do is start with a LARGE one. Well, I didn't HAVE a large fortune. But I knew how to con friends and bend the rules of law.

By 1971, predictably, I had failed in the racing business - and lost a nice inheritance from my beloved mother. I had to use it to pay off the creditors I had conned into loaning me money under false pretenses. I damn near ended up in jail over that fiasco, and would have if the inheritance hadn't arrived just in time - and the fraudulent loans got repaid.

The cops were never called - the victim just wanted restitution.

I still had a few bucks and my house and family, so it was not a total disaster. But I knew I had dodged a big bullet. Cost me $200,000! 1972 dollars. (That's about two million today.)

The wags are right. Crime don't pay! As I learned the hard way.

Curiously, it never occurred to me at that time to wonder what the source of that borrowing and conning - and the seeming "miracle" - of a timely inheritance - actually was!

I still labored under the illusion that I was in control of my life.

Despite all that evidence that was mounting - to the contrary.

I believed my *thinking* was the evidence that I was in control - instead of looking at Reality.

Later - as I began to examine the "evidence" I used to "prove" there was a me in control - with the help of wise and loving beings I call teachers and friends - any real "proof" that I was "in charge here" would be found utterly absent!

Meanwhile, though . . . my saga continued.

15. Livin' High On The Hog In Tinsel Town

In 1972 I opened a Ferrari agency on more borrowed money. (Stupid is as stupid does?) I had almost unlimited backing from my old friend Carl Haas (Newman-Haas Racing.) That business flourished magnificently for a quite a long while.

In one month in 1973 we sold something like 24 Ferraris, and grossed about $500,00 (1973 dollars – that's like FIVE MILLION today!) - but it all went up in smoke.

Why? Because I spent way MORE than even a whole lot. I loved shopping, buying crazy stuff like a dozen pairs of Gucci shoes, a couple of Rolls Royces, and a Mercedes Limo!

And, the more money I made the more the desperation was in my face. I "had it all:" Beautiful wife, wonderful little son, gorgeous home with five bedrooms (for three people!?) – we had the pool, the pool TABLE, the amazing food and wines, the Good Life.

So how come I was miserable? I didn't ask – I just kept buying more stuff (instead of paying my creditors.) And then drugs took me over - big time.

I would get up at six AM, look over my ads for Ferraris in the Los Angeles Times, and pop a couple of amphetamines – my wife's diet pills. Speeding up, I would then ingest several cups of coffee. Out of bed, dress in jeans and a funky shirt, comb out my shoulder length hair and scraggly beard, hop in a Ferrari and zoom off to the shop. Then once ensconced in my luxurious office, I would get my hippie secretary to bring more coffee while I rolled a few joints from some very pricey seedless marijuana to get down from the frenetic pace of the speed high – what a freakin' roller coaster. Of course I thought this was just completely normal – a high roller Hollywood lifestyle.

As the addiction to "more" continued and I tried to fill the bottomless despairing emptiness I felt, I was back in the mode of the con man – as I adopted sleazy business practices and ended up once again lying to borrow more money to buy more Ferraris and make the business grow – in the mania I remained convinced that more more more would eventually bring happiness – despite the overwhelming evidence to the contrary!

So I conned more and more money out of others - even my loving but naive little sister! This was NOT a Nice Puppet! Just your basic spoiled brat.

Finally, since I was doing more and more drugs, lying and conning, in June of 1974 the whole house of cards fell apart.

Carl and my sister lost a bundle in the ensuing meltdown. I am still amazed that they both found the willingness and the heart to forgive me and I love them both deeply.

16. Death Of A Salesman

How did the "Great Meltdown" happen?

I was keeping my Ferrari business creditors and bankers at arms length, lying about how great the business was. But in fact, we had gone from selling 20 and more Ferraris a month to selling only three or four - because in the aftermath of the gas crunch of 1973 the two leasing companies that bought all my paper went out of business overnight in January of '74. But I still had the overhead of a dealership making the large sums that sales of 20 plus Ferraris had produced. Revenues shrunk, but the overhead kept on and it was killing me.

One morning in June I got into a Ferrari 365GT 2 + 2 that I was road testing and using as a demonstrator, and started in to work. I had a vast array of unpaid bills, un-honored drafts for car purchases, cars that had been sold and not paid for. I was exhausted from trying to keep all the balls in the air.

I stopped for breakfast and then began to have very strange experiences. There were voices in my head telling me that everyone in the coffee shop was totally aware of my lies and the house of cards I had built, that I was a cheat, a phony and a loser that was about to really end up in jail this time unless another inheritance arrived to bail me out. Problem was, there was no more inheritances to be had. The givers were long gone. I was REALLY on my own this time - and I did NOT like that at all.

I got the hell out of there, and sat out front staring at my right eye in the Ferrari's rear view mirror. I don't know exactly how long I sat there, but my sense is it was at least an hour. I had totally lost it. The mind just was ground down to a halt. My lack of honesty and integrity was finally gonna bite me in the ass, but good!

Finally I forced myself to drive the remaining few blocks to my agency. Once seen by many as the best exotic car dealership in the United States, the business I loved was about to go up in smoke. Arriving at my store, "Salon Ferrari," I parked out back, got out of the car, and sat on the curb, staring into space. I was struck dumb. Near paralyzed physically - totally paralyzed mentally. Next to me was my briefcase, filled with damning evidence of all the lies and half-truths and unseen debts.

I could not think or move. I was just ... stopped. Dead.

My brother-in-law Ed - also the Service Manager for Salon Ferrari - came out after a half hour or so - he knew I was a bit weird so he didn't bother me till he became convinced that something was seriously wrong and this was not Charlie being "eccentric" again. I remember dimly he asked if I was OK. I think I said no. In any case he saw what was needed and bundled me into the car and drove me straight to the doctor's office. The doc took one look at me and told Eddie to take me to a Mental Hospital/rehab place in Whittier, California.

I had no resistance to any of it. I was like a lump of tofu at that point.

I was in that hospital for a month. People in there were really crazy! Me included of course. Then after the first week, my wife informed me that the business was going into bankruptcy (she was the president of the corporation so she didn't need my permission - which I would not have been able to either give or deny anyway, at that point.)

Evey was handling all the angry creditors, trying to explain what she didn't really understand, and generally being an angel about the whole damn mess. That is one fine lady - I really blew a great marriage - but did I actually choose ANY of that? Later that would become a burning question for me.

(At the time though, I didn't realize that Evey was in the process of falling for the body-builder hippie guy that worked for me detailing Ferraris. Which I had stupidly precipitated by having a brief affair with a neighbor - Evey walked in as we were doing the nasty. Adultery. Was there NO sin I would not commit? No.)

I was realizing along about then that I was, in a word, still upright but dead - but REALLY DEAD – again! My new life as a Ferrari dealer - life as I knew it - was gone.

My wife would leave me shortly after this - and with no business, no job, little money and no prospects, I was to be on my own - a stranger in a world I had no clue about how to manage.

It was a living hell. I had gone completely around the bend. I was dead as a doornail. I had gone from Ferraris and Rolls Royce's to an old VW and was finding life to be an incredible struggle to stay alive and survive. Poor, poor me - such a sad sad story I believed was ME. Yuck.

Part Two

Waking Up From
   The "Nightmare" Of My Life:

Beginning The Purging Of The False -
   And The Remembering Of The Real

17. Awakenings

While I was in the Mental Hospital a sort of strange awakening occurred - although I did not see it as such.

I just thought I was crazy . . .

Sitting in a therapy group, another patient began to speak and I had the clear and unmistakable experience of being not just me any more but rather being HIM - AND ME - with NO separateness.

That knocked me for a loop! It was my experience that it was *me* - speaking *through* that other body-mind apparatus - I was over there inside HIS head.

I knew what he was about to say a split second before the sound was heard. I - as a separate entity - had disappeared and there was nothing but space, in which thinking arose and sound arose ... for no one! Unicity!

But not having - at that time- the least idea of what this might be pointing me to - I dismissed it as a Looney-Toons Moment and went right back to being "someone, a person, separate and alone" - a "thing" - with no sustained awareness of the unity I had glimpsed.

No Separation - I Am Both Me And The Other Guy

I later learned that this was what was referred to in the East as Jnana (or 'The Experience of Jnana,' a Sanskrit word meaning true Wisdom, pronounced 'yah-na.') Or pure knowing without a "knower."

Also known is some Christian mystical literature as the "Impersonal Life" at the heart of creation.

After that moment I saw quite often that what I had thought was "me" was actually a sort of "perpetual-thought machine," running on endlessly, producing one furball of thought after another.

And this machinery of nattering negativism also plagued just about everyone I met! And I saw that its favorite thing to think up was this apparent "me!" A "Poor suffering me."

Therein began compassion – for others and for myself.

My Sweet Lord

Then, while still in that mental ward, I found a record by George Harrison singing this "Love Song to God" called "My Sweet Lord."

It sent me straight into ecstasy! My Sweet Lord!! Another kind of awakening. It was what I later learned was a taste of the unconditional, pure love of God, or Oneness. Bhakti in the East, Agape in the West. I listened to it over and over. Hallelujah - Hare Krishna - I LOVED it!

At this point some new energy surged up. I lost weight, exercised, and quit smoking, much to the amazement of the doctors and staff. They thought that I was miraculously cured.

Well, it did seem that way. But I was to crash big time from this "enlightenment" after leaving the cocoon of the hospital.

From Ferraris And Rolls Royce's To An Old VW

I had come into the hospital as the owner of a Ferrari dealership, with a 3000 sq. foot home, a beautiful wife, a charming six-year-old boy, a Rolls Royce, a Ferrari and a Mercedes. I came out into a cold, damp apartment in a redneck orange county town, driving a clapped out ten-year-old VW.

Something of a shock. Especially when I found out later that my beloved wife had fallen in love with that foxy-looking mechanic man and as noted before, I was soon to lose her as well.

Blame happened - big time. There was much resentment - until I remembered, "hey, Charlie, YOU were the one who was caught screwing the neighbor lady!"

Paybacks are hell.

Anyhow - after being discharged, while still on heavy medication for depression, I was steeped in resignation and despair, sick as hell and pretending as best I could to be OK. I got a job selling used Volkswagens, and forced myself to go in to work every day, living a suffering miserable existence. Poor me! Sheesh. It was the never-ending story - with NO happy ending - or so it seemed at the time.

18. Praying To Die

I was "praying and waiting to die" when came across a book called The Tao Te Ching. It was unfathomable. I thought, *what bullshit!*

Then I heard talks by "Baba Ram Dass" AKA Richard Alpert, PhD, former Harvard Professor, friend of and fellow "Spiritual Traveler" with Timothy Leary, dropper of much acid. Ram Dass traveled to India where he found his Guru, Neem Karoli Baba.

I bought and pored over Ram Dass' book "*Be Here Now,*" which I found confusing - and strange - but something in it rang a bell. Quite a lot of it rang a bell, really.

Finally, while still on heavy medication for depression, I was exposed to the teachings of the Great Sage of India, Sri Ramana Maharshi.

Ramana's books made NO more sense that the Tao Te Ching, and the practice Ramana suggested - asking "who am I?" - led only to dullness and headaches. I didn't last long with it - it was too soon. Later it would really hit home.

Then in December 1974, while selling second-hand Volkswagens, I overheard a customer tell another salesman that he needed the used VW van he was buying to be ready by Saturday so he could go see his Guru. My ears perked up and I went over and butted in as the other salesman was closing the deal - a real no-no in the used car biz - and blurted out, "Guru!? Did you say you have a Guru?"

The fellow smiled and said, "Yeah, my Guru is coming to Los Angeles for a Satsang on Saturday night. Would you like to come see him too? His name is Baba Muktananda."

I later learned that Swami Muktananda – affectionately known as "Baba" - was an Indian Sage who had been touring the world teaching meditation and chanting - practices designed by the ancient Guru-Sages to reveal the non dual God-Self - Being, Consciousness Itself, which is the essential nature of all mankind.

I was stunned. I knew I needed a Guru - and here one was - finding ME! I quickly agreed and this wonderful guy - whose name was "Gurudas" which means "One who serves the Guru" - gave my the location. I had no idea what a Satsang was. But I didn't care. I knew I had to go to it - whatever "it" was.

So my wife, my brother-in-law, and I all drove up to L.A. for this meeting with the Guru - getting loaded on cheap pot on the way. Naturally. I was so bloody stupid – in "my thinking," that is.

When we walked in Gurudas greeted us with a smile and said, "Turn On." I wondered if Timothy Leary was appearing with this Muktananda guy.

The evening started with a droning chanting sound - a small group up front singing, then the audience responding in the same sound. I couldn't understand the words - it was like listening to a mudslide. Later I learned that the sound being sung was an ancient "Mantra" used to awaken the sleeping dream-character we think of as ourselves out of its slumber, into the True Nature of Pure Being, unbounded and ever free in its Self.

The mantra sung was "OM Namah Shivaya." This is said to be an ultimately meaningless sound - it's the *vibration* that does the awakening job - destroying the belief in false thoughts of a separate identity – the "me." But since the mind loves meanings, a meaning is ascribed - I Bow To Shiva, My Own True Self, Which Is All Existence, Consciousness and Bliss.

That vibration worked some magic, even on the old stupid stoned Charlie thing, that night! Something bit me. I learned later that this "something" was called "Shaktipat" Initiation – a kind of Heart To Heart "Transmission" from Guru to Seeker - that resonating energy-transference which is pointed to in the ancient texts of India, Japan and Tibet, and sometimes in the Mystical Christian texts.

Much later I heard an American Sage, Wayne Liquorman, point to this "transmission" - I'll paraphrase: When a Guru-Organism and a seeker-organism meet, the True Guru is made manifest – in the space – as a space of resonating Love.

In India - and increasingly in the West, at this time - this is commonly called "Advaita" - nondual spirituality. The word "Advaita" means NOT TWO. Or Oneness if you like that term better. Or God, Source, Noumenon. Or Tao.

I finally came to see that any truth that can be spoken or known – by a "knower" - is NOT the Real Truth. The Tao that can be spoken is not the Eternal Tao.

19. My Head Goes Into The Tiger's Mouth

Much MUCH later I heard a pointer from the Sage Ramana Maharshi, who said (approximately) - "take comfort in the fact that your head is in the tiger's mouth." In other words, understand that the spiritual path has opened; you have become a seeker, though no choice of your own. And, to paraphrase Rumi, the one who brought you here will take you home.

In the metaphor the tiger is what is usually called God - or Oneness. Oneness has put "your" head in the His -The Tiger's - mouth of Oneness - and Oneness will chomp off that head in due course. We are finished, in a way - final liberation is assured. We need not worry about when.

Fast Forward - Over the nearly thirty-two years of dream-life from mid-December 1974 until early July of 2006, I forgot and remembered - and forgot and remembered - this point Baba Muktananda stressed from the git-go:

"The One you are looking for is the One looking." And his successor, Swami Chidvilasananda, once said directly to me:

"*You* Are *The Self.*"

Yes. I was beginning to glimpse some truth - that this One Looking for THAT is the Nondual Godhead - THAT is The One-Without-A-Second.

That Is the Real. That is All. This is sometimes pointed out this way: The I Am that I Am and the I Am that You Are - are NOT TWO. There is but ONE "I Am." That only becomes clear - "once upon another time" - called The Timeless NOW. Just Now. Just Here. Just This.

Stop. Know THIS - BE *THIS*: "I AM The Self. I Am The God I Seek."

Paradoxically - I could not do that – know that - and never ever would be able to - because in Truth there is no "person" that could do that - or anything else - in the human body-mind organism! And yet – it DOES HAPPEN! Don't try to grasp that with the mind.

For the seeing of this, however, there had to be "preparation" - or so it seemed. That turns out to be another false story - a myth!

Meanwhile, back at the ranch . . .

20. Go Directly To Jail. Do Not Pass Go.

In April 1975 I was still peddling Volkswagens, now new ones, and still looking for answers.

Despite having met Muktananda.

The stubbornness of my ego was boundless!

One day I read in the paper that another Indian Guru named Maharishi Mahesh Yogi was scheduled to appear on the Merv Griffin TV talk show that night.

I was working a late shift so I shrugged it off, figuring I couldn't get away early enough to get home to watch - there were few VCRs and no TIVOs in those days!

But at about seven PM, I found myself walking into the manager's office and telling him, "I have to leave. There is something I have to do." He looked at me strangely and said, to my surprise, without any resistance, "Oh. Okay. See you tomorrow."

I hightailed it home and eagerly turned on the television - and was blown away but what I saw and heard.

I was completely taken by the Loving Presence exuding across the airwaves from the Maharishi - and doubly impressed that Clint Eastwood - "Dirty Harry!" - was on the show as well - it turned out stars Mary Tyler Moore and Clint were doing the meditation that this Maharishi was teaching all over the world. Mary was no surprise really. But Clint Eastwood? Unimaginable. (I met him years later in a Ferrari store in Monterey, California. It turns out that the tough guy thing is of course just the crafting of a character by a helluva good actor - his was a really clear and pleasant presence to be with.)

Anyway, when Eastwood walked on stage clutching a flower to give to the Guru - rather than his customary Smith And Wesson 44 Magnum! - I was bowled over.

Right then and there, I decided I had to learn to do that meditation.

So I did. I had to wait a couple of weeks because I was a dope smoker - I needed to be off all drugs for 15 days, before they would teach me.

But finally, on 3 May 1975, I learned "Transcendental Meditation" or "TM" as it became popularly known - and practiced it diligently twice a day.

I figured my life was finally settling down, as I was working at the meditation and enjoying some long periods of deep peace.

But Then - "Reality" Bites Again

After a month-long meditation retreat, doing advanced techniques and yoga, and watching like thirty videos of Maharishi, I was "blissed out" and happier than ever before in my life.

But when I came home to my tiny Corona Del Mar, California, apartment, I found a business card in my door from a Santa Ana, California Police Detective.

A hand written note on it said, *call me.*

I did. After a perfunctory *"thanks for calling in,"* the detective announced, *"we have a warrant for your arrest for Grand Theft Auto. Would you like to come in or do we need to come get you?"*

SHIT. Suddenly I had a WHOLE NEW DEFINITION for SCARED!

What the hell? I thought. I didn't think I had actually done anything ILLEGAL. Not THIS time, at least. I was just - unethical. But it looked like THIS time I WOULD go to prison. Paybacks are hell . . .

Anyway, quaking with terror inside, I drove my old VW to the police station, and the detective informed me that a leasing company I had done some business with and who had left a Dino Ferrari on consignment for me to sell had claimed - falsely - that I had sold a car that belonged to them, *without* their permission. The car *was* sold - and had of course *never gotten paid for* - because the account was caught up in the massive debts I had that ultimately necessitated declaring bankruptcy.

So - despite the fact that I DID have the car on consignment and had NOT "stolen" it from them but was in fact selling it on their behalf, the leasing company had gone to the District Attorney with a complaint. In short - they lied. The D.A. believed the lie and decided to prosecute me for Grand Theft Auto.

At this point the business had been closed for a year and a half so I couldn't figure out what was happening. Because I NEVER sold a car that I didn't belong to us unless I had a signed agreement consigning the car to us for sale. But that argument fell on deaf ears at the police department.

And a search of the records proved that most had been lost or otherwise fallen through some cracks in the system.

So the next thing I knew I had made my one phone call to a lawyer friend - HELP! - And was being trundled off for a strip search and a stay in the Orange County Jail.

Man, that was scary. This was a BIG dark almost windowless place full of very nasty men.

I remember sitting in a corner of a cell that also contained five or six other guys, all of whom looked like murderers to me. To say I was terrified falls way short. I could hardly breathe. The television was blaring, and all sorts of strange sounds were echoing off the very not acoustic walls. It was a cacophony.

The sounds of madness and lawlessness. And the feeling of absolute, stark, raging terror.

I have lived on the lip
of insanity, wanting to know reasons,
knocking on a door. It opens.
I've been knocking on the inside!
Real value comes with madness
ecstatic one below, scientist above.
Whoever finds love
beneath hurt and grief
disappears into emptiness
with a thousand new disguises.

- Rumi

21. I Escape From Hell - For A While

After a very long day in that hellhole jail cell - what grace that it was ONLY one day! - Finally late in the evening a guard called my name. Hayes! Up. You are out of here. Whew!! I am amazed that people can endure for years in such places.

My lawyer had gotten it done, and I am OUT on OR release - on my Own Recognizance, no bail! - Release. Freedom - at least for now. I guess they figured, what the hell - since I turned myself in I probably wasn't gonna run. It was sure as hell not that I didn't *want* to flee - I just had no place to flee TO.

Over the next few months I sold Volkswagens again and made enough money to pay the lawyer while we prepped for trial. I was sweating bullets at night - and thanking God for TM which smoothed the way somewhat.

Then, Grace Happened: Somehow we found the (honest) guy who had given me that car on consignment when he was working for the leasing company. I don't recall how - but we located him up in Seattle, by some miracle!

As it turned out it was someone else who worked for that leasing company that lied in court about the car having been sold illegally. The nerve, I thought, forgetting how many damn lies I had told in my time!

And so, my attorney - a great guy named Art Folger, a former prosecutor who knew everyone in the system - went to the District Attorney with the news that this fellow had surfaced, and asked the D.A. if he could make the false charges go away. The guy essentially said, sure - just have the witness call me to verify - no need to go to trial and drag the witness down from Seattle.

Wow.

That is Grace - Big Time - for lack of a better concept.

And so it unfolded that I found myself in court listening to the District Attorney say, "In light of new evidence the State moves to dismiss all charges." The judge said, "So Ordered." And I was free to go.

22. Gate Gate – Gone Beyond!

After a few months of selling cars and making decent money, by March of 1977, things had calmed down.

I was doing Transcendental Meditation twice a day, and enjoying the moments of peace that this practice provided.

Then on a chilly mid-March morning - Nothing happened.

It's Timelessness - similar seemingly to the way it had in the race car crash - but this time it was not due to trauma.

I am sitting in meditation

and all at once

I disappear!

Gone.

Nothing.

Blank.

In fact not even that

ONLY after "I" came back did "I" realize –

"I" had been completely GONE.

No words No Space No Me No Other-Than-Me

The Absence Of Absence of Absence ? ? !

23. Back In A Material World

A day or two after this "disappearing and reappearing" of me, I got a call from Carl Haas, who had lost a ton of money in the meltdown of Salon Ferrari. What made Carl be the forgiving and patient guy he is I will never know To my great surprise, he invited me to be his guest at the April 1977 Formula One race in Long Beach - to discuss a job with him.

Grace.

I was in heaven at the F1 race! The sound of a Ferrari Formula One engine, revving to god knows what, screaming as the thing was driven right on the absolute limit by Gilles Villeneuve - sent chills up and down my spine. I was finally at home in the world again – after the long nightmare – or so it seemed.

Carl had the kind of passes where you could practically walk out on the track itself - so it was as close as I could get to World Class Racing without actually driving again. Amazing.

I will never forget seeing old pals like Teddy Mayer and Stirling Moss, and meeting people like Bernie Ecclestone, the czar of Formula One then and now. Carl knew everybody and everybody knew and respected him. As they, as we, should. He is great.

Big Money Again - But No Joy

So I moved to Chicago to work as Carl's Race Car Sales Manager. The money was great but the perks were really extraordinary. Imagine flying into Indy for the 500 in a private plane, then having (again) the best passes you can imagine. But there was still this ache in my heart. No matter how great the outer was, the inner was empty. And no amount of external satisfactions could ever fill the hole. It was bottomless.

Then I started buying and selling Ferraris on my own, cutting Carl out of the deals. I even stole one of his customers! Gradually as the "programmed mind" of putrid integrity came back and took over, I got more and more crooked again, and of course more and more depressed - despite making a large amount of money - both with Carl and on the side.

Nasty little boy, that "me."

Finally in December Carl and I talked. I said I wasn't happy, he said it was not working for him either. Besides, I hated the Chicago winter weather!

So I moved back to the West Coast. I think Carl knew about my side deals, but never asked for any recompense. Carl is that kind of man. The best.

This finally set me firmly onto the spiritual path. I knew I was an asshole. I knew that I didn't seem to be able to act like a decent human being - I seemed unable to be kind to myself or anyone else. I did not seem to be able to win without cheating.

It felt like everything I touched blew up or died or left.

I felt I was both a victim and a perpetrator - no matter what I did someone ended up getting hurt and suffering.

Especially me.

Escaping Into Meditation

So I came back to California in a deep funk, and started a ten week long in-residence meditation course, with TM.

From Late December 1977 until mid March 1978 I meditated about eight hours a day and learned an "advanced meditation" called the "TM Sidhi Program" - based on the teachings of the ancient sage Maharshi Patanjali.

I met a beautiful (but married) woman on one of the courses and we had a brief illicit affair, until she saw the ego and arrogance that ran me, and got out of Dodge. That left me suffering more desperately than ever - the pain of loss of love and the frustration of feeling, "I just can't do anything right!" had me near suicidal.

I would have done anything to get out of myself! So on the recommendation of a friend who was a former TM teacher, I took Werner Erhard's two-weekend "enlightenment intensive" that he called "est."

est (the word was always written in all lower case) is Latin for IS, or It Is. Very Zen! Anyway, I thought, "Maybe est will be the last thing I need to erase my pain and suffering." *Hope Springs Eternal . . .*

24. Werner Erhard, 'est,' And Integrity

At first the est staff told me I could not take the seminar because I had been in the mental hospital. I said, bullshit, I am doing it. They said not without a doctor's OK. So I said I will GET the doctor's OK. I did. I conned a naive psychologist in Laguna Beach into signing off on me. I was a great liar!

'est' was two long weekends, in April 1978. 9 AM till 1 or 2 or one night 3 AM. That was interesting! Brutally a ball busting of the ego. Big time.

It stared out with the trainer announcing, "You are all assholes." That was no big deal; I KNEW I was an asshole. But I found depths of asshole-ness in myself that I never could have imagined existed. It was like taking the lid off the cesspool. But - I found out I *could* go six hours without taking a pee despite really needing to!

I also learned not to drink coffee before the sessions started.

That sucker was Spiritual Boot Camp! I hated and loved it. But I did not get IT. Whatever IT was that I was supposed to get.

Nevertheless, as with the other things I had tried, something bit me there - I felt - and still feel (rightly or not, who knows?) that Werner was – IS - a sage, and that his work has deep roots in Zen, The Tao and Advaita.

And - unfortunately for an ego - in the concepts and practices of Integrity and responsibility. Bad place for a spoiled brat to hang out, hey?

Then I ended up meeting Werner himself at a race! Surprise. Here was an ordinary appearing guy, but he had a radiant Presence. And magnetic charisma. A sparkle in the eyes.

I immediately wanted to hang out with him. As it turned out that would happen! Werner had started a team - Breakthrough Racing - as a project to delve into deep principles of what it is to be human and work in or as an organization. I was the perfect candidate to be one of his "Coaches" for the project, as a former world-class driver. So I moved up to San Francisco and joined the project.

I spent several months in San Francisco and was loving it - until I went broke (again).

I simply spent more than I had - like a ton more.

Though I was officially a member of Werner's est staff, I was like a dollar-a-year guy, an unpaid volunteer. Just like the wealthy men of my youth – friends of my father's in Washington - who contributed that way to the war effort in the 1940's.

That was fine with me; I would have paid to hang out with the man. He was that cool. Silly, huh?

BUT! I was NOT wealthy! Duh . . .

Anyway, deep down I knew that some energy of Aliveness was cooking me from the inside out. Wiping the ego out little by little.

I was hooked.

For about five months, I worked side by side with Werner - but he was like, *not there*. He was - IS - Space. Unconditionally loving all that is - even me! Of course I loved him deeply. I still do!

Nevertheless, the "IT" to be "GOT" eluded my attempts to capture and own it. (Of course.)

A glimmer happened though – as the est training said over and over, there is nothing to get.

Advaita - as expressed through Tony Parsons - goes further – there is no person who can get or NOT get anything.

When the iron bird flies and horses have wheels, the Dharma (Teachings of Nonduality) will move west.

- Ancient Tibetan Proverb

25. Muktananda Redux

While I was working for Werner and est, Swami Muktananda once again appeared in my life! I am reminded of the old saying, "When the student is ready the Teacher appears."

Werner knew Baba – and loved him deeply. He also endorsed Baba's "Siddha Yoga" teachings – and so, off I went off to the Oakland Ashram to meet Baba again. This time sans marijuana! Clean and sober, I was really excited to see him again. I visited several times and really enjoyed the chanting and meditation, and the "Satsang With Baba."

Then I ran out of money and had to quit est and get a proper job with a real income - so in March 1979, I took a job selling Ferraris in Monterey. Around March 15th 1979 I went to the Ashram for a program. Baba had announced he would be giving a weekend Intensive - in which he would bestow "Shaktipat" - divine initiation - to all attending. It cost $150, if I recall. I couldn't begin to afford that. So I settled for just coming to an evening program a couple of days before the Intensive

What happened next was unimaginable. I remember it like it was yesterday: I sat along the wall in the meditation hall and stared at Baba with huge intensity, saying silently over and over "I cannot afford the intensive, please, give me Shaktipat tonight." Over and over for an hour I chanted this in the mind.

Then it was time for Darshan – the chance to go up and meet Baba - so I purchased an orange to drop in the basket as my offering and got in line. By now I had given up my inner begging - I just wanted to get a hit from the peacock feathers and then drive back to Monterey and sleep.

As I approached Baba there was a palpable silence and deep resonating love surrounding everything. It felt like – heaven.

It was all just a sublime dance of Love.

I knelt and bowed my head with respect, dropped the fruit, felt the feathers, and started to get up to go. I was halfway up, one leg cocked, and then Baba looked straight at me. The energy made me turn to look at him and our eyes met.

Then the world stopped. Everything just STOPPED. It was like a freeze frame.

The movie of life just stopped - in a single timeless moment - and nothing moved. Nothing - perfect stillness. It was like a movie still - a freeze frame.

I don't know how much time elapsed . . .

It seemed like hours but was likely only a second or two maybe - but that was One Eternal Instant.

Then Baba looked away and the spell was broken so to speak. I nearly fell over as I was in an awkward posture, half up and half down. I remember as I stumbled and swayed all the swamis (teaching monks Baba had initiated) and the others close to Baba burst out laughing.

I finally made it up onto my feet and began to walk away - and then a flood of horrible thoughts and emotions and self-hatred and critical judging started to happen. I was inundated with the most horrific negativity - beyond imagination really. It was a waking nightmare!

A few days later reading about Baba's own experience when he received initiation from Bhagavan Nityananda - in his book "The Play Of Consciousness" - I belatedly realized I had in fact been given what I was longing for, and that this Shaktipat gift had "removed the lid from the sewer" of me-thoughts that had been roiling inside since the idea of "me" first arose - if you are relating this to your own "me story" maybe you'll grasp this.

In any case, I was a jerk big time, a thief (literally) and a con man, a womanizer, all that terrible stuff one imagines to be what we are. As this "character" in the play, "strutting his hour on stage," I had rotten integrity, NO real friends, and was a cowardly but aggressive punk in a large body.

I was lucky I wasn't called on my bullshit in a bar or at a race. I couldn't fight my way out of a paper bag!

And yes all that is a story but at the time that seemed to be who I was.

Anyway Baba (or the Energy!) broke the dam and lowered the floodgates and wow. The next six months I was a total basket case - BUT I WAS aware that I had received the great gift of direct divine initiation - Divya Diksha, or Divine Initiation into a Spiritual Path.

Over the next few years intense experiences of suffering continued to happen. But I moved back to Los Angeles - and then Baba reappeared in Santa Monica in October of 1980. I avoided him like the plague until

December, but the energy pulled me back to him! So I attended five consecutive Intensives from December 1980 through April 1981.

There are many more stories associated with those events - but perhaps for another time. All these stories may seem amazing - but they're not really important to the realization of Self - that True Nature.

THAT is the nonduality which is being pointed to ultimately in this book. And the seeing that all is done is just happening – and is not done by a "person." The doing was happening through the body-mind – which was nothing more than a puppet.

Speaking of which, Baba was a non-dual teacher in many ways. Consider this - "God dwells within you AS you. You are what you are seeking. What can you really attain? (Nothing, you are already That.) "

"All there is is the Play of Consciousness. "Etc. And the biggie? "THERE IS NOTHING THAT IS NOT SHIVA (Consciousness.)"

So it seemed to the mind that I didn't "get it." BUT: After that I began to slowly but surely recover some integrity.

Little by little I reached out to those I felt I had caused pain and suffering for.

I asked for forgiveness, and requested that they tell me what I needed to do to make up for the mess I had made.

Some were willing to forgive, some were not. But all seemed to appreciate that I was making an effort to straighten up and fly right.

Over the next twenty-five years I worked to clean up things as best I could, using whatever means and teachings I could grasp.

But I continued to make a few new messes too. It really did seem hopeless. I would never be a decent human being, I thought.

And I was afraid - of just about everything.

So I decided to confront my *worst* fear - that of falling from a great height.

26. Rationality Is Gone. There Is Only Terror.

I am standing on a tiny step, attached to the wing of a perfectly good airplane. It's 3000 feet above the ground, and I am frozen in terror.

It is a Now called Summer of 1979.

I have a parachute strapped to my back. There is a line attached to the aircraft that will pull the cord and open the chute.

I do not care how safe it is. I do not care that this jump school has never had a fatality or even a serious injury. I am scared shitless. Thinking – THIS WAS NOT SUCH A GOOD IDEA AFTER ALL!

All there is, is wind noise smoke fumes exhaust flimsy wing rocking airplane tiny step terror. All thinking and rationality is gone. There is only terror.

The jumpmaster is staring at me with a red face – veins stand out on his neck. I hear a shout GO! I freeze solid. I'm stopped dead.

I'm thinking, *"No way. I am NOT going. Anywhere. NOT EVER! I will hang onto this goddam wing forever. "*

Again, he shouts GO GODAMMIT GO! You are gonna miss the drop zone, you stupid asshole! GO GO GO GO.

I have NO choice. I must choose.

I cannot! I cling.

Letting go suddenly happens. Choosing is done for me. In one instant I die.

Rushing violent wild white noise black space. I am a single point of terror in a black timeless eternity of stark terror.

No thinking. Just this terrible experiencing death knell sounding impossible loudness of unbearable wind tearing at me. Murdering me.

BANG

All is quiet NOW. All serenity NOW.

I Am.

I Am.

Nothing else.

A body floats swaying gently in air-space. The ground is far away, far below. There is a daytime moon. A world is born – it is indescribably beautiful.

I am Home. There is only pure silence.

Then the ground starts to get larger. I look up in amazement, a white tent appears above my head. I notice I am gripping the straps that grow down toward me from the canopy. Then I notice the ground is coming up from earth awfully quickly now!

I remember the ground school training; don't look down to predict when your feet will hit the ground! The mind will LIE to you and you will break both your legs.

I look straight out at the horizon – feeling the earth, at the instant that my feet actually touch the ground.

I let the legs buckle, roll, and sigh in relief and joy as the chute tumbles to earth beside me.

I am alive in a whole new way.

But it was a temporary high and soon, it was business as usual.

So still, I practiced for endless hours in TM and TM Sidhi Meditation. And chanted mantras I learned from Muktananda, who died in 1982 but appointed two successors to carry on the Teaching.

It all helped – and I would experience bliss. Then I would get up to make coffee and the despair would return.

I worked as a salesman, then a sales manager, and made pretty good money. But I still felt deep down that I really was a con man. And suffered pangs of guilt.

Then in 1983 I received the Indian name "Ishan" from "temporary" Muktananda co-successor Swami Nityananda - Nityananda was later "retired" from Siddha Yoga - due to his allegedly breaking his vows of celibacy with young ladies living in his ashram - leaving Swami Chidvilasananda as sole heir to the role of Guru.

But I got the name first - and I loved it. Still do.

The name Ishan is said to be a name for Shiva, the Hindu god that destroys the ignorance of ego.

It was SO wonderfully spiritual!

I spent lots more time with remaining Muktananda successor Gurumayi Chidvilasanda, and diligently studied Kashmir Shaivism, through a Course called "In Search Of The Self," written on the command of Gurumayi by a devotee of Muktananda's.

Then in late 1983, I found myself once again nearly broke and out of a job, so I decided to move into the Ashram in Los Angeles. I could be "spiritual" AND live on the cheap at the same time! It seemed perfect.

The ashram was amazing – and I was happily (for the most part) immersed in practices, meditation, chanting, Guru-Seva (service to the master), doing Puja (worship ceremonies) and whatnot. But there was still no real peace. I would still get pissed and throw temper fits - even in the ashram. I became known as a guy to avoid - other seekers were not fond of these antics!

Eventually I ran out of the little money I had left. I sold my car to make the small ashram rent and board, and kept hoping for a miracle. But it sure seemed like there were no such things as miracles, despite my urgent prayers and firm beliefs!

I MUST AND I DO TRUST GOD

That was my password to a fleeting peace.

But no miracles came.

Until later.

27. Down And Out In Beverly Hills

Suddenly it's 1984.

Finally I am virtually out of money again. I am down to about twenty bucks and cannot pay even the tiny amount of monthly room and board rent at the ashram.

And so, I move out onto the street.

I start walking south toward Orange County, where I have family and friends. I do have twenty bucks so I know I can eat for a day or four.

I am clad in layers of clothes, carrying nothing.

I walk from Santa Monica as far as the hillock overlooking Los Angeles International Airport, until, exhausted, feet beginning to blister already - I've led a very soft life until now - I climb up on the grassy hill and sit. Rest. Take my shoes off and let the breeze cool my feet. "Cooling my heels."

I stare out at the beautiful jet planes taking off and landing, thinking, "How the hell did I end up here, broke, beat, old and alone? I am damn near fifty years old and this is how I end up?"

I am thinking, "Jeez; I used to be ON those airplanes. How did I end up here!?"

I had been flown to Japan - First Class no less - as a guest of Nissan Motor Company - and tested their racing cars for them at Fuji Speedway.

I had flown to London, Paris, Nassau, the French Riviera - you get the idea.

God, I hated what I had become.

I had a real mastery of self-pity!

About three in the morning I prayed like I never had. I was praying to die. I said aloud, Lord, take me to my Father's House. I was as down and dirty as anyone could be and I begged for death.

Death did not happen (obviously!)

A few minutes later, I found myself getting to my (now badly blistered) feet, and starting back in the direction from which I had come.

I had a new respect for the guts it took for people who lived their lives out on the street to keep going day after day. After just one such day I was physically and emotionally devastated.

I limped up the road, wondering what forces were propelling me - having no sense that I had any control over any of this nightmare. Finally at about six am I dragged myself into the ashram, and plunked my last twenty down to buy one night of bed and board. I gratefully ate a huge breakfast and then slept the sleep of the damned till about noon.

28. Back On Top? What A Roller-Coaster!

When I came down the stairs for lunch I spotted a friend and asked for a loan. He readily agreed and I had a hundred bucks. Five more days! Then another devotee found me a place to stay for no rent - I would just be doing some menial paperwork for a car leasing company the woman who owned the house worked for. I got room and board and a few bucks - and I had a chance to let my feet heal there.

It was strange - the room I was in had been the scene of a suicide earlier. It felt awful - there seemed to be a really dark energy in that whole house, but especially that room. As soon as I was able, I got myself out of there and back in the ashram.

Then another ashramite friend offered me a job driving some diplomats around L.A. while they visited the Olympics. That friend in the ashram worked in the Brazilian Embassy.

Man, what a TRIP.

Here I had been out on the street, and three weeks later I am driving the personal Physician to the President of Brazil, who had come for the Olympics! A few days later my wallet was full and there I was, shaved and spiffed up - standing in the lobby of The Beverly Hills Hotel - shaking hands with the President of Brazil.

Really.

Bizarre. No screenwriter in Hollywood would have dared make this up. True story. Yet not believable as a plot for a film . . .

Next I got a job manning a table in front of a supermarket for a political campaign. That ended but many more friends and odd jobs found me and I was surviving, and then I left the Ashram in early 1985 and lucked into a great job in racing. I started as a sales rep, and then became the National Marketing Manager, for a racing parts business.

I was back on those airplanes, smoking big cigars and driving a company car. Fat city. Or so it seemed.

But the "longing for Home" was always under the surface no matter how "good" things looked or seemed.

I was still a dreamed character try to become a "better dream character."

29. The Never-Ending Seeking

Over the next several years an enormous collection of concepts and teachings and meditations and Bhajans (devotional songs and chants) accrued to the "me" I thought (knew) I was. All of which left me highly educated in spiritual matters. Educated - and still IGNORANT.

However, Ramana's and Baba's teaching had been germinating for all that time, while I searched through many teachings, seminars, gurus, books, tapes, meditations and other "spiritual practices."

I spent much time in Muktananda's ashrams. Like Baba, Gurumayi taught, over and over as mentioned earlier, "The One you are looking for is the One who is looking."

But I STILL didn't get it.

For years and years I kept seeking - and I was getting older and more tired - as it seemed endless and fruitless.

But something always kept me going - despite the fact that I was resigned and in despair that I would EVER know "Who I Really Am."

The ego is one stubborn non-entity!

I also read and studied "A Course In Miracles" - and that was quite a challenge to my ingrained sense of who I was. The impact was almost like violence - as though I was identified as the cage in which I was a prisoner, and when these pointers - said to be channellings of The Christ - came at my cage - it felt like it was destroying me and if kept on with it I would die.

At the time I said a lot about wishing to die, wanting to die, being suicidal and so on. But the more true thought was - I damn well did NOT want to die - no matter how awful my life was.

Years later I met Marianne Williamson, the author of a book based on the principles shared in the Course - "A Return To Love." I was struck by her inner beauty, her great wit and bright intellect, and her very attractive form - but I was REALLY knocked over by her expressions of such absolute integrity and authenticity that I became newly inspired to clean up the mess once and for all.

Part Three

True Awakening

Coming Out Of The Never-Ending

The Dream- Story Of *A Separate Suffering "Me"*

Once again, Ramana's Teachings Find Me - And a

Nonduality / Self-Inquiry Phase Of Seeking begins anew

30. Arrogant Ignorance

Around the year 1999, despite so many years of studying things as diverse as Ayn Rand's Objectivism, Baba's Kashmir Shaivism, A Course In Miracles, Advaita Vedanta, Sufism, Hinduism, Buddhism, Zen, and Mystical Christianity, who I was - so to speak - for myself and most people that knew me - was still a stubborn, arrogant individual.

I was opiated, opinionated, self-righteous and domineering, a control freak, a pissed off tantrum-thrower puppet that was convinced that it was right about almost everything it knew - or thought it knew!

Somehow during this time - from 1986 through 1999 - I was able to leave my marketing job and start my own company.

(Actually I got fired! I refused to alter my spiritual seeking schedule to accommodate my bosses' request that I work an unscheduled trade show in Canada. So he said, "Okay. You are not working here any more.")

It was - as all is ultimately seen to be - a great blessing. Every single thing that happens is for the best. As it happened, I ran a quite successful sports marketing agency, working with racing drivers and teams to help then find sponsorship.

However, this was a person for whom there was always something wrong, who felt out of place, alone in a hostile world and trying to figure life out in order to survive.

This person, as others knew him, was almost a wild kind of zombie, raging around seeming to be alive but actually numb and dead inside. That me was rarely *experiencing* life and livingness.

I was a true believer in the story of ME.

And the suffering became more and more intense

Despite all the apparent "accomplishments" I took credit for, my deep down inner "mantras" were, "Something is WRONG with me," and "I CAN'T do anything right!" - and "I'm NOT good enough - in fact I am BAD." Not only that, "I don't fit in ... anywhere!" And finally, the Death Sentence ... I am on my own in a hostile world" - no doubt about THAT! This world and it's god killed off my father and my favorite uncle early on! All words forming into sentences - death sentences.

And all ultimately totally false, just beliefs, sprouting from the core belief, "I'm ME! And no one can ever tell me otherwise!!"

I put on an act of being happy but inside, I was a tired, sad, lonely guy, and once again praying, waiting and wanting to DIE.

And it seemed close - to the dismay of my son Charles - as I was very run down and had seriously clogged arteries.

I was - perhaps - a few weeks away from a heart attack - being on massive medication that didn't work any more and barely able to function physically.

Then Grace Happened. In December 1999, after suffering these ever-worsening conditions for about 15 years, I was resigned to poor health and my immanent demise. As a last ditch effort to complete my spiritual quest, I went to visit Baba Muktananda's Successor, Swami Chidvilasananda (Gurumayi.) She was in Ontario, California for a New Year's retreat - about an hour away. So once more I made the trek to the Master's Abode. After receiving her "Darshan" through two very intense "glances" on New Years Day 2000, I returned home ready to die.

Then, out of the blue, a few weeks later I received a phone call from the brother of one of her devotees offering what had been impossible to get - health insurance. Since my son Charles had made his love for me and his desire that I stay on the planet for as long as possible very clear, I accepted the offer rather than just let go and wait for the heart to stop. Charles is SO incredibly loving - and that love is in large measure why I am here today.

In any case, this salesman didn't know Gurumayi and was not a practicing yogi. He was just a regular guy who sold insurance. He had no idea I knew Gurumayi until - at my apartment to complete the paperwork - he saw a picture of her - and said with an astonished look, *"No way! Wow. My sister lives in her Ashram in upstate New York!"*

We were both stunned - and I mentally bowed my head in honor of this incredible-seeming Grace that brought what would be an impossible-to-predict physical healing that enabled this organism to be sitting here six and a half years later pecking a computer keyboard with two fingers. This insurance enabled me to get Quadruple Bypass open-heart surgery in April 2000.

Without the operation, this body would have dead.

Amazing Grace. But I STILL didn't totally" get it." Because there was still a "me!" I was still doing the sports marketing thing, but my heart wasn't really in it any more. So I was going to seminars with Landmark Education, a company formed by the employees of Werner Erhard's organization when Werner decided to leave the business. I was still looking for answers.

Then I received initiation as a Reiki Master Teacher, in 2001, from a dear Australian lady named Ruth Magdalena Smith. She was - and IS - a wonderful teacher and a very good friend. Becoming a Reiki Master was a breakthrough into a healing, freedom and joy that I had sought since 1974.

So I quit my business and began teaching Reiki full time.

I found it was pretty easy to make a small fortune teaching Reiki. Just like it was in racing. All I had to do was start with a large one - but I didn't have a large one or even a small one by now.

I was slowly going broke - and it seemed a piece was still missing.

That piece was Nonduality - or "Advaita."

Until the teachings of the Ancient Sages took over, there was still a "me" making the claim that "I am free."

That ain't freedom.

That is the egoic idea only of someone who is free.

And the arrogant idea that he can heal and free others.

It's the fabled "enlightened person."

It's totally false, despite the absolute conviction of belief in it's own reality. When that belief is still in play, then suffering is bound to return. As I was about to find out the hard way. Because there are, quite simply, no "enlightened people!"

It was like the parable of the wedding feast in the Bible - tossed out of Paradise once again - there would be much weeping and wailing and gnashing of teeth!

It would come back - like that rubber ball on a string tied to a paddle - no matter he peaceful and blissful I got, the string of self-centered identification would pull the ball back to Ground Zero over and over and over and over. And it would sneer, "*Welcome back to Hell. You belong here.*" An evilly grinning faceless being - some call that Satan - would say - "*there is NO escape - you belong to meeeeee ......!*" I needed an exorcism!

31. Paradise Found, Paradise Lost

In May of 2002 I had another deep awakening with an Indian meditation and breathing-yoga teacher called "His Holiness Sri Sri Ravi Shankar." One of my Reiki students was a devotee and invited me to meet him. I accepted out of respect for my student - I was not really looking for another Guru. But Sri Sri was definitely VERY charismatic - and really powerful.

Sri Sri, who draws 200,000 or more to his satsangs in India, had come to Los Angeles during his World Tour promoting his global service programs and his breathing course, "The Art Of Living."

I was quite taken with this charismatic little Indian guy in his white dress with the long hair and beard. He sure LOOKED the part of the Guru.

And as he was leaving the stage in a large public program, he beckoned me to come and carry his basket of chocolates, which he was playfully tossing to the immense crowd of seekers that had come for his "Darshan."

So for about forty-five minutes I was literally jammed up against him by the crushing crowd of seekers that were desperate to get close enough to touch his feet. It was really trippy! The energy - what the Indians call the Shakti - was incredibly intense. It was an energy of a HUGE LOVE. Incomprehensible yet the most real thing I had ever known.

Then at the end of that dance something shifted and I was no longer seeing the world as apart from me. I was One With All. I became convinced that THIS was the "enlightenment I had been seeking since 1975! I was ecstatic!

It was as though THE BIG IT had finally happened for real

I had gotten IT at long long last!

I was Enlightened! Me! THAT turns out to be the ultimate oxymoron. BUT - for a few weeks I felt whole, complete and ecstatic.

What was still not understood and seen was that the Experience of awakening " for a "me" - is NOT the final step. Because any experience, by its very nature, MUST end.

And so it did. Once again, there was "much weeping and wailing and gnashing of teeth".

I had seen the Promised Land and then gotten ejected.

The "I" was still very much in play – and took that temporary experience as "its own."

So there was no finality.

Soon the suffering was back and worse than ever.

Paradise had been found. But "I" was still there - and that - as I soon found out the hard way! - ain't paradise. Because any personal experience - no matter how "spiritual" or sublime - has duration in time, but no permanence!

And what is called enlightenment is totally IM-personal. But I didn't know that - nor did I know that there was something about all this that I didn't know.

That's blindness. So paradise would soon be lost.

The Devil in me would smirk one more time: *"I told you - you are MINE. You will NEVER be free."*

> *God and the Devil were chatting one day over Espresso, looking down at Creation, when they noticed an old man - all alone in a ramshackle hut - who was glowing with the Absolute Unconditional Freedom Of Divine Love.*
>
> *After decades of seeking and practices he had just given up the seeking and meditating - and BANG! He was Liberated - there was Self-Realization!*
>
> *God and Satan both saw the man had found the Absolute Truth - there was no doubt about it.*
>
> *So God said, "See, now look at him - he's found the Truth. He's FREE. So what are you gonna do now?"*
>
> *"Well," said Satan, "I'M gonna help him ORGANIZE it!"*

- Thanks, Tony Parsons!

32. No Way

The suffering continued, so I planned a trip to see Sri Sri in Northeastern Canada - a trip that ended up in terrible depression, and was cut short by several days. What was supposed to be some sublime enlightening liberating Satsang with the Master turned into a freaking nightmare. I was physically and mentally sick as a dog, and so totally frustrated that I could not get out of that place fast enough.

Sri Sri came out to the car I was sitting in waiting to be taken to Montreal Airport, and seemed concerned. But all that light and love I had experienced "from him" in Los Angeles was totally gone. There was just this nice little Indian guy in his white dress and long hair and beard, talking to me, telling me "you'll be okay." But it made no impact, and all I was left with was the immensity of despair and the conviction that once again, I had allowed myself to be conned!

There seemed to be no light at the end of this tunnel of despair – except the train that kept running me down.

Then in August 2002, on a recommendation from another devotee of Sri Sri's, I went to meet Wayne Liquorman, the author of a great book of spiritual poetry called "*No Way*," written under the pen name Ram Tzu. Wayne also authored "*Acceptance of What Is*," and "*Never Mind*."

I started attending his meetings and reading his books, and those of his Guru, Ramesh Balsekar (former translator for the Indian Master Sri Nisargadatta Maharaj), and a few other non-duality authors.

Then I got a copy of *I am That - talks with Sri Nisargadatta Maharaj*.

I fell in love with it right away, but it was a bit confusing, because Maharaj could say two apparently contradictory things, sometimes to the same seeker.

I asked Wayne about this confusion. He cleared it up by pointing out that Maharaj was not PRESCRIBING METHODS for 'gaining enlightenment.' He was in actual fact DESCRIBING the occurring of the process seekers can go through - and the process differs for different seekers.

With this new interpretation, I sailed through the book, and there was no more stumbling on concepts.

Like earnestness of seeking: My interpretation that "I" must be earnest and sincere in order to gain understanding became, "There may or must be for seekers, earnestness and sincerity."

I began to understand that all of that arises - if it does - but the seeker does not cause it.

"*You must be earnest.*" No. "There (usually, but nothing about all this is cast in stone) *must be earnestness.*

As Wayne once said, "What force makes you think you can manufacture Grace?"

Good question.

33. I am That

When Wayne Liquorman said he could not get through I *Am That*, the book of Nisargadatta Maharaj's talks, I was mystified. Because for me *I Am That* was THE BOOK – a true blockbuster of the authentic, ancient Non-Duality! Advaita Vedanta.

I had read and re-read the book and found it utterly inspiring! So I began to wonder about whether Wayne could actually "take me across" the sea of Samsara (suffering.) But his Satsang was close to my apartment and I was hoping it would produce an end to the suffering. I figured hanging out with a sage was better than just reading books.

I was so damn tired! I had been seeking forever! So hope kept me going back there despite the lack of any real help or good advice - at least to me: by many accounts Wayne has helped a lot of people - I just wasn't one of 'em! What I wasn't getting from Wayne was HOW I could investigate - how to get at whatever it was that was making me miserable. Much later I realized that in an ultimate sense there's no "how to" - because there is no doer.

During this time I offered the "Guru Seva" service of working on getting some really precious talks on Non-Duality preserved on the computer. I had the privilege of transferring to PC, and editing, about 200 audiotapes of Ramesh Balsekar taped by Wayne while Ramesh was teaching in America in the nineteen-eighties, which I then converted to Audio MP3 files so Wayne could make CDs to sell on his web site. I also did some of Wayne's talks in various places.

To do this, I had to listen fully, to see what need to be enhanced for sound quality, and for loud unnecessary noise spikes or long silences that Wayne said needed to be deleted. Through this thorough immersion in The Teachings, I finally became unalterably convinced through the words of Wayne and Ramesh - as well as Nisargadatta Maharaj and a few significant others - that that this enlightenment "I" was seeking all those years is utterly IMPERSONAL and is NOT something a "person" can "attain."

In a way this was VERY bad news. I realized that for thirty years I had been looking under the streetlight for a key that was lost by the door, but, you see, there was no light by the door so I kept looking for "it" where it ISN'T. There was still an "I" that owned this "understanding" - the mental comprehension that is the "Advaita Booby Prize!"

Hearing The Teachings did lead (seemingly) to a period of peace and prosperity I never could have predicted. What happened was, by April of 2003 I was running out of money again, and in desperation I looked for a car sales job. I landed in a Cadillac agency and ultimately became an Internet Sales manager, with a fabulous income. But that ended in May of 2004 a fit of temper and an argument with the General Manager!

Did I "choose to get fired?" That became a stimulus for fresh looking: Who is doing what I call "my life?"

But the Universe had banked a pretty good chunk of cash for me - on which the body could be fed and sheltered for a good while.

Which was great because the frustration, longing, and deep despair hit again ... big time. I could not have worked at that time.

34. Getting kicked Out Of Satsang

There IS Endless Suffering –

So of course I blame Wayne!

HE was supposed to "take me across." (So I said to myself - WAYNE never made that promise or any other promise to me.)

In any case, whatever was happening there, it wasn't working - I was suffering more than ever! So I started a new practice - a meditation called The Ishayas' Ascension. I liked it a lot – still do. But I still had the sense that it was not a "final path" - at least, not for me.

Then a <u>long</u> period of deep suffering ensued, which I hoped a final four-day retreat in Sedona, Arizona with Wayne would put an end to. No such luck! The retreat was more hell than heaven as the suffering only got worse and frustration and outrage mounted. The only thing that kept me from total insanity was Ascension meditation.

I was more miserable after that trip than ever! So I wrote an e-mail to Wayne, and told him, approximately, *"I am simply, very, very tired of living. This path is crap. I am getting worse and worse. Every day, I pray to die. I don't know when or if I will see you again. At this point I have no plans of any sort for any activity whatever.*

I suppose I was really hoping the retreat would provide whatever is missing for me to be happy, prosperous and productive but obviously that hope was empty. As usual, it seems, after 30 years of the same old same old seeking, I'm finding only ultimate disappointment and despair. I guess we will have to wait and see what my destiny is. I sure don't know. I do know I pray to die, and I am sick and tired of feeling this despair."

Wayne did not respond.

Later I read in "No Way," "*Ram Tzu does not give advice. Whom would he give it to?*"

Very Very Very Zen.

Finally, in late 2004, the Ego-Mind-ME got TOTALLY fed up, frustrated, and exhausted. I was SUPER pissed. And I let Wayne know I was pissed.

And suicidal and frustrated in the extreme at him for his lack of empathy.

I was heavy into the Blame Game - being a self-righteous victim - without being really aware of that.

Wayne responded by summarily ordering me to never come to his Satsang in Hermosa Beach ever, ever again!

That was PERFECT as it turned out! Because it opened NEW doors along the path - that made a huge difference.

Ultimately this led me to my "final teachers" - John Wheeler, "Sailor" Bob Adamson, Byron Katie, and Tony Parsons.

Anyway, at this stage the only book I could really stand to read any more was *I am That*. I thought, yeah, Nisargadatta definitely knows what the hell is Real – and what is NOT. But, the guy is DEAD and I need someone who can cut into the crap and answer my questions.

At this juncture I had been a "Spiritual Seeker" for over thirty years. Tried everything, most of it twice. And I realized that I had had more gurus than girlfriends - that suddenly became ludicrous. (I had not had an intimate relationship with a woman for 18 years at that point!)

So I guess it is safe to say that I had gotten pretty damn disgusted with the "Spiritual Path."

I searched the Internet for painless ways to kill myself - for over a year. But I simply didn't have the balls to go through with it. And sometimes when suicidal thoughts would arise, the Ascension meditation phrases would also arise and quell the disturbance - for a while at least.

But the crap always came back.

It seemed that there really was NO escape - as Tony Parsons has been pointing out for years.

I need to listen.

I needed a friend.

And along came Tony - right on timeless time!

35. Endless Fruitless Seeking - Then Here Came Tony

After 30 years of this endless fruitless seeking, while living a life of not quiet, but very LOUD, desperation, I happened onto a website for an ordinary but utterly charming British gentleman named Tony Parsons.

There it was! I newly discovered a Loving Presence that exuded from behind the words - I call that "resonance." Some of this resonance had occurred when I was working with Werner Erhard in 1978-79, and Baba Muktananda as well - and I had heard the term from various Advaita teachers - but it was only a dry, useless concept, at best a memory.

Until Tony.

I bought a CD from his website straight away.

I had wished and hoped to one day really get, really *experience*, that delicious resonance, and aha! Here it was, arising unsought, through his CDs of meetings - as I sat listening to this regular guy talking with other regular gals and guys, there was a sense that arose, this might just be IT, and this light at the end of the endless tunnel might, just might, NOT be the damn TRAIN again! Tony's words resonated in me and the natural Space within ME that Tony was pointing at just knocked me sideways (Tony's term) – right into a deep experience of pure Love. I thought finally, there IS someone besides a dead sage who knows what this is and is talking clearly about it!

The only problem was, he was in England and I was in California, so going to sit with him was not very practical. Despite that I nearly went over for a retreat in Wales anyway, but it filled up and I could not get a place. So I had to settle for tapes and books and CDs, but those actually resonated very deeply with me. (They still do - I love listening to Tony!) I KNEW without a doubt that Tony was the Real Deal! He KNEW this. If HE knew it I could know it too! Hot dang. Light at the end of the tunnel? Maybe this time - yes!

Since Tony was so far away I was still looking around and found a site where books on nonduality were offered - and one of the authors was a nice fellow named John Wheeler - who was in Santa Cruz, California.

So I connected with John and we talked, e-mailed and met - and there was another crisp and clear awakening. But there was still the flip-flop in and out of that state - at least, so it seemed to "me."

36. Depression and Awakening

After meeting with John Wheeler, I was once again thinking, "*I have got it.*" That is - it's seen that there is NO "me" - the person is a phantom. Unreal. But there was still some suffering from time to time. Why, I wondered.

I called Tony at his home in England to see if I could get this last seeming issue handled. Got a voice mail, so I left a message, telling him I really hoped we could talk.

Truthfully, I did not really expect him to call me back.

But much to my very pleasant surprise Tony DID call, on New Years Day of 2005. To para a phrase, he blew "me" - not "away," but HERE. Tony's Heart blew me nowhere. Now. Here. Wow.

I told him I was a fake. He laughed. Then we talked about being half-baked - trying to teach from an unfinished place - and how this identity of a separate "me" kept coming back in and making me miserable. Tony pointed out that this is a kind of addiction - the addiction to being "me." But it wasn't the words that I loved - it was the Space. Tony clearly is not there - as an identity. He - and you - and I - ARE that Space.

After that brief but glorious conversation with Tony there was another long period where there was freedom - Being Nothing and Everything. That was another undeniable Awakening Into that Eternal True-Nature. Once again I was HOME.

However - that persistent "I-sense" was still there. There was still a "me." CLAIMING, "Now I have GOT it!" And I can give SATSANG. I did. But nobody came! Nobody really was buying that "Charlie is now a sage."

Then through 2005 I continued to dialogue with John Wheeler, who also introduced me to Joan Tollifson, another source for Non-Duality. Her book "*Awake in the Heartland*" is highly recommended.

I was worrying that taking anti-depressant medication would inhibit the unfolding for me. So e-mailed Joan to set up a phone conversation because for some reason I thought she knew about that stuff.

Her reply by e-mail, before we ever spoke on the phone was that she "*saw no contradiction between Prozac and clarity.*"

Then when we spoke it sank in. The body-mind is a machine. Machines need stuff, like cars - fuel (food) and sometimes "Additives" for old engines. Medication for body - heart stuff for example - and brain - like antidepressants for those of us who have either DNA such that the brain does not produce seratonin or when there has been a brain injury. Both were so in my case! But arrogant and stubborn pride had me thinking that it was something I "should" be able to "overcome on my own with no professional help." Dumb? Oh, hell yes.

But that was a terrific conversation with Joan, as we discussed depression and those sorts of seeming barriers. When Joan said again, something like, "*None of that has anything to do with the Clarity*" something else dropped off and there was more peace.

Nonduality author Leo Hartong helped tremendously at this point. Here is a dialogue that took place around that time in Leo's newsletter - this appeared on www.awakeningtothedream.com. An insight happened that turned out to be somewhat pivotal: Here is an e-mail I sent at the time ...

Leo, in your latest newsletter, I read, *first I would advise you to make sure that there is no mental or physical reason for the way you feel. Perhaps you ascribe it to the seeking while it also could be a chemical imbalance in the system. Who knows what your travels have done to the body.*

Indeed! This was an issue here - this body-mind had been brutally abused for much if its 68 years by hard living, including that serious head-banger back-wrenching crash in a race car. And a number of life-threatening illnesses including a heart issue that required quadruple bypass surgery. Plus many years of drug and alcohol abuse.

When examined by experts it was found to *absolutely require* medication. But the ego resisted medication thinking it was not "spiritual."

Since resuming that medication, gradually all the confusion was seen for what it is - a mechanical breakdown.

The engine of a car needs oil and gas.

This old body-mind machinery needs medicine, as it needs food. That would be that way until it wasn't.

And by 15 July 2006 - it wasn't that way any more.

Grace.

Leo's post went on with, "Awareness sees the thoughts appear as bubbles in a glass of sparkling water, all by themselves without a thinker pushing the bubbles into existence."

I wrote, Leo, this describes just exactly what has been unfolding here. Seeing with no seer, hearing with no hearer, thought appearing with no one thinking. Just this. Ordinary beauty. That devastating sense of a suffering "me" has faded and all there is, is This. But even AS the suffering occurs on occasion, there is a knowing that even the "suffering" is Oneness appearing AS that! *That too.* Oneness is all there is. NO exceptions. Poof.

And, *You say that "a life is being lived through this body" - I am not so fond of this "living through" concept and prefer to say that Life appears AS the body mind; just like clay does not appear through the shapes it assumes, but AS those shapes.*

What arises here is to say that there is elegance, glory and affinity in "your" articulation and gentle pointing back to what is. Just Beautiful. Thank you!

Thank you so much for the gift that your eloquence and clarity is to other seekers who may have this issue and not even be aware of it! If it comes up to share it with others feel completely free to do so. I have no secrets.

I so appreciate the Wisdom that you and Joan and Tony share!

I Love You, Leo. As the Self that we are in Truth.

37. Control

For me, this spiritual path stuff is all very like racing. For example, spinning out at 180 MPH in a race car. After the ride is over people say, "Wow, you did a great job controlling the car!" Bull-pucky. NOBODY CONTROLS ANYTHING. We are just along for the ride.

I look for the one in charge. What is it? Where is it? There certainly appears that *something* is causing it all. But that ain't "ME." I have no claim to be in control of ANYTHING. How can Nothing control anything?

Okay, I get it ... It is all Oneness. Whether it is "experienced" at the moment or not. Oneness Just IS. ALL that Is. There is no "me." And that "me" that thinks it IS "me" is Oneness "Me-Ing." It is my clear understanding now that all of it – the whole manifestation, including the wisdom AND the ignorance, IS LOVE. And sometimes Love looks like Not-Love! But, *Am "I" Finished? NO.*

> *A knowledge of Sanskrit is of little use to the man trapped in a sewer.*
>
> - Anonymous

No "I" can ever be "finished." That is what I have heard over and over. But it is not yet real for this one. It is a knowledge of Sanskrit but I am still in the sewer. My mind is still busy claiming that it - me - is the managing director of my life - and man, does it suck. Because I know better! Shit, and two makes eight.

There is still something wrong.

Nisargadatta said, nothing is wrong. *Yeah, well, he didn't live in MY head,* I think to myself. In an endless loop-de-loop of circular grooved in thinking about the fact that I am here and separated still, and that me has something seriously wrong with it. I am guessing, I am just a hopeless case, no wonder Wayne kicked me out. Yeah baby. What a whirlpool. Life sucks still. Thirty goddam years of this spiritual crap and what has it gotten me? Old and broke. So something IS really bad wrong with me - and this world. I look around and all I see is suffering.

I am suffering.

Death and taxes. Love comes to pass, never to stay. I am tired of waiting and want to drop, but I cannot do a damn thing about this seeking that now has me in its grip so completely that I couldn't even freakin' kill myself!

To be or not to be! That sleep of death sure looked good from my head. And I shore nuff did want to go to sleep and not wake up.

I can imagine what any who is reading this must be thinking. Jeez, why <u>didn't</u> he kill himself?!?

GOOD question.

Despite feeling like a rag doll in the mouth of that cosmic sheep dog, or "Tiger" - the "One doing the Work" – it continues. Life living me – so to say. Wayne one said, something like, once the anti-virus of Advaita gets into you it is like Cancer. It spreads until it eats you alive. Replaces you with Itself - Oneness.

Here at the time it was more like getting burned almost to death. And not being able to get to actual death, release.

Now I know what they mean by "eternal hellfire." It ain't over there or down there. It's HERE. When it is.

But somehow I trust the Unfolding that is occurring, not because of "me" but in spite of "me" - with help from John Wheeler, "Sailor Bob Adamson, Byron Katie, John Wheeler's friend John Greven, and Tony Parsons - I have a faint glimmer of that light at the end of the tunnel.

So how come I am still here trying to convince myself?

Jeez, it is tiring having to pretend to be nothing!!!

38. The Final Truth?

There IS no such thing.
Period.
This Is It.
Is it?

I Do Not Know.

(Maybe THAT is the "Final Truth.")

I don't know.

Is anyone in control here?
Or wherever *you* are right now right now right now?

39. Final Understanding - NOT

As I was sharing my experience on my website and blog - a seeker asked, *Is The Search Done For You?*

I replied, Short answer ... yes and no.

REAL short answer ... NO.

Accurate answer: There is no seeker, never was. (Bullshit. But really lovely bullshit!)

Does exist. Cannot be expressed. - David Carse

So Spirit has grabbed me by the ass today and sat me in front of this stupid laptop and pecks away. This will go on as long as it does and whatever appears here will be MORE bullshit.

OK? Ohhh ... kay ... here is my Bullshit Long Answer:

See, I spoke earlier today with a guy who has been reading and listening to "Advaita Teachers" for a while now. He called to talk about the "understanding" or "enlightenment" - whatever label one likes - and I told him that so far as I am concerned, I am not "enlightened," and that there are no "enlightened people." He liked that ... hell, he's a New Yorker. Certain lack of bullshit in that culture, ya know whaddimean?"

Here is my take on this spiritual trip: there are people who seek "Self Realization" or "Ultimate Understanding" - been there done that. Got dozens of trophy pictures. And mantras. And practices. And a zillion books. I throw 'em all out or give 'em away, then buy the same goddam books again! Duh. (But wait ... WHO "does" all that?") Oh geezus MORE Advaita-speak! * I * freakin' do that!

But what the hell ... of course I believe in free will. See, I have no choice in the matter!

There are other people who seek for years and reach an understanding that, to paraphrase, "I am nothing." But there still is, sometimes at least, someone who thinks or believes he or she is Nothing. Lot's of so-called "Satsang Teachers" have that one going - also been there and done that.

Then there are some famous saints or sages, like Ramana Maharshi.

Sri Nisargadatta Maharaj. Buddha. Jesus. Shirdi Sai Baba. Nityananda of Ganeshpuri. The Real Deal.

At least so I believe! But they are dead, so we can't go "get what they got." Some of us go walk around their statues or tombs or the mountain they called their Guru, and worship that as the Guru. Been there, done that. Got the t-shirt. Even got a little $120 (!) statue of one of these dead sages! Don't get me wrong - I love that little "murti." But is that statue really the Guru?

How about sincere devotees of LIVING "Sages / Saints /Gurus" - say, like Maharishi Mahesh Yogi, or Gurumayi Chidvilasananda, or Sri Sri Ravi Shankar? Or various "downline" Sages - or wannabe sages - from their "traditions?" Or the DEAD ONE'S traditions? Been there done that got the orange clothes and the red dot. The fat belly and the suspenders. The Sanskrit vocabulary.

Or worse yet, how about those sincere devotees of apparent "Saint/Sage/Gurus" who then get totally crazy and did/do things like have sex with their devotees – or worse, with children - or bug the shit outta their followers for money, and build huge monuments to themselves in one way or another?

And they keep justifying that crap by saying, "Oh, it's ALL just the Play of the Oneness, the Totality." The truth (even if true) does not justify a goddam thing. Advaita? NO. It's Bullcrap.

Then there are the deluded dream characters who are very articulate and have brilliant clarity and express the non Dual Teachings with eloquence, wit and wisdom AND with whom their acolytes or followers rave about the "CLEAR POINTING" and subtly keep their dream-self alive by worshiping them in some way or another. Been there done that played that game no joy in mudville.

Then finally there are people who seem to have "Become Liberated" or who no longer have any sense of being an entity. But how the hell can we - as dreamed characters that are sleepwalking through "life" - know who or where or what they really are?

There seems to be no "reliable test" for who is authentic and who is not. See, some very good hearted, sincere, caring people end up talking about this stuff and sharing what they have come to understand or realize or "see." But in so many cases, there is still a "person" with a (sometimes very subtle) hidden agenda ... he or she wants "you" to "get" what "they" know.

These are the ones who are so good at pretending that they even fool themselves! At least for a while.

Been there done that got the burned bridges and emotional scars!

But ultimately, the clear space of the One TRUE Self must reveal that there are tendencies that remain, in the organism. Call it conditioning, or programming, or ego, there is still a subtle little feeling-sense of a separate me, where the True Sages see NO separation.

Self has done that here (in the Charlie organism) a number of times. People cringe, then shrug. Whaddya gonna do? Rocks are hard, water's wet, and the dance is the dance. It IS as it IS.

Anyway - while chatting with my friend this morning - what came out of my mouth was the truth as it is "for me". I said, yes, I still have a "me" sense. Granted it is faded and hardly believed in any more, but ... or perhaps AND ... it still shows up. Tony Parsons calls this an (apparent) process that happens over (apparent) time. He makes a distinction: In concepts, "Awakening" - clear seeing followed by falling for the lies of the mind-ego that "I" that still exist (or seems to) as an entity - and "Liberation" at which pointless point there is literally nobody home. In the latter there IS NO separation, no entity, no creation, no dissolution, just The One, Awake, seeing its dream AS a dream.

So the long answer to the question, is the search over here, is ... sometimes. And that ain't hay. Life is a helluva lot more peaceful (less mental chatter, more clear seeing) - but it is understood here that this state of affairs, while pleasant and peaceful, is NOT the "Final Understanding" as Ramesh Balsekar has called it, or "Liberation" as Tony calls it, or "Final Truth" as Ramana Maharshi dubbed it, or "Awakening to the Dream" as Leo Hartong puts it, or "Nobody Home" as writer Jan Kerschott puts it. Or "The Natural State" (which I understand as NO state at all) as quite a few are putting it these days. So - there is deep comprehension - of these "spiritual concepts/precepts" - here. So what? So nothing. That and three bucks gets ya a fancy cuppa coffee. The "Understanding" the Sages point to has got nothing to do with comprehension!

The search has ended for Charlie in that there are no questions that the "Teachings" don't spontaneously answer. So there are really NO questions any more. And I understand perfectly, as wonderful guys like Nathan Gill point out, that all there is is space, and in the space stories arise.

Then the me which is itself a story keeps believing it is real, an entity, THEN believes that IT is enlightened and now can "show others the way home."

It becomes one of those deluded dream-toy puppets, one of many a dream character that is very articulate and has brilliant clarity and expresses the nondual teachings with eloquence, wit and wisdom. But as Tony Parsons tries to remind us, CLARITY HAS NOTHING WHATSOEVER TO DO WITH AWAKENING, OR LIBERATION.

LOOK ... IF all there is, is Oneness, who the hell is there to show anyone and who the hell is there to be shown?!? "We has met the enemy and he is US." (Comic strip character Pogo, by Walt Kelly.) So who to listen to? Who to trust? Who to believe? Who to follow? NO ONE. Trusting, following, talking, believing, awakening, liberation ... like the tides coming in and out, happen when they happen. If at all. And, I hear tell, they happen to no one. No person!

A former friend, the outrageous Wayne Liquorman (who kicked me out of his Satsang, thank God), puts it this way: "This process is like having sex with a 500 pound gorilla. You ain't done till the gorilla's done." In other words, you and me, we is SCREWED.

So: Let's you and me go have a cuppa coffee or a martini or a brewskie and see if there's any good lookin' single women around who wanna get frisky tonight. Since I have had more gurus than girl friends, I got some catching up to do!

Meanwhile, if you still believe there is someone to awaken and someone who is awake, you can explore the various Teaching expressions linked on www.awake-now.org. There are a few that I trust based on my own direct experience. But that does NOT mean that if you see or hear or meet them or read their divine bullshit, that you will get whatever the hell it is that is happening here to the Charlie machinery.

So Seek On.

Go ahead.

You have no choice but to "exercise your free will." Just don't get any on the walls.

40. IT Happens

Meeting Tony Parsons by his CDs - and meeting John Wheeler in person in December of 2004 - seemed like it was the kind of the beginning of the end of all the suffering and searching for the Eternal Stateless State of Reality.

However doubts and confusion still seemed to return again and again to overshadow the simple awareness of Being that John, Tony and others had had pointed to as the "Natural State" which the seeker longs for.

Therefore I engaged that stuff, over several months of frustrating dialogue, plagued by persistent-seeming doubts. Amid my frustration John suggested rather strongly that I get my butt down to Melbourne to see HIS Teacher, "Sailor" Bob Adamson. John threw enough loving and compassionate heat my way that I finally figured, screw it if I go broke, I have GOT to get to Australia!

So, I finally went to Melbourne, in September 2005. What happened there was reported in the book "From I Am To I Am, With Love." I rejoiced in the clarity.

Back home, I was certain that "I had seen the promised land" - yet I remained somewhat frustrated - and then I began convincing myself that "I Finally Got It."

Ooops! Time for a Reality Check! This "IT" cannot be possessed by the person – as would become abundantly and painfully clear. I knew that! But it still caught me out.

After returning to California, there were dialogues with Bob, and with John Wheeler's students John Greven and Annette Nibley.

But I continued to labor under a delusion, "I've gotten freedom for real," or the opposite, "I am still not home." Through no fault of theirs, of course. All any friend – or sage – can do, is point from where they are (nowhere) to that which the seeker might be missing.

Now I was seeing - In the quiet space of my bedroom at three AM I know - either "I am" or "I am not" "enlightened" are false ideas - and yet there was no real freedom and the often-pointed to "Uncaused Joy Of Being." Not here.

I could convince myself that I Am That for a while.

But that always bites me in the ass - sooner or later. I was certifiable but couldn't admit it.

The con man cons himself.

Then on around July 7th 2006 the search ended. Again? Oh dear - what does that actually mean? Just this. The clear understanding that all questions are answered and all doubts essentially resolved - or dissolved.

It was not that I found what I was seeking. What I found is that there is nothing to attain and no one to attain it. I Am - Being, just that.

Nothing was wrong any more. There never was.

That lasted for four months this time. But it faded again – and then it starts up all over again - thoughts tell me there is a me and that there is something that should not be as it is!

And at this stage I am comforted by the fact - if that happens now – that I have the understanding of what is Real – and I have Self-Inquiry!

Asking Who Am I?

Or The Work of Byron Katie.

Waking up to the dream, all there is is . . .

What Is. As It Is.

Full non-conceptual freedom, just That.

Unattainable - because it IS what we are.

No cause - no effect. Just - This.

No one wakes up!

No one is actually asleep.

Wherever we go, whenever it is – here we are, as we are – and that is all there is to this journey's end.

Loving to be.

41. Night Dreams, Waking Dreams, Reality

Who, or what, awakens a dream character from the dream at night? Can that character know he is a dreamed character? No. Only the body-mind dreamer can awaken and see that it was in fact only a dream, not real. And that the subject-character and all the objects - scenery, other characters etc - were never actually real at all. It only seems real to a dreamed character, never to the body-mind dreamer.

So who awakens the "person" to the realization that what he thinks of as his or her life is actually only a dream, exactly like the sleeping-dream, except with more seeming persistence and solidity? Can a person... a dreamed character arising in the Self - the Dream-er in this metaphor - ever wake itself up?

Upon awakening in the morning, perhaps a vivid dream is remembered - sometimes even with fondness for the characters. (I recall a number of such dreams where there were wonderful lovers!) But there is no delusion about these characters having any substance or existence whatsoever.

I also recall a series of night dreams where there was a seeming continuity - some character from previous dreams reappeared, and all sorts of prior dream-events were remembered, giving seeming continuity to a story that seemed real and alive. But only to the "me" in that dream.

This waking dream is precisely the same with the added dimensions of apparent persistence and solid sensible continuity. This appearance, called Maya in the East, is the magical dark woolen veil of the Dreamer pulling the wool over the eyes of its own True Nature, so to say. Why? It just happens.

No one can answer why (though many try, doomed to the ultimate realization that it is a mystery of magnificent proportions.)

In Reality there is no dreamed character. How could there be? The "you" that you think you are blows totally away in the seeing that all there IS, is the Dreamer - the Self - and nothing else has any actual solidity or persistence, any more than the at-night-asleep-dream does.

The search for joy and peace, or liberation, is all over then.

The play continues as long as the organism lives. But there is no possibility that once the Dreamer has awakened to its Self so to speak, that any belief that all of this play is real and separate from the Dreamer can be sustained. Even if a delusion arises it is quickly – or eventually - seen as what it is - by the Dreamer - as insubstantial.

And Poof. It's gone. (Again, 'so to speak;' the Dreamer is not separate from what is seen; words always fail!)

The pointer is that all efforts by a dream character to wake himself or herself to what REALLY IS cannot possibly succeed, any more that a nighttime dream-person can satisfy an urge to empty the bladder by peeing into a dream toilet. (I have had the experience of attempting that as a dreamed character many times; fortunately the body-mind wakes up and shuffles off to the bathroom just in time to avoid ruining the bed sheets!)

The dream-reality at night is only real to the dreamed character, never to the body-mind dreamer.

The bigger longer more seemingly connected event-by-event called the "waking state" is exactly the same only much more elaborate. That's all.

When the Dreamer wakes her Self to her Self, then it becomes a celebration of aliveness, but not for the person. There is no enlightened meat. Only the Dreamer - Oneness, The Self, True-Nature, whatever concept you like, can know that there never was a dream.

The Dreamer Her-Self arises in thought as Self Inquiry. Asking the last question, the one that counts, dissolving Her dream - Who Am I?

We think <u>we</u> do it.

And so it does seem! The belief that we cannot do it is leads to just as much suffering as the belief that we can, in the so-called process.

In fact, we do nothing. But that - as a belief - can create a load of despair.

Doing happens. Including for some fortunate patterns, Inquiry. Call it Grace, or any other label - it is simply Self arising to see Self, One becoming many, folding back into One ... the Dream of the Source.

Paradox.

Beautiful stuff, this apparent creation.

Literally incomprehensible in magnitude.

To me, awe and humility are inevitable when this Magnificence arises and there is no one to see it.

Loving to be. Just that, and all is well.

Wakey wakey.

> There seem to two kinds of searchers: those who seek to make their ego something other than it is, i.e. holy, happy, unselfish (as though you could make a fish unfish), and those who understand that all such attempts are just gesticulation and play-acting, that there is only one thing that can be done, which is to disidentify themselves with the ego, by realizing its unreality, and by becoming aware of their eternal identity with pure being.
>
> - Wei Wu Wei

42. Awakening To The Original State

Do I exist? Space-like Awareness, evident and real, before time or thought - IS. Then a thought, arising to represent - RE-Present in another way - THAT Space - Consciousness - Oneness - pick a label!

THAT which I am and YOU are. That non-thought is a silent YES.

Then aloud, there is only YES. I am aware, I have never NOT been aware.

As I write this, I am calm. I have nothing to convince you or myself of. I am, to borrow a phrase from Ramesh Balsekar, *Anchored In Peace And Harmony*.

I see that doubts or old patterns and fur-balls of thought arise from habit, from my sixty-odd years of conditioning. But as these energy patterns are seen to form from nothing at all, they are simply seen and they dissolve. Without disturbing the peace.

In the past when I had an awakening, and then a crash, and there were many such events, there was a real, deep despair that totally took me over. Sometimes I would sleep 18 hours a day and be barely be able to function.

That had not been occurring during this unfolding. All that happened was that a worrying mind activated.

One morning at about 3 AM a Non-Event occurred.

I awoke to a warm sensation in my chest, which was exactly like being deep in love but with no object of affection. I enjoyed this for an hour or so, and went back to sleep. When I woke again at about Seven AM the sense of separation was no longer there.

The seeker was simply no longer there except as a remnant, a sort of holographic transparent identity that was never real. Seen through, it is now just an appearance, and what is seen is the Always Radiant Light that gives the Holographic apparent entity the appearance of a thing. It is seen as only an APPARENT object with apparent properties.

But it's a character formed of nothing by no one with no author and no audience.

That character would return again and again to claim its own absence.

However - there is always that love and unshakable peace as the background Awareness on which the dance of life is seen and loved.

<u>Whether it is noticed or not</u>!

In a way of speaking it - this is a deep space of impersonal knowingness itself. Regardless of how life shows up.

I hit my ankle on a footstool the following day, and there was an "OW," three unprintable words, and it was all over in a few seconds. And then there simply the presence of pain for no one. After a half hour or so the pain had just melted away.

For me this has to be a new record for the shortest temper tantrum EVER.

In the past that incident would have produced a half hour of suffering. (Thoughts, seen as real for a real me, would take over and there would be a long inner dialogue about the stupid idiot I was who could never anything right, such a freakin' loser and on and on. Feelings of helpless rage. And a deep sadness and despair would often set in. And more Yada Yada Yada Yada Ad Nauseaum). This time there was NO suffering.

As I get accustomed to this seemingly new presence-awareness, it continues to delight and enliven me in unpredictable ways. <u>Being</u> this Oneness - I don't HAVE it, NO ONE HAS IT - IS The Peace That Passeth Understanding. THAT - What Is - IS Impersonal Awareness Presencing.

Anyway, being - dwelling as - this unshakable peace - is sort of like riding through a ghetto in an armored Rolls - and at the same time realizing it is all a movie and there never was or is any danger to That which we are. That truly IS invincible Eternal. Untouchable. Unbreakable.

THAT is solid infinity - that always was-is-will-be THAT IS EVER FRESH - THAT was-is-will-be - in THAT there is no past, future OR even a "Present!"

This IS wholeness, completeness. Space. Infinite. Being.

Alone (all one.) There is NOTHING missing. (And NOTHING Present!) There is nothing wrong any more. There never was; it was all a soap opera.

Nothing is good or bad, right or wrong, except that thinking makes it appear so

– Paraphrasing Shakespeare

Nothing is Sacred. So Is Everything! No one sees that. It never leaves. It cannot - IT is the Energy that is keeping the stars apart. One of my good friends calls it "Creative Intelligence." That Intelligence that becomes intelligent when Consciousness becomes Conscious.

All this naturally unfolded as the insight became a firm conviction, for no one, that whatever is happening IS the Understanding WORKING. Perfectly.

43. The Eternal Is

The Eternal
IS
Our Natural
Self-Luminous
Always So
Awareness-
Presence-
Affinity
How Does Awakening
To That Unfold?
Through Looking?
I do not know.

44. The Unborn

who
is Un-Born
on a summer-winter Day?
what is this "me" with a "name"?
a concept.

what is a concept?

Something formed in the mind; a thought or notion.
conceit, fancy, image, coinage of the brain,
brain-creation brainchild, notion, idea . . .
And what about . . .
Awareness-Presence
before conception/conceptualizing?
that IS . . . NO - me
!

45. I Think Therefore I Am. Really?

I am That

You Are That

All Of This is Nothing but That.

So the sages tell us.

But what the hell is this THAT they keep yakking about??

Yakkety Yak! Don't Talk Back!

The sages tell us all kinds of stuff.

Are we supposed to just believe these sweeping statements? So then we can go around thinking "I am That" and offering "Satsang?"

Been there. Done that. Got a dozen red Sanyasi style t-shirts. No joy there. Just a "me" claiming loudly, "I am Nothing." Hey, so long as there is a me that thinks it is nothing, that ain't nothing. Is it?

That is something busy *pretending* it is nothing! Right?

So some of those same guys tell us, "Inquire" ... find OUT Who You Are. *Then* you will discover "You ARE That."

"You must LOOK and look deeply within." So I did that. For thirty some years in many bizarre and exotic ways.

After all that was done with, there was still a "me" claiming either "I Got It" or going the opposite way, "I Do Not Got it" ... and variations... "I had it but I lost it" and "I always had it but it is obscured" and all such bullshit.

It's all about "me" taking up the oxymoronic idea that there is a nothing (a thing called no thing!) to "get" and that "I CAN get It."

As a heard one guy who always says, "Everything is Consciousness" say, "If you chase your own tail long enough and hard enough you MIGHT disappear up your own asshole."

Yeah, sure.

So after all this stupid seeking for something or someone that would settle my hash so I could be free and happy, what have I got to?

This:

Just This - As It Is.

All the questions about Spirituality, God, Self, Self-Realization, Enlightenment, Advaita, Non-Duality etc etc ad Nauseaum are answered.

"I know this shit."

And, if questions come up like "What is Real," What Is My True-Nature," Who AM I?" - the questions CAN loop right back to one of these "sayings of the sages:"

"I am That," "All There Is This," "whatever is IS, as it is," "All there is is Consciousness," and my personal favorite "In my hut this spring, there is nothing, there is everything."

All of which along with three bucks gets you a Latte at Bucky's. Which at least will get your blood moving!

So what?

So this: Having a look at the frustration and the despair of thirty some years getting nothing but still being someone who is there claiming "I am Nothing," I began to look at a whole nother thing.

Who is this "I" that thinks IT is Nothing (or something or a body or whatever?"

"I Think Therefore I AM?"

El Toro PooPoo.

Who Am I?

I don't know.

Good answer.

Better one - "It Is Known." By no one.

Best One?

s i l e n c e

>"Whereof one cannot speak,
> thereof one must remain silent.
>
> - Wittgenstein

46. Who Is Thinking?

I am thinking (WHO is Thinking) that the unseen MATRIX of all of this may lie in the assumption that this Descartes dude was "right."

But what if he was just another "me" claiming to be right about something that may in fact be totally UN knowable?

I think therefore I am answers the questions neatly. Because now I KNOW what am, because a thought I AM tells me that I am a thought!

So I am the thinker. Clearly. Right?

The box that thinking comes in is this sort of Core Thought, invented by some GUY who had nothing better to do than sit around and make this up.

"I think therefore I am."

And what if that too is bullshit?

OK. Now maybe I am onto something ... I get a little excited about it. But who is excited? And where is this "I" that thinks IT is excited?"

I am crazy but I cannot see that I am crazy because when I see I am crazy I am sane. Catch 22?

Sheesh!

Well, OK, what again is thinking?

Oh god. That is a whole nother can of worms. Ask anyone who has read Martin Heidegger.

Is faith the secret?

Right back atcha:

WHO or WHAT is it that THINKS IT IS TRUSTING IN FAITH?

No hope, no joy there either. Oh, maybe for a week or two, while the glee that permeates all these "Spiritual Highs" lasts. But then it is right back to the default state: "Life Sucks. Then you die."

So NOW what?

Nothing. This is just a RANT. It is not going anywhere.
I think therefore I am.
I am therefore I think.
It's all machinery. Mental masturbating.
IT goes, Think think think!
Think think think!
That stuff is like a computer program.
Running amok.
Is any of it TRUE?
Who says it is?
Who says it isn't?
Who?

Be . . . In Not Knowing . . .

47. HOS: Human Operating System

It's like the body is a computer and the mind is the Operating System. Like DOS - Disk Operating System.

Let's call it HOSS.

Human Operating System Stupid.

HOSS is built with endless loops: If this GOTO that. If That GOTO another LOOP which says IF this GO to END. If End GOTO Begin. Etc.

In other words, it loops endlessly back in on itself with NO true END. The label END takes it back to BEGIN and the whole goddamn rigmarole continues: "World Without End Amen."

Amen I say to you, we is royally screwed.

Royally.

Trying to get out of the loop by thinking makes as much sense as trying to end a program by rebooting the computer. There might be silence for a while the machinery resets itself, but it can never last.

OH, by the way, THIS hardware, the so-called human body, is the sort of computer that is self-starting, self-running, and self-rebooting. It is a perpetual motion machine that needs NO external power.

How do we STOP? Well- If I knew that I would open an ashram in Lucknow or Mountain View.

Who is gonna STOP? The I that thinks it is me?

That sucker is only a thought.

Freakin' Descartes.

It's not even MY thought!

What If: You and I have never EVER had ONE original thought?

Where does thought come from? Who wrote the Source Code for HOSS?

That, dear boys and girls, is a freakin' MYSTERY.

What if there IS no author!?

So that is all there is to say about that.

48. A Fake Seeker And A Fake Sage

My rant continues with a made-up dialogue with a Sage:

Note - there ain't no sage - this is actually a monologue, I'm just calling it a dialogue.

It is a conversation of the programmed mind with itself. Like the so-called talks with god preachers claim.

Kaka PooPoo.

It has NO point or purpose; it's just a RANT!

For ease of reading the "*Sage*" *will appear in Italics.*

OK, here we go:

Sage: You are all there is. You are the Self of All. You are freedom itself.

Me: Oh yeah? Then how come I don't have a good job, if I am all that is? I should be able to 'create' any job I want if I am what YOU say I am.

But all that is includes the job or no job, my son.

Oh bullshit. What possible value can this information have for me? I am old, depressed, tired and going broke sooner rather than later. Haven't you got some answers for me? I need to know how to make my LIFE work!

Ahhh. You need to do self-inquiry, my son. Who is it that needs to know? Who is it that CAN "make "your" life work?

Shit. Well, OK, I have tried everything else. I got more Gurus than girl friends. I know more Sanskrit than English. What the bleep, go ahead. Now what?

Just look at these questions as I say them and see what arises in the space. Take a good long look, and then tell me what you observe. First Question? WHO is thinking?

Well, I am. I am thinking.

Alright, STOP thinking.

Hunh? How do I do THAT? I can't stop thinking. Oh crap! Now I am thinking, "how do I stop thinking?"

Very good. Now: WHO is thinking?

I told you, I am.

All right. NOW who is thinking?

I am! I AM. What the hell is the POINT of this? It's the same endless loop!

Fine, you are doing fine. Do you see that this loop always goes right back to "I" when you ask, "Who is thinking?"

That's what I just said! Now I am really getting pissed. This is just more of the same bullshit I have been going through forever. WHAT is your POINT?

Excellent. All right, now, WHO is "Pissed" Who is angry.

I am! Oh, crap, there it is again. It is ALWAYS there. There is ALWAYS that "I am" whenever there I am. See? There it is again. There is no escape! I am an endless LOOP of I am Thoughts. How do I get out?

You don't.

What? Oh shit. You are kidding, right? I thought enlightenment or whatever you supposedly teach was supposed to set me free?

Nope.

(long silence)

(Much Thinking. Feeling. Hearing. Seeing. Experiencing.)

Then: OmIGod. I am trapped!
Quite right, my lads and lasses. No Way Out.

B A N G !

It's All Over.

49. Nothing Matters – Everything Matters

That is to say - Nothing As-It-is, A Priori Consciousness Presence Awareness as its Self alone (All One) .... Is Matter-ING.
Right Now - Here. (NoWHere.)
Nothing does NOT <u>become</u> Everything.
Nothing <u>IS</u> Everything.
Do you Comprehend? Forget it.
Is there Seeing-Knowing-Being This?
"You/me" dis-appear as the One Impersonal Silence
 of I-Consciousness Its Self
Then these No-things ARE this. Appearing. As. This.
What is to know? Who would know it?

   w h o ?

The journey from Here to Eternity
Is the journey from here to Here
From Something Looking to Nothing Seeing
From Now and Then to Now and Before-Now
The Seer before See-Ing Happens
No Yesterday No Tomorrow No Today
Not Now Not Then Not Not at All
Beyond thought of Being
Beyond Self or Other
There is Only Eternity

Lies! Lies! The Truth cannot be Languaged.
It is hopeless. It is an impossible task
Only a fool like me would try.

                              No way, Jose'

50. Stay With That Lovingness Of Being

A friend said, *Stay with that which lovingly allows for everything to appear in peace that cannot be disturbed. Allow it to show you the depth of its void and the fullness of its emptiness.*

Thanks, John Greven.

This moment,
That shows itself to me
and bang. There is no more me
Never was there a me
It was merely the phantom
Of "my" soap opera
And then there is no one to suffer.
No questions? No. No questioner.

51. YOU are Here, Be-Ing.

This Awake-ness is always so. It is a Timeless spaceless IM-personal awareness of '*I Am*' AS the Eternal Moment - a nano-second before language seemingly traps That in an illusory conceptual cage of two-ness.

This simple Awareness-Moment is a re-cognizing of The Natural, Eternal Instant. THAT is Pre-Conceptual, Cognizing Emptiness: The 'a priori' Full-ness of Eternal Love.

Don't believe any of this. Nothing any so-called sage or Guru has EVER said or will say is "the truth." Truth is not a new better belief that I am all that is.

True-Nature is the Absence of *any* belief - OR believer.

There is nothing - appearing Now as simple Awareness and all the 'content' of Awareness- Oneness. Not Two (A-dvaita.)

Period.

52. One Fine Day - I Met Byron Katie

We talk about Love and do - together like partners of Oneness - the method of Inquiry that she calls The Work.

It is very deep and profoundly beautiful - the serenity is priceless. And now - always right here under the noise of the confused mind - there is Grace - the Grace of inquiry.

She says, Ask you

1. Is it True?
2. Can you absolutely KNOW that it's true?
3. How do you react when you believe that thought?
(what do you do, when you believe those thoughts)
4. WHO would you be without the thought?

Then - Turn it around.

I am a separate individual - a me. Is it true?
I don't know.
Can I know absolutely it is true?
No, I cant'- not absolutely.
How do I react when I believe that idea?
I feel vulnerable, and insecure - shaky and often sad, lonely and scared.
Who would I be without that belief?
Free. At Peace with myself and the world.

Turn It Around:
I am not a separate being.
Is that as true or truer?
Yes. And I feel different when that idea is in play! Much more at peace.

The experience is of not knowing. This leads to a dissolution of the false "knower" - and a natural unconcealing of the Actual - non-conceptual Self - Being, Just That. Peace that surpasses understanding.

The best part of meeting Katie 'in person' is the realization that her Work is about being our OWN Guru. And there was absolutely NO need to meet her in person - and, there is absolutely NO need to meet her in person again. And yet I love being with her.

She makes it clear that she is not a Guru in the classical (dualistic) sense of the 'Guru-disciple' relationship. Her Work is about finding the Guru Here, where we are - and that is her unique treasure (for me.)

Ask four questions, turn it around ...

Visit the website and try The Work for yourself at

www.TheWork.org

Thank you - Katie
From the Heart of All.

Argue with reality and you lose.
But only 100% of the time.

- Katie

53. Inquire Within - Here, Now

Is there really a separate, discrete 'ME?"

I am ME. I believe in ME.

Is that true?
Yes. I think I am therefore I am. Right?

Is THAT true? Do you think? Or is there thinking happening?
I THINK.

OK. Is that true
Yes. There are always thoughts in my mind. Constantly they chatter away like monkeys in the trees. They should shut up and leave me in peace.

OK. Is it true that thoughts should not be?
Right. These thoughts should not be there. This thinking...

Hold on - Are you saying thoughts and the thinker should NOT be?
Yes. That is exactly what I am saying.

Well then. Is that true, that thoughts should not be? Can you know beyond a doubt that thought and the thinker should not be?
Well, I have heard that it is possible to be in a thought free state.

Is that true?
Uh... hmmm
I don't actually know.

OK. Is that a no?
That is a no.

How do you react when you believe this thought, thoughts and the thinker should NOT be?

I am frustrated. Angry. Depressed. And afraid ... I don't know why I am but I am afraid.

What else?

I feel tense all over. My chest tightens, and my muscles tense, I even get cramps sometimes. I guess you could say, I suffer. A Lot.

Can you give me a stress-free reason not to drop that belief? And, I am not asking you to drop it...

No.

Thank you. OK, who or what would you be without that thought, that belief?

Nothing. I don't know ... Nothing.

Close your eyes, please and look deep inside. Who, or what, would you be without that those thoughts? The thought that thinking and the thinker should NOT be?

<eyes closed>

<eyes Open>

Just ... aware. Just ... here. Present. Hearing sounds. Peaceful. Serene. Awake ... alive. Just ... living, aliveness itself. .... FREE.

OK, lets turn it around.
Thoughts and the thinker SHOULD be?

Yes. They are, aren't they!? And when we want them to NOT be we are arguing with reality. And when we do that we lose. But only 100% of the time...

And - 'the me is real?' Is THAT true?

No. There is the thinking that there is a me but without the thought of a me, that does not exist anywhere I can find it.

Yes. Good.

Well now ... if there is no 'me' who is thinking that " I exist?

That is a good question.

Without the thought, "I am thinking" where is the me?
Am I at ALL?
I AM!

Is it true?

Part Four

Pointers From The Sages

54. The Absolute Truth Of All Timeless Time

The Self alone exists;
    and the Self alone is real.
Verily the Self alone is
    the world, the "I" and God.
All that exists is
    but the manifestation of the
    Supreme Being.

Self is only Being -
    not being this or that.
It is Simple Being.
    BE, and
There is the end of ignorance.

> *If one can only realize at heart what one's true nature is, one then will find that it is infinite wisdom, truth, and bliss, without beginning and without end.*
>
> — Bhagavan Sri Ramana Maharshi

Wherever you go, here you are.

55. Pointers From The Avadhut Gita

Sri Dattatreya Avadhut was The Primordial Guru Of The Navnath Sampradaya Lineage Of Masters, of whom Ramesh Balsekar and "Sailor" Bob Adamson are the Primary expressions in the world currently.

This is his Pointing to the True Way.

"One's own Self is one's chief Guru. By knowledge of Self [in] communion one gets the great bliss." –Sri Dattatreya

The Self Alone Is

How can I salute the Self, which is indestructible, which is all Bliss, which in Itself and by Itself pervades everything, and which is inseparable from Itself?

I alone am, ever free from all taint. The world exists like a mirage within me. To whom shall I bow?

Verily the one Self is all, free from differentiation and non-differentiation. Neither can it be said, "It is" nor "It is not." What a great mystery.

This is the whole substance of Vedanta; this is the essence of all knowledge, theoretical and intuitional. I am the Atman, by nature impersonal and all-pervasive.

That God who is the Self in all, impersonal and changeless, like unto space, by nature purity itself, verily, verily, that *I am*.

I am pure knowledge, imperishable, infinite. *I know neither joy nor pain; whom can they touch?*

The actions of the mind, good and evil, the actions of the body, good and evil, the actions of the voice, good and evil, exist not in me (Atman). I am the nectar which is knowledge absolute; beyond the range of the senses I am.

The mind is as space, embracing all.

I am beyond mind. In Reality, *mind has no independent existence.*

How can it be said that the Self is manifest? How can it be said that the self is limited? I alone am existence; all this objective world am I. More subtle than space itself am I.

Know the Self to be infinite consciousness, self-evident, beyond destruction, enlightening all bodies equally, ever shining. In It is neither day nor night.

Know Atman to be one, ever the same, changeless. How canst though say: "I am the meditator, and this is the object of meditation?" How can perfection be divided?

You, *Atman, were never born,* nor did you ever die. The body was never yours. The Shrutis (revealed Scriptures) have often said: "This is all Brahman." [The Self.]

You are all Brahman, free from all change, the same within and without, absolute bliss. Run not to and fro like a ghost.

Neither unity nor separation exist in you nor in me. All is Atman alone. "I" and "you" and the world have no real being.

The subtle faculties of touch, taste, smell, form and sound which constitute the world without are not yourself, nor are they within you. You are *the great all-transcending Reality.*

Birth and death exist not in the mind, not in you, as do also bondage and liberation. Good and evil are in the mind, and not in you. Beloved, why do you cry? Name and form are neither in you nor in me.

Oh my mind, why do you range in delusion like a ghost? Know Atman to be above duality and be happy.

You are the essence of knowledge, indomitable, eternal, ever free from modifications. Neither is there in you attachment nor indifference. Let not yourself suffer from desires.

All the Shrutis speak of Atman as without attributes, ever pure, imperishable, without a body, *the eternal Truth.* That know to be yourself.

Know all forms, physical and subtle, as illusion. The Reality underlying them is eternal. By living this Truth one passes beyond birth and death.

The sages call Atman the "ever-same." By giving up attachment the mind sees neither duality nor unity.

Concentration is not possible either on perishable objects, on account of their mutability, nor on Atman. "Is" and "is not" do not apply to Atman either. In Atman, freedom absolute, how is Samadhi [state of inner union] possible?

Birthless, pure, bodiless, equable, imperishable Atman - This you know yourself to be.

Then how then you say: "I know Atman," or "I know not Atman."

Thus has the Shruti spoken of Atman; "That You are." Of the illusory world, born of the five physical elements, the Shruti says: "Neti, neti" (not this, not this).

All this is ever pervaded by you as Atman. In you is neither the meditator nor the object of meditation. Why, mind, do you shamelessly meditate?"

I know not Shiva [it can mean Brahman and high awareness], How can I speak of Him? Who Shiva is I do not know, How can I worship Him?

I am Shiva, the only reality, Like absolute space is my nature. In me is neither unity nor variety, The cause of imagination too is absent in me.

Free from subject and object am I, How can I be self-realizable? Endless is my nature, nothing else exists. Absolute Truth is my nature, nothing else exists.

Atman by nature, the supreme Reality am I, Neither am I slayer nor the slain

On the destruction of a jar, the space in it unites with all space. In myself and Shiva I see no difference when the mind is purified.

Brahman alone is, as pure consciousness. In truth there is no jar, and no jar-space, no embodied soul, nor its nature.

There are no worlds, no truths, no gods, no sacrifices, no races, no families, no tribes, no nationalities, *no smoke-path, no shining-path*.

Some there are that prize non-dualism, others hold to dualism. They know not the Truth, which is above both.

How can the supreme Reality be described, since It is neither white nor any other color, has no qualities such as sound, and is beyond voice and mind?

"I eat," "I give," "I act"; such statements do not apply to Atman, which is purity, birthless and imperishable.

Where the one Brahman alone is, how can it be said "this is Maya [by which the phenomenal world has been brought into existence]", or "this is not Maya", "this is shadow" or "this is not shadow"?

I am without beginning and without end. Never was I bound. By nature pure, taintless is my Self. This I know for sure.

From subtle substance to formed creation, there is nothing but Brahman; most clearly do I see this. Where then is the division of any kind?

The absolute void and its opposite, all am I everlastingly.

Atman is not male or female, nor is It neuter; neither is It happiness or suffering. How dare you pervert It?

Atman is not purified by the six methods of Yoga. Absence of the mind makes It no clearer. The teachings of a Guru reveal It not. It is all purity, in Itself, by Itself.

I am neither bound nor free. I am not separate from Brahman.

Neither the doer nor the enjoyer of the fruits of karma am I. The pervader or the pervaded I am not.

As a volume of water poured into water is inseparably united with water, so, I perceive, matter and spirit are one.

Why do you call Atman personal and impersonal. Since you are neither bound nor free?

Pure, pure you are, without a body, unrelated to the mind, beyond Maya; why are you ashamed to declare: "I am Atman, the supreme Reality"?

My mind, why do you cry? Realize thy Atman, Beloved; drink the timeless great nectar of non-duality.

Knowledge born of the intellect am I not. By nature Truth eternal am I. I am perpetual immutability.

Neither formless nor with form, described by the Vedas as "Not this, not this," free from separation and unity, the true Self reigns supreme.

There is no father, no mother, no kinsman, no son, no wife, no friend, no prejudice, no doctrine. Why are you disquiet, my mind?

Why do the wise imagine the bodiless Brahman to be a body? In It there is neither day nor night, neither rising nor setting.

Since the imperfections of attachment and the like are not in me, I am above the suffering of the body. Know me to be infinite, like unto space, one Atman.

My mind, *my friend, many words are not needed*. In a word, I have told you *the essence of truth: "you are Truth, you are as Space."*

56. The Avadhut Says, Learn From All

Do not hold the immature, the credulous, the foolish, the slow, the layman and the fallen to have nothing good in them. They all teach something. *Learn from them.* Surely we do not give up a game although we have mastered it?

Think not lightly of your Guru should he lack letters and learning. *Take the Truth he teaches* and ignore the rest. Know well that a boat, painted and adorned, will carry you across the river; so also will one that is plain and simple.

The higher intelligence which without effort pervades the movable and the immovable, and which by nature is all peace and consciousness, that I am.

How can the one supreme consciousness which without effort rules the living and the inert and is all-pervasive, be other than I?

I am subtler than primordial substance, beyond elements and compounds, free from birth and death, above duality and unity.

As space cannot be compared with another space, so Brahman being above duality, cannot be compared with any object. Brahman alone is perfection, taintless, all knowledge. It walks not on the earth, the wind cannot move It, the water cannot cover It, It stands in the middle of [inner, subtle] Light. It pervades space-time. Nothing pervades It. From limitations ever free, *eternally the same, with nothing outside It and nothing within,* It abides.

Atman is most subtle, beyond perception, without attributes, {and} must be realized step by step, and not by sudden violence. *There is but one antidote to* the poison of *highly dangerous passions,* which beget infatuation, and that is to *return to the state of Atman.* Atman is unapproachable by the emotions, is ever formless and independent.

Like the full moon is Atman. See It in all. Duality is the product of defective vision. As there is only one moon so there is only one Atman in all.

No duality can touch Brahman, because Brahman Is All-Pervasive. The wise who teach this acquire boundless patience, and their disciples can never be too thankful to them.

The wise discover that Atman is not seen either by the study of the Vedas, by initiations, by shaving the head, or by being a Guru or disciple. That God, Atman, by whose power the whole universe is born, in which it abides and to which it finally returns like bubbles and waves in the sea, is realized by the wise.

In It there is neither knowledge nor ignorance. There is neither unity nor duality in Atman, nor unity-duality, neither smallness nor greatness, neither emptiness nor fullness. All these exist in the mind, and the mind is not Atman.

57: Not This Not That

More from the Avadhut Gita -

My Friend! There is no cause for disquietude since you are not the body. You are imperishable and eternal, then why do you cry? Rest in peace. Space-like, immortality-giving knowledge absolute am I.

Why are you troubled, friend, since avarice, lust, attachment, are not you? Realize This Now: "Space-like, immortality-giving absolute knowledge I am."

Why this craving for power, companion, when in truth wealth is not thine. "Mine" and "thine" are not in you.

In your heart there is no meditator, there is no Samadhi, nor is there any possibility of meditation in Atman. Time and causation never existed in you.

I have told the disciple the essence of Truth. There is no "you" nor "I," no world, no Guru, or disciple. Know that by nature I am freedom absolute. I am transcendental Truth.

When Atman, the absolute existence, alone is, and It is I, then where is transcendental Truth, where is bliss, where is knowledge, secular or spiritual?

Unknown to fire, water and earth, motionless, all-pervasive as space, knowledge absolute - THIS, know your Atman - Your Very OWN True Self nature - to be. By nature all-pervasive as space, knowledge absolute are you.

The whole universe is a projection of the mind; therefore it is a mode of the mind. The true nature of the mind is bliss, and when the mind is stilled, bliss absolute is revealed.

Consciousness absolute, being unknowable by the mind, how can speech explain it?

The Self is free from day and night, and therefore the conception of its pilgrimage in time and space is no true one.

No sun illumines Atman; the fire and the moon cannot shine therein. It is not equanimity or even desirelessness; how then can action exist in it?

Neither can it be said that It is to be known by the absence of action. It is neither within nor without. It is nothing but bliss absolute.

How can it be said that It is the first or that It is the last, since It is neither element or compound, nor emptiness nor fullness? Eternal, ever the same, the essence of all is Shiva.

The statement that Atman is describable or indescribable cannot stand. Neither is It the knower nor the known. It cannot be imagined or defined. How can we say that It has a mind or any of the senses?

Space, time, water, fire, earth, constituting the world, are a mere mirage. In truth the One, imperishable, ever blissful, alone exists. There is neither cloud nor water in It.

As there is no possibility of birth and death in It, so no conception of duty nor dereliction of duty can be applied to It. That undifferentiated, eternal, all-pervasive Shiva alone is.

The modifications of primordial matter and of individualized consciousness are in the realm of cause and effect. When there is eternal all-pervasive Shiva alone, how can there be matter or spirit therein?

There is in It no suffering, and no possibility of suffering, because It is free from all attributes.

There is no duality in It. How can there be age, or youth, or childhood in that One eternal principle?

Atman is dependent on nothing and is unlimited. The law of cause and effect touches It not. How can the buddhi [intellect-ego-me], which operates only in duality, and which is perishable, discern It?

It grasps not, nor is It grasped. It is not born nor does It bring forth. We can only say that in It there is no destruction.

In Atman there is neither manhood nor womanhood, because such conceptions cannot exist in eternity.

There is no pleasure in It, and no faculty of enjoying pleasure, since It is free from such defects as attachment. Equally free from doubts and suffering, one and eternal is Shiva; thus the conception of "I" and "mine" do not apply to It.

Neither is there Brahman in It, nor the absence of Brahman. Since It alone exists and is eternity, it must follow that It is free from pain, and also from freedom from pain.

There is no gain and there is no loss. Infatuation and worldly wisdom have no place therein. When the eternal consciousness alone exists, how can discrimination or wisdom, or any such thing be contained in It?

In It there is no "you" and no "I", therefore family and separate castes or races exist not therein. It is neither true nor untrue. Neither is It of this world nor of the next.

How then can one pray to It?

The body itself is imagined in Atman, as is the whole universe. Atman is free from all differentiations. Then since I am Shiva, there can be no idea of prayer or worship.

Presence-Awareness - The Absolute - has no body. It cannot be said that It is without a body or attributes. All that can be said is that It is bliss absolute, and that bliss am I. This is the height of worship, and this is the culmination of all prayer.

All this world is a magic show, like a mirage in the desert. Concentrated bliss, alone and secondless, is Shiva and that is the Avadhut.

The wise do not strive for anything, not even for Dharma [good conduct and righteousness, etc.] or liberation. They are ever-free from all actions and movements, and also from desire and renunciation.

What do they, the pundits, know of such beings?

Even the Vedas cannot speak of him perfectly. That bliss absolute, ever indestructible, but a source of bliss to all, is the Avadhut.

Blessed am I; in freedom am I.
I am the infinite in my soul;
I can find no beginning, **no end.**
All is my Self.

Parts of this were gleaned from
http://geocities.com/advaitavedant/avadhutagita.htm
There is no copyright listed.
This note appears after the text:
Please feel free to distribute and download these texts.

58. Self-Liberation - Pointers From Buddhism

Self Liberation Through Seeing With Naked Awareness

From The Ancient Sage Padma Sambhava:

Appearances are not erroneous in themselves, but because of your grasping at them, errors come into existence. But if you know that these thoughts only grasp at things which are mind, then they will be liberated by themselves.

Everything that appears is but a manifestation of mind. Even though the entire external inanimate universe appears to you, it is but a manifestation of mind. Even though all of the sentient beings of the six realms appear to you they are but a manifestation of mind. Even though the happiness of humans and the delights of the Devas in heaven appear to you, they are but manifestations of mind.

Even though the sorrows of the three evil destinies appear to you, they are but manifestations of mind. Even though the five poisons representing ignorance and the passions appear to you, they are but manifestations of mind.

Even though intrinsic awareness which is self-originated primal awareness appears to you, it is but a manifestation of mind. Even though good thoughts along the way to Nirvana appear to you, they are but manifestations of mind. Even though obstacles due to demons and evil spirits appears to you, they are but manifestations of mind. Even though the gods and other excellent attainments appear to you, they are but manifestations of mind. Even though various kinds of purity appear to you, they are but manifestations of mind. Even though (the experience) of remaining in a state of one-pointed concentration without any discursive thoughts appears to you, it is but a manifestation of mind.

Even though the colors that are the characteristics of things appear to you, they are but manifestations of mind. Even though a state without characteristics and without conceptual elaborations appears to you, it is but a manifestation of mind. Even though the nonduality of the one and the many appears to you, it is but a manifestation of mind.

Even though existence and non-existence which are not created anywhere appear to you, they are but manifestations of mind. There exist no appearances whatsoever that can be understood as not coming from mind.

Because of the unobstructed nature of the mind, there is a continuous arising of appearances. Like the waves and the waters of the ocean, which are not two (different things), Whatever arises is liberated into the natural state of the mind. However many different names are applied to it in this unceasing process of naming things, With respect to its real meaning, the mind (of the individual) does not exist other than as one. And, moreover, this singularity is without any foundation and devoid of any root.

You Cannot See It

But, even though it is one, you cannot look for it in any particular direction. It cannot be seen as an entity located somewhere, because it is not created or made by anything. Nor can it be seen as just being empty, because there exists the transparent radiance of its own luminous clarity and awareness. Nor can it be seen as diversified, because emptiness and clarity are inseparable. Immediate self-awareness is clear and present.

Even though activities exist, there is no awareness of an agent who is the actor. Even though they are without any inherent nature, experiences are actually experienced.

If you practice in this way, then everything will be liberated. With respect to your own sense faculties, everything will be understood immediately without any intervening operations of the intellect. Just as is the case with the sesame seed being the cause of the oil and the milk being the cause of butter, But where the oil is not obtained without pressing and the butter is not obtained without churning, So all sentient beings, even though they possess the actual essence of Buddhahood, Will not realize Buddhahood without engaging in practice.

If he practices, then even a cowherd can realize liberation. Even though he does not know the explanation, he can systematically establish himself in the experience of it.

(For example) when one has had the experience of actually tasting sugar in one's own mouth, One does not need to have that taste explained by someone else. Not understanding this (intrinsic awareness), even Panditas can fall into error. Even though they are exceedingly learned and knowledgeable in explaining the nine vehicles, It will only be like spreading rumors of places which they have not seen personally. And with respect to Buddhahood, they will not even approach it for a moment.

If you understand (intrinsic awareness), all of your merits and sins will be liberated into their own condition. But if you do not understand it, any virtuous or vicious deeds that you commit will accumulate as karma leading to transmigration in heavenly rebirth or to rebirth in the evil destinies respectively. But if you understand this empty primal awareness which is your own mind, the consequences of merit and of sin will never come to be realized, Just as a spring cannot originate in the empty sky.

In the state of emptiness itself, the object of merit or of sin is not even created. Therefore, your own manifest self-awareness comes to see everything nakedly.

This self-liberation through seeing with naked awareness is of such great profundity, and, this being so, you should become intimately acquainted with self-awareness.

Profoundly sealed!

How wonderful!

As for this "Self-Liberation through Seeing with Naked Awareness" which is a direct introduction to one's own intrinsic awareness, It is for the benefit of those sentient beings belonging to the later generations of those future degenerate times.

That all of my Tantras, Agamas, and Upadesas, though necessarily brief and concise, have been composed.

And even though I have disseminated them at the present time, yet they shall be concealed as precious treasures,

So that those whose good karma ripens in the future shall come to encounter them.

SAMAYA! Gya! Gya! Gya!

This treatise which is an introduction to one's actual intrinsic awareness or state of immediate presence is entitled "Self-Liberation through Seeing with Naked Awareness."

It was composed by Padma Sambhava, the Master from Uddiyana.

Until Samsara is emptied of living beings, may this Great Work of liberating them not be abandoned!

(On the full moon day of the eight-month of the Wood-Ox year, this Terma text entitled the Rig-pa ngo-sprod gcer mthong rang-grol, belonging to the Zab-chos zhi-khro dgongs-pa rang-grol cycle of Rigdzin Karma Lingpa, was translated by Vajranatha in the hope that it will enlighten and benefit all beings.

Sarva Mangalam!

Guru Rinpoche, Padma Sambhava, was an Indian tantric sage who brought Buddhism from India to Tibet in the 8th Century AD. Invited from India by Tibetan King Trisong Deutsen, Padma Sambhava ("The Lotus Born" Guru) converted the entire country.

This text was found at
http://www.buddhistinformation.com/tibetan/self_liberation_through_seeing_w.htm
There is no copyright listed.

59. See For Yourself

Wherever You Go - Here You Are

In This Clear and Obvious Presence of Livingness its Self, Everything is That - One-Self Not-Two.

The "ultimate pointer" IS...
There is NO Oneness.
There is NO <u>Not</u>-Oneness.

Despite all your valiant efforts of reading, hearing CDs, practicing meditations, and going to satsangs and retreats, do you still feel something is wrong? Or that something is missing in your life?

Are you frustrated by the endless search for true peace? This is unnecessary suffering!

Who is suffering? Find out, and the knowing arises, right where you are, that there is nothing wrong or missing any more.

And there never was! All is Being, appearing *as* "you" and "other-than-you."

Wherever you go, Here, You Are.

This reveals that You Already ARE the Being that 'you' seek.

60. The Original State

The Eternal can never be that which can change. Bodies, minds, feelings, experience - even neat spiritual ones - can never be THAT which never changes.

What is Eternal? What NEVER changes and never did? And never could? ONLY your simple being, awareness, your very own always-so never missing knowingness of your original state, which arises as the awareness that "I am Present and Aware. Period."

THAT never changes.

THAT has always been with you AS you. Remember any time or place hwere you were and there must have always been the pure pre-conceptual sense 'I am" - see this now. Before there can be any thing, thought, memory, feeling, perception – that awareness must be there first.

That is before Time and Before cognition. That is the Cognizing emptiness itself ... the subject-less objectless Is-Ness that is always right with you, AS You, whenever and wherever you are.

Dwell in That. Abide AS That. The eternal is ... that which knows you are. Like deep sleep, That is knowing before there is a knower.

Before Time You Alone Are. After Time You Alone Are. NOW You alone are. Awareness of Being. Just That. Period. Game Over. You are That I am That. All there is, is That.

There is NO separate 'you' or 'me.'

Try to find that me - a separate self - there isn't one. There is an unshaken space: timeless-unchanging, untouched, always so. *That, you are.*

I am You Are Present-aware-period. One No Thing called Love.

It is just that simple.

Welcome.

61. A Priori

What IS - Always On - Always Awake - before language?
Before Language there is not-language
What is before not-language? Not language - Not no-language
What?

> *"Language Is The House of Being."*
> - Martin Heidegger

No Language no Being?
No Being No Language?
Which Came First?
Both. Neither.
NOW What?
What is the 'house' of Language?
Silence?
(No. Not That. Nor THAT! Stop wording.)
The *word* silence is not *Silence.*)
Then - What?
?!?

> Even a good thing is not as good as nothing.
> ~Zen Koan

If a tree falls in the forest and there
is no one there did the tree fall?
What forest? What tree?
Moot.
Mu.

62. Nothing I Say Or Write Is "The Truth"

This originally appeared in the book "From I Am To I Am, With Love." It bears repeating.

"Nothing I Say Or Write Is The Truth"

What does that mean? Simply this: All words are concepts, language, letters; at bottom just sounds. Is the sound in your ears of "water" ever going to quench your thirst? No. The word water, no matter how loudly or lovingly said, will never BE water. The word water is a representation of a substance known to be clear, wet, thirst-quenching.

Similarly, the concepts in this book represent certain "spaces" which cannot be captured by concepts or sounds or pictures ... because the SPACE is BEYOND all such forms and formulations. So look where the concepts point; never taking the concept to be the Real. *The truth cannot be captured by words and images*

> *The Tao that can be told is NOT the Eternal Tao.*
> – Lao Tzu

What does that mean?
Who asks that question??

> *Only those who have no knowledge of the Source of destiny and free-will dispute as to which of them prevails. They that know the Self as the one Source of destiny and free-will are free from both.*
>
> - Sri Ramana Maharshi, "

63. To Believe Or Not To Believe

My dear pal Werner (Jack Rosenberg) of est seminar fame said, in a little booklet given to me as a graduate of est, "*Don't change beliefs, transform the believer."*

Almost no one I know understood that - including myself.

What was Werner pointing to?

Any belief requires a believer. An "I" who says, "This is what -I- believe."

And that "I" is itself nothing more than another belief - a core belief, if you like.

What is it to "transform a believer?"

There is a problem right off the bat – with the word "transform" itself! Because most dictionaries offer a definition that smacks of change, an alteration of the appearance of a thing while its substance remains unchanged – or some outright claim that transform is change, period.

That is not what my friend Werner was trying to elucidate. I guarantee that – I hung around the man long enough to hear him say over and over and over that transformation is NOT change.

No matter how often he said it, we stuck in the great maw of the mind, which ONLY knows from change. The mind says, "Oh, I used to be this way, now I am that way."

The mind cannot grasp "transformation" because in fact transformation, as Werner used the word, actually pointed BEYOND the mind stuff to That in which the all the mind stuff appears – the Emptiness of Pure Space-Like Awareness. And THAT emptiness is the very fullness of Being, loving to be all that is.

So perhaps we can clarify, in the Light of Nonduality expressed through Advaita Vedanta, this misconception of Werner's pointer, in this way:

Don't change beliefs. See that the believer is not even there.

That I, as is pointed out in this book, is a phantom. Look for any separate "I" and you always come up empty handed. Yet, you still exist! As in deep sleep, the Real You – Presence, Being – is NEVER absent. That is what you are.

So don't take all this on as yet another belief. Instead, see if you can get down to the source - the core of all beliefs – the believer. The THOUGHT of I as separate from other-than-I.

Once you investigate thoroughly and find that "I"-person to be absent, then there is no longer any need to adopt, change, discard or embrace ANY belief. The whole issue of this vs. that belief is moot.

This is Absolute Freedom from suffering – simply seeing, what I Am is Presence-Awareness. Nothing but that.

Okay? Good. Now don't believe any of this either! Look for yourself. Transform the believer – into no thing – And BE what you are, as it already always is.

64. The Advaita Diet

Written originally with tongue firmly in cheek.

And yet it works. How wonderfully odd!

Hey? If you keep your tongue in the cheek - you can't stuff more food into that pie-hole!

How rude.

Who cares?

Look. The author lost 62 pounds in five months - and is still slimming down - with this diet. Of course, the massive change from burgers-fries-caffeine to eating only veggies, fruits and soy, plus drastically reducing caffeine - <u>and</u> taking up an exercise practice - might just have a little something to do with it.

But what was the SOURCE of that change in diet and lifestyle?)

Ta-Da! The Advaita Diet!

Read On - what have YOU got to lose? (In body-pounds that is?)

This is the simplest diet in the world.

There are only two chapters.

Chapter One

Are you hungry?

WHO is Hungry?

Who Says Burgers Taste Better than Salads?

WHO says one is better?

Who is the ME that is "hungry?"

Quite Possibly - The body needs a LOT less food than us obese Americans feed it.

Who is hungry?

A suffering "me" that on investigation is NOT actually there!

What if nearly ALL food is Comfort Food?

Don't we eat 'way more than necessary for livingness itself?

Who is being comforted by larger and larger portions?

Who is comforted by a fatty burger-fries diet?

Who is stimulated by endless coffee and caffeine sodas and gobs of sugar?

Find that one.

Bring it to me.

Where is it? Absent. It's a story of a hungry me.

Looking right now, where IS the ME that is hungry?

Chapter Two: An Exercise

Go to the kitchen Open the fridge door.
1. Look at sugar-caffeine sodas and fatty foods.
2. Ask, WHO wants to be comforted by fatty food?
3. Ask, WHO wants the stimulation of caffeine?

What's wrong with salads, veggies, soy and non-caffeine tea or soda Unless you think about it?

Who is this YOU that thinks?

Now: Just One Question To Ask yourself!

Who is hungry?

Ask it! Ask it whenever "hunger" arises. Check in. Is the body needing food?

Or is the little "me" wanting comfort or a caffeine rush?

Who is hungry?

This question is dangerous that an ego-mind that is always hungry for more and better of this and that, believing that food or caffeine will bring it satisfaction.

It will NOT. You know this deep within. As Eric Hoffer put it, *you can never get enough of what you don't really want.*

Ask your mind: "WHO'S HUNGRY? WHO AM I?"

Ask that of your mind-self 24/7, and lose – not only your excess weight – but all suffering as well.

Go for it.

I Love You.

Nothing more to say.

The End.

65. The Truth That Sets Us Free

The truth that sets us free is that there is no person to BE set free. It's simply a thought of a me, taken on as the "real me," while ignoring the actual simple beingness that must be there for any thought or feeling to appear.

In deep sleep is there a me in that body-mind machine? No. Yet the heart keeps on beating through the night. No me beats that heart – the heart is being energized and beats due to the energy of beingness itSelf.

We are redundant.

Other definitions – pointers – to this freedom that I enjoy include:

The final Truth

> *There is neither creation nor destruction, neither destiny nor free will, neither path nor achievement; this is the final truth.*
>
> - Sri Ramana Maharshi

Enlightenment

> *Self-Realization or Enlightenment is nothing more than the deepest possible understanding that there is no individual doer of any action - neither you nor anyone else. Also you are not the thinker of any thoughts, nor the experiencer of any experiences - they happen. When IT happens, no bright lights are likely to flash in your head!*
>
> - Ramesh S. Balsekar

> *There is no such thing as enlightenment; the appreciation of this fact is itself enlightenment.*
>
> - Sri Nisargadatta Maharaj

> 'Sudden Enlightenment' means precisely the immediate apperception of all that in fact we are. 'Enlightenment' is 'sudden' only because it is not in 'time' (subject to sequential duration). It is reintegration in intemporality.
>
> - Wei Wu Wei

> Don't become anything, even enlightenment is becoming something.
>
> - Papaji

Liberation

> Liberation (Moksha) occurs when the individual soul (human mind/spirit) or Atman recognizes its identity with the Ground of all being - the Source of all phenomenal existence known as Brahman.
>
> -Hinduism

Being - Livingness

> *The Self Is Existence-Consciousness-Bliss.*
>
> -Ramana Maharshi

That last one fits the impersonal re-cognition of the Naturalness of our very undeniable unavoidable Being - THAT IS what YOU ARE.
Period.
Stand as That, and nothing else.

Part Five

Dialogues With Seekers

Finding Truth
Within - And All Around

66. It's Oneness ringing the bell to Oneness

Q: *I know I exist. That's impossible to deny and never fluctuates. So for the sake of keeping a consistent vocabulary, let's call that undeniable knowing that I exist - "Awareness of Presence." I'm not sure if that's the common definition, but that's how I'm using it in this conversation.*

A: That is a fine pointer to That Inexpressible Isness that IS Is-ING as all that IS.

In addition to that, I certainly notice that sometimes there's an "I" who feels likes it's doing things, and sometimes things are just being "done" without any thought of a doer. So clearly that "I" is impermanent.

Clear and undeniable!

The thing that still isn't clear to "me" is that what I AM is that "Awareness of Presence." I'd be happy to just take your word for it, but somehow I think that would be missing the point.

<u>Don't take anyone's word for it</u> - look for yourself at WHO that isn't clear for. The I AM that I AM and YOU ARE is NOT a concept to be taken as truth!

If there is anything you can do or say to help this become clear, I would be eternally grateful. And please don't say that the "me" that wants to be clear about this, never will be, because it's just a phantom thought, and thoughts can never be clear about anything. I know that, but there is still suffering here.

Why do you ask for the false rather than the True? YOU ARE THAT. And that "me" doesn't even EXIST as a separate thing! So it – a thought of me – can NEVER "be clear!

Stop fooling yourself. The mind serves up all this crap and you believe it! That is the ONLY issue here.

That "me" is ONLY a thought! Who is claiming that THIS Simplicity Itself is unclear!?

I feel like I'm at the end of my rope. While I've been dangling here, I've been diligently continuing the inquiry into who I am, but that inquiry has been feeling more like a "practice", which I'm afraid might defeat the purpose.

Let GO of the rope. That rope is the false idea that there is something "wrong" about the Sage's pointers to DO the Self-Investigation!

There is NOTHING WRONG WITH PRACTICE!

Some bullshit artists claim that a practice of Self-Investigation is going to defeat the purpose. That is ego at its most self-egregious and self-justifying – hanging on for its very false crappy suffering life!

I now tell you in compassion for your plight, <u>cut the crap.</u>

Just keep asking that question - "Who Am I?" - and dwell AS the pure I Am. It was good enough for Ramana Maharshi to suggest. And for Sri Nisargadatta Maharaj. It works. You Are - and That which you are IS always already free. ALL that is required in this "end game" is to keep digging in and uncovering what you are not.

What you ARE is Presence-Awareness. The Pure I AM.

What you are not THE THOUGHT I AM, NOR anything at all that follows this thought or subtle sense of "I am."

The only true statement - pointer - the mind can think or say is - I AM. All else is FALSE. Period!!!!

Awareness of Presence is translated by the IDIOT MIND into a thought "I am" followed by I am Me! It's just your ignorant mind speaking that bullshit – and that is NOT who you are! See it now. Cut the rest away with the inquiry. Now get back to work and call if there are doubts, angers, upsets, feelings of being insulted, or any other ego crap that is keeping you in inexorable suffering!

Take up this pointing - with the mind at first - and let it destroy all the subtle senses of separation and identity as a bound soul!

Who Am I?
I AM.
Who Am I?
I AM.
Who Am I?
I AM.
Who Am I?

Who Am I?

(silence.)

Wake up. You ARE That I AM. Nothing else!

Stay in touch until that false "me" DIES and the Freedom You Are shines unshakably! I Love You.

<u>Follow-up:</u>

Wow! Thanks, Charlie! What you said really hit home (although for whom, I'm not sure). Out of curiosity, when something like what you said "rings true", is that just another illusion, or is some deeper understanding occurring somewhere for some one (or perhaps "no one")?

That is a very good question!

The "ringing true" happens as Oneness Re-Cognizes ItSelf - when a pointer destroys ignorance. Well done. Enjoy The Now.

The bad news is you cannot cause awakening.

The good news is you cannot prevent awakening.

It happens - unless it doesn't.

67. Finished

Last night it all clicked and I saw that all my suffering is wrapped up in this fantasy I keep watching and believing on some level, seen for what it is there is then only this presence and no suffering lingers. The "I" is part of the tale in these mind stories, and the reason it has been so hard to see through them is I have had a life time to practice watching them and acting out of them. As today unfolded, I saw a lot of old fears float to the surface, very old memories and experiences. Yet today was filled with just this one mind, this Big Mind.

The little mind kept on trying to gain back its position, but I kept on seeing it for what it is, just a passing scene in my imagination. Thoughts arise in it, the world arises in it. I do the next thing that comes up, it all happens by itself. The person apparently doing things before was this "thought self" that has no actual substance of its own, now I connect completely with everything because I am that same substance.

All I know is that I AM (this single mind that contains all and is not contained itself), that is the only truth outside the ramblings of my imagination. It is so simple, no wonder I have missed it for so long. Asking who doubts and who is questioning seemed to be the key, it just opened up.

Now, there is no one to doubt here, nobody to ask any bloody questions. John [Wheeler] talking about a 180 degree turn in looking and seeing what was missed really says it all. The stories of suffering always have this "me" involved, seen as the BS stories that they are. No suffering exists at all.

There is NO "I" here. Just this.

A: This is the best news ever.
Welcome Home, no-person!
Happy UnBirthday.

68. It's Not Luck - it's Commitment

Q: I am still working on that "end of suffering" thing. But getting a lot better at it and am trying to finally tackle the "special love relationship" thing - ouch - Never had the courage to try just "BEING" in that until now - I'm getting lots of pain and many past unhealed thoughts are coming up for processing.

Here is the Truth of the matter: There is NO processing of healed thoughts or other so-called " conditioning" or past hurts – there is NO past. There may be pain. But without a me to think it's MY pain there is NO SUFFERING!

All you are doing is telling yourself a STORY here and now - and believing it. Where is any past without a story? They call that History – HisStory or HerStory.

And it keeps getting easier. Wish me luck, okay?

I do not wish you "luck," dear One. I wish you Commitment. A steadfast no BS commitment to getting at the core of suffering and rooting it out once and for good!

Just ask yourself right now: "Can I actually truthfully deny the FACT that I Exist? That <u>I AM</u>?"

<u>That I AM is the ONLY Reality.</u> The THOUGHT I Am is a pointer to That. The words is never the thing represented BY the word. The concept is not the actual. The menu is not the meal.

That – the pure simple I AM - IS what you are – and the I Am that YOU are, and the I Am Ramana Maharshi Is, and that I Am, are <u>NOT two - or many different - "I Am's!"</u>

Ask yourself who thinks or believes otherwise?

You start that sentence "I *am still working on ... etc."*

STOP at I AM. "Still working on...." etc is a story appended to that pure sense of Being Awareness – I Am. Discard all that follows I Am and stay with That.

If doubts arise, whose doubts are they? Investigate the one who thinks she thinks or owns doubts or is working on anything or doing any action or feeling.

WHO AM I?

Ask yourself this until you drop. Take no answer as real. Only the Question counts!

Go for it with earnestness and total commitment.

Stay in touch. Finish this seeking and Rest In Peace!

69. Decisions Decisions - Who Makes Them?

An e-mail comment from a visitor at a meeting here arrives:

Q: *A decision came along - that this "I" decided to not remain identified with thoughts, feelings, and self-narrative stories.*

Excellent!!

Who decided (typical nonduality addict question)? I don't know. Maybe I did or it just happened. Why does it matter? It feels more right to say, " I decided" rather than "functioning of totality" to me.

That's fine. And yet that notion that "I decided" IS totally false. Decisions appear – but they are nothing but thoughts! There is NO individual "thinker" – either in you or in anyone else. Once that is seen, and that "I" is no longer considered to be who you are, however, then it's fine to say I decided – just so long as the energy of belief isn't going to that "I and marking it as separate from All That Is.

"Feeling good" feels much better that "knowing something that most other people don't know".

Yes indeed! That knowing *about* is crap. What we're pointing to is THE BEING OF NOT-KNOWING.

Do I absolutely know that "I" doesn't exist? Is that true that the I doesn't exist? - thanks, Byron Katie

I've met Katie twice. We have done The Work (Inquiry) together. She is a love. But don't confuse her pointing and method by trying to figure it out in the mind. Her pointers are for anyone - those still stuck in the false psychological paradigm of separateness and those for whom there has been awakening but not yet liberation.

You are beyond the psychological stuff now. As you always were in fact – just now, though, I sense that it's kind of landing inside for you.

Ultimately, what Katie is pointing to is the undeniable FACT that You ARE. You DO exist. As the Totality - arising as Presence Here Now.

It is only a false entity that seems to creep in and generate suffering - and that "entity" does not have any independent power or freedom apart from then TRUE Natural Freedom of Existence ItSelf.

That - is ALL.

It's a pleasure to see many people get help from your friendly pointers. Not many nonduality teachers do that at that personal level. Thank you Charlie.

You are very welcome – yet just know that it is Nothing Special. All this bubbles out from NowHere.

70. Do NOT Believe This - Or Anything Else

Q: This "I" that keeps coming up represents presence awareness translating in the mind as 'I am'. This awareness is not 'personal' however memories, ideas, and a body and eyes looking outwards appear in it, confusion apparently appears.

That's just fine as a pointer. However DO NOT BELIEVE this - or any other pointer! That's how the Sage's pointers are turned into dogmatic crap religions and philosophies.

Q: Does this sound about right?

NO. NOTHING is "Right." Right or not right are mental judgments! All these words - they are all just more story. A nice "Advaita-story!"

The story arises in What You Are - Presence Awareness. Drop all the trying to clarify or figure it out conceptually.

Just BE.

"If you can take it, then take it and just BE. If you can't, then go about other people's business, and do or undo unto them until you drop."

- Ramesh Balsekar, paraphrasing e. e .cummings

71. Why Accept The False As True?

Q: *Why do I accept the false as true -?*

That is ONLY due to an incomplete investigation. Keep going.

You say, "That which thinks, types, speaks and reads is this living presence. The thought is not sentient, it is not conscious, it is not living and does not have being."

That is an enlightened ego (there's an oxymoron!) talking. Who owns all those answers? An as yet un-fully-examined YOU. STOP with the answers!

The answers you come up with all just are more bullshit!

Who knows that crap? Only the ego is embarrassed. It will die of embarrassment - when you keep after this with the inquest!

Who the bleep am I? Who is yakking on and on with endless questions and answers?

ASK WHO AM I? - UNTIL YOU DROP.

Can I make it ANY plainer or simpler that THAT!?

Upon further consideration, there is no one to do any of the things we discussed.

Asking again and getting a talking to, I cannot defend the existence of anyone doing anything here.

There is just this. All my answers and talk was doodoo.

Stay with That.

Follow-up: It is very clear to me that what I have always referred to as "me" is part of a story that goes on in the apparatus of the mind (Me T.V.), it is that character that has been the center piece of an imagined life involving what this Me wanted and didn't want his whole life.

If I lose myself in the T.V. show I become the show.

If I realize it is only make believe then I still know who I am.

I can see that everything is impermanent except that in which all things arise, this timeless moment - often called awareness or a sense of being - knowing that I AM.

The knowing that I Am is NOT the Final Knowingness. In THAT - Being ItSelf - there is NO knower of that I Am.

There is ONLY Is-Ness – Arising AS - I AM!

It Is – This Is - Pure Non-conceptual Being.

I ask the only question there is and I get back only the contents of my story as answers, none of these qualify as a core self I can point to. When these answers are seen as missing the mark, then what is left is this impersonal knowing of existence.

Again, that is false. It is a nice-sounding "Advaita concept! It's just crap!

There is no "impersonal knowing of existence!" All there is, IS existence EXISTING as all experiencing – devoid of experiencer and object of experience. THAT is just plain ordinary aliveness.

I cannot find a thinker of thoughts, the thoughts come up and I often respond to them (the thought of ice cream, and 5 minutes later I am chowing down on some).

Who thinks the thought? WHO? Who chose ice cream? WHO wants the solace of comfort food!? WHO*?*

What About Feelings? Those Aren't Thoughts, Are They?

Feelings arise with the story of MY life, always about what this character in my drama wants and doesn't want. This body has no place to call the essential ME, it seems to be a place where consciousness is present and in which the thoughts and feelings flow through.

There is NO consciousness in that body. The body-mind is an appearance IN Consciousness!

Having said all this, I think as you pointed out to me on the phone, there is this subtle feeling of being less than completely baked (still some doubt and suffering left, I guess still some belief in a separate self that ironically cannot be located).

It will never be located. It doesn't exist!

It seems like there is not a total conviction that the contents of the mind are mere fantasy, that I cannot quite see the whole appearance as unreal. Urgh! Any thoughts or help you can give me would be greatly appreciated. I have this question with me all the time now, it is always there.

What question? The only question that will help take you beyond the need for help is Self-Investigation. Ask who is typing? Who is reading? Who AM I? Who asks THAT question!?

Stop all this mental masturbation and trying to figure it all out - and simply stay in the sense of I Am - That alone is a real pointer to the Real.

The thought "I am" is the closest to the ACTUAL I Am.

Bring it all down to That. Abide as That - disregarding the endless gymnastic gyrations of the mental machinery. STAY WITH THE I AM. THAT will show you the depths of silence and perfect non-conceptual stillness.

Now, see if you can formulate what your absolute FINAL question is that seems to leave you subtly suffering! Ask me THAT one. Take a few moments to look then write or call - look right now. Keep me posted.

Follow-up #2:

Q I just checked and read your message. Is there anything or anyone that can be called Me that can be hurt, suffer or be diminished? I suppose it comes down to that, I have still some belief in my life being something I can think about, direct and control in some way or form.

NO. There is NO Me that can be hurt. There is an organism that can feel pain and pleasure. But it is the false identification - the thought that "I am a body in a world" - which is taken on as our consensus-believed-in reality - and that alone IS the root cause of suffering.

We are being conned by a mind-thinking mechanism that we didn't invent. Until Inquiry takes hold.

The stubborn hanging on to this I-thought as the real you, and accepting the false as true, expresses in your message this way:

"I suppose it comes down to that, I have still some belief in my life being something I can think about, direct-" etc.

It is all bullshit.
WHO keeps saying I HAVE SOME BELIEF etc?
Stop and look. WHO AM I? What thinks - says - I?
Who are you?
Stop and Ask:
Who is thinking speaking typing reading?
WHO THE BLEEP are you?
STOP Dear One. Ask Who? Keep at it until you drop.

Who Am I? Who Am I?

Who Am I? Who Am I? Who Am I? Who Am I? Who Am I? Who Am I? Who Am I?

Who Am I? Who Am I? Who Am I?
Who Am I? Who Am I? Who Am I?
Who Am I? Who Am I?
Who Am I? Who Am I? Who Am I? Who Am I? Who Am I?

<u>Follow-up #3:</u>

Please keeping calling me on my bullshit, I am in your debt. It's all crap isn't it? Good lord! My whole deal is bull shit. There is only this, this I AM, I exist. There rest is fantasy island.

No Debt. Just keep going with the Self-Investigation!

Until it all drops - then it will be seen - nothing mattered ever. Doing inquiry, NOT doing inquiry - all that was just happening. To no one.

There never WAS a doer in the machine.

There is no wizard of Oz!

It's a MOVIE, Dorothy.

I Love You.

72. This Is Seen - BUT

It is seen. But the I comes back at times...

That I comes and goes WITHIN THAT.

THAT - Being-Awareness-Presence - is inescapable - and - undeniable! AND UNIMAGINABLE.

The puppet-I arises in the space of awareness. So this "I" will always come and go. There is no problem in that at all. Simply stop giving your focus and energy of belief that this thought of I is the Real I that You Are.

The last bit is this:

The I disappearing and then coming back is Oneness - it's the Divine Dance.

Me-ing and be-ing are BOTH Oneness - Being me - Being no-me.

That's the end of the seeking - there is already always only All-That-Is.

Not Two.

73. Clarity & Non-Clarity Both Arise In Being

Q: I have no clarity that being is never absent

You say that you have no clarity that the Presence of Being is never absent. And yet, that very "no-clarity" arises here and now right within that Being! This Awareness of Being is inescapable!

Who cannot see that they must BE to claim, "I am not clear that I am being?"

Q: As I type this there is an awareness of sadness - a heaviness...

That sounds alright but I sense a red herring here. You claim, "There is awareness of sadness." If you really are simply seeing that as your phrasing indicates then there would be NO problem whatsoever with the simple arising of sadness and heaviness or depression or anything else the puppet-you experiences. The issue is where your focus is. You focus on the sadness and want it to be gone – rather than on that Awareness in which it arises.

Pat phrases and correct Advaita-speak is just more ignorance, dear One. See right now that ALL your knowledge – especially 'Advaita-spiritual' knowledge – is pure IGNORANCE. Ignorance is a word pointing to the IGNORING of what you are and believing what you are not – an entity that can suffer!

Claiming to be independent of sadness and heaviness is the mind co-opting the Understanding of the Sage for itself.

It's total crap. The mind feeds you this crap and you believe it to be real. That is all that is happening. It's a puppet show. You dance on the ends of the strings of the puppet-mind and take on the belief that the puppet is YOU and that this puppet IS what you are. YOU – the authentic YOU – is neither puppet nor puppeteer – YOU are the space – being – in which the whole show arises. And the show is also You - Being "the show."

Are you needed to beat the heart and grow cells in that body during deep sleep?

What you ARE is That which is Being – in all states of consciousness AND unconsciousness! Who cannot see this?

I ask, "Who is feeling sad? Who am I?" The pain doesn't immediately lift but probably by the time I finish writing this letter I will be aware that the sadness/heaviness is gone. But I want everlasting peace not this roller coaster ride of crisis ... noting crisis ... inquiring ... disappearing of crisis ... new crisis and on and on.

The problem is that "I" that "wants." It is taken - by mistake - to be a "person" who wants what isn't. That's craziness! This desire for a better future is the trap of the mind-stuff that is always on about "someday."

Keep peering into the space for the Source of that "I". You cannot simply play around at Self-Investigation. You have GOT to take it on with a no bullshit commitment to end your own suffering. No sage can make a difference. YOU must take this up like a warrior takes up a sword against her enemies and vanquishes them in bloody battle! Nothing less will do it. That can be tough to hear. But the wish for someday MUST be cut at the root!

Who is stuck in a program? Keep looking 24/7. You as that mind are dead to what is Real. Your Aliveness is unavailable to the mind!

There will NEVER be any unending knowing where you are looking for it. The unending knowing is what you ARE – so looking for it can only happen right Here inside of That which you are - the simple, ordinary, unimaginable yet undeniable, existence of being - That Which Thou Art! There is no possibility whatsoever of knowing that knowingness! That knowingness is inconceivable simply owing to the brute FACT that IT is the conceiving itself. You can never see your Self. You ARE that Self.

Your suffering can continue ONLY due to lack of FULL TIME investigation. NEVER LET UP. You indulge the mind's bullshit. This mind's like a mushroom grower - it feeds you manure and keeps you in the dark. You have simply GOT to get real with this. It really does help to speak with One who is beyond all suffering. There is a vibratory energy that arises when there are two organisms in close contact – especially in the end game so to say.

74. Paradise Is Here - Now

A Friend Writes - *Paradise is here and now.*

Not in Utopia, subterranean fields,
Or some secreted island, Heaven knows where!
But in the very world, which is the world
Of all of us, - the place where in the end
We find our happiness, or not at all!
- Wordsworth

Thank you, Charlie! I've been reading the correspondences, etc.....
Lead, Kindly Light - lead on - thou Presence/Awareness.
-M

Thanks for this, M.
It's a privilege to be used by Aliveness this way.

75. Still a perceived 'I'

Follow-up: Unfortunately, nothing has been seen yet. There is still the perceived "I", as always. Nothing has changed, except I have lost all desire to read books and to watch and listen to DVDs and CDs about all of this. The "one simple fact" you refer to will either be grasped or it won't. There seems to be little "I" can do about it, self-inquiry or otherwise. I wish I had a good "the I has disappeared" story to tell you, but no such luck.

The "one simple fact" – that what you are the undeniable beingness that must be here for all this to be said, including the self-denial of being - will never be grasped. The one simple fact is that You ARE. THAT can neither be grasped nor lost.

You are this only, nothing else: I AM.

Not just the thought I Am. The space IN which the thought appears - and AS which the thought appears. Not Two.

WHO wants to grasp - or WHO believes "It will be grasped someday!?"

Who are you?

Anything thought or said after this simple knowing, I AM, is crap.

Give it ALL up.

Stay with That Beingness - your own undeniable I Am.

76. There Is No 'Time' - It's A Mental Construct

Follow-up: Q: *Thank you, I think I catch your drift. I get the impression the I am the fish tank and all these things are coming and going inside me. Which is better that just no thing I guess. Anyway I will delve into my Advaita-Schizophrenia more this afternoon.*

Don't wait for some other time then now. RIGHT NOW look and see, is there any time unless there is the belief in a 'person' in there thinking that the thought 'I' is the actual I and that the thought 'this afternoon' is actually some other 'time' than Now? Right NOW stop. Look. Listen. While making tea, who is here that makes tea? While having a dump, who sits here and grunts!? Who writes who reads who?

Get after this like you have one minute to live and this - Undeniable Being-Awareness - Natural Seeingness-Knowingness- MUST be found to be what you are and all else be found to be false. Die before you die! Get with the program!

Focus on the fact that you are That - all differentiation is ideation ONLY!

Is any idea true? Can we know absolutely that ANYthing is true?

Is there any truth to know?

No.

All that separation is, is a thought. What you are is I Am - and yet the thought I am is NOT the real I AM - which is BEFORE thought or OUTSIDE of creation. This endless timeless actuality is here now. Wherever you go you are - you ARE - Here. Whenever the mind says later that thinking arises only NOW. This is the inescapable final truth - you ARE this Timeless beingness - livingness. Just That. Now - STOP.

A funny thing just happened, a cute young teenage girl just rang the doorbell, must be a Jehovah's Witness or something.

She had a flyer in her hand and I got a big grin on my face when I read the headline. THE END OF FALSE RELIGION IS NEAR!

And that's another great load of crap. DUMP IT ALL. There is NO end and NO beginning of any damn thing! Why do you keep on believing this bullshit!? Find out by investigation - who the BLEEP believes this stuff? Who are you? Find that what you think is 'you' is a phantom - a thought only with absolutely no physical reality to it - and let the belief in that thought as a real 'entity' die NOW.

Die before you die.

That - ego-death - Is Eternal Life.

77. The Idea 'I Am This Body' Is False

Q: I saw into the 'issue' of their being no person/doer this evening, thoughts just arising, choices even intellectual ones just happening.

Excellent!

This has been kind of a sticking point for me. Anyway, there kind of was like a subtle level of freaking out because, everything that can be seen or experienced is from the point of reference of my body.

Who says so? Who thinks these thoughts? Keep looking for that one who talks and types, thinks and drives, feels afraid or happy – WHO?

This idea 'I am this body' is totally false. The reference point itself is only a thought-feeling – a sense of BEING "my body." That is the ignorance we are dealing hammer blows to with the pointers – which arise from OUTSIDE of creation to impact the suffering by removing the false belief in separation. But you have GOT to use the tools!

Driving of a car (body object) as a movie - is happening, you cannot stop the film. If there is no controlling entity. Why is this happening?

Why is the earth here? Why is the sun burning? Why does a spider be? ALL your why questions are simply the storyteller – the I-thought – adding to itself. It's the never-ending story.

Seeing through to the True Nature of what you are as the Being-Awareness in which these thoughts of a me who wants to know why why why - and seeing that the I is ONLY itself another thought-story - puts paid to the whole thing. But you have GOT to stop asking all "why" questions and ASK: WHO wants to know why? Who is asking why? Who? Who are you? I've said to you a hundred times, stop and ask, "Who Am I" that thinks there is any why - and any cause - of all the effects in the dream.

If you want answers to the why question - consider a pointer from Zen:

Why did you write me?

You wrote me because you wrote me. Period.

I would appreciate your insight on this. I think I see that expecting to be enveloped in a loving THAT upon 'realization' is a delusion, who would it happen for? Maybe the mind is just begging for something to cling onto.

Give up all expectations. Give up "someday."

Give up the search! You ARE – Being.

Just that.

Allow That to show you its depths - without striving for any outcome whatsoever!

Inquire.

Who thinks ANY thought is true?

Thoughts are like a snake in the road that on close examination proves to be only a rope.

We fear these thoughts - or resist them - when they are not even real.

Craziness.

Use Inquiry and set yourself free.

78. This Is The Good News

Follow-up -Q: *I have been working with the "WHO?" questions as you suggested [in e-mails and the <u>book - 'From I Am To I Am, With Love'</u>].*

Excellent!

First result is that it removes all tendencies to try to understand or work things out intellectually, because it kind of short-circuits those thoughts.

Exactly. Now you see directly in your own experiencing of This - the enormous Transcendental Power of this simple Self-Investigation. The question Who Am I arises from, is brought into creation from, OUTSIDE of creation. By You - the Real You, not the ego-thought of a separate 'you.'

This is a good result because that has been a habit in the past - to try to understand. It is now clear that understanding will not help. There is no intellectual answer that can achieve anything.

Yes - you are well into it now. Keep it up.

Second result is that each time a WHO question is asked, there is a kind of stop, and there is just present awareness, a kind of empty looking. It's a kinda of curious looking, interested but disinterested. There is seeing and hearing etc. very clear, very present, and nothing much else. Then usually thinking starts again and then asking "WHO?" again.

Great news! Now you see that what you are is that Perfect Silence - the "stop" reveals what was already always there - YOUR REAL SELF-NATURE - <u>AS</u> THAT SILENCE.

So asking the "WHO?" questions seems to clear everything away, leaving just a knowing aware presence.

That just is quietly aware of its own knowing presence. Nothing fancy, just a quiet looking. In fact that quiet knowing looking is there as things get done. It seems to dispassionately watch what the body is doing - like making the tea or taking a leak - and in that, everything is very clear and alive and bright.

Spot ON. That Clear And Present Brightness-Aliveness IS what you are. And Now you know That. Always Now. ONLY Now.

The thought arises: "well this doesn't feel blissful or special like others have written about" but then that is just a thought or words on a page in a book. None of that is what this is, here, now and that's the only thing which is real here, that knows itself to be.

This is a terrific bit of insight. The idea of something (some thing) blissful or special is the delusion of the false Guru who claims to have something you don't have. Now you see that it's all crap. GOOD.

So I can only stay with that knowing presence and see what arises. I pay no attention or time on the content of any thought, but just return to this present awareness.

Good job of sharing the seeing of the Actuality and exposing of the false.
That is IT - just as you so clearly and beautifully articulated it. Very well done.

79. The I That Gets It - Or Not - Is A False Entity

Q: I've been searching on and off for years) in different ways not just "spiritual". I stumbled across Advaita 2 years ago. I've read the lot - traditional, neo etc. Then came Nisargadatta - well what can you say - breathtaking.

The authenticity of any TRUE Lineage IS breathtakingly clear, no doubt. As the Lineage of Nisargadatta harks back to The Avadhut called Dattatreya, and the Lineage of Muktananda harks back to the Avadhut called Nityananda Of Ganeshpuri - these expressions are always available. It's a sort of "Back Door" out of the programming of Maya - the Grand Illusion. The Matrix. The Avadhut is The Eternal Liberating Oneness appearing in various forms through apparent time.

MOST fortunate are we who are led to that Grace.

Mind you, there is actually NO requirement that there be ANY lineage whatsoever. Three <u>great</u> examples of sages who had no lineage of Master-Organisms are Ramana Maharshi, Byron Katie, and Tony Parsons. Read the accounts of how all three "died before they died" and this gets very, very clear. Same with Eckhart Tolle, Karl Renz, Nathan Gill, Richard Sylvester, Unmani Lloyd, Leo Hartong, and others. The story that a "Guru" and a "Lineage" are "required is just - well, bullshit! Oneness is the Guru. Only Oneness. Your True Self is the ONLY Guru in actuality.

It took some time but slowly it all began to make sense and sink in. I have to admit though, have said got it intellectually on several occasions only to discover new understandings later.

The I that gets it or doesn't get it is false. Investigation – in any form that works for you – can and likely will reveal that "I" to be utterly insubstantial: It is ONLY a thought arising presently in your undeniable beingness. The investigation that works for many is a simple question: Who Am I? Accept no answer. Knowing "I Am That" is useless as a concept. Who is the one who believes it knows "I" Am That – or believes it is NOT That!?

Find out. Ask the question "Who Am I" until "you" DROP.

And that still goes on. Over 2 years there has been tremendous progress and also an understanding such a thought of progress sends "me" off in the wrong direction!

There is NO progress. There is no person to progress. All ideas of progress or lack of progress are a story the "I" thought adds onto itself to keep its (false!) sense of identity. Who wants or believes in progress? Who are you? Ask yourself, my friend. Don't stop until the whole illusion collapses under the fire of Self-Inquiry. As Nisargadatta pointed out, what is needed is to "Give up all questions except one: Who Am I?" Why bother with all this other stuff?

Nisargadatta said do it. Ramana said do it. I say do it.
I tell you it works – on my experience - NOT hearsay. So?
Just DO it.

I know and appreciate at the end of the day it is not an intellectual understanding that matters.

And yet it can start there, with the intellect. Nothing wrong with that at all! But NOW it's time to go DEEPER – seeking the source of that "I" thought by Self-Investigation.

But (yes I know there should be no "buts") two main points keep niggling. The first is time just being a concept. There is change so how can change occur without time? The 2nd is nothing existing outside my immediate consciousness so when I go to sleep the world ceases to exist. Any pointers to assist?

The "should" is the ego-mind claiming that something is wrong – with me, with it, with this or that. It is the delusion of a thinker that believes in its own thoughts and stories, and makes them real due to the lazy lack of investigation. That's all. So? So get to work. Forget all that and just ask, first off, who is asking these questions or holding to some need for answers?

Then take it Home with the great question: "Who Am I?"

80. This Is It

Follow-up: Hello again... You asked me to keep you posted, so here goes. I can locate no person that the name ***** is referring to, only stuff coming and going and that which it all takes place in. There is thoughts, feelings, emotions, drama, memories, hope, pain, anger, joy, the world, everything as before.

Beautifully said. Stop Here. Now look: We say joy and anger arise. What do they arise IN? Uncaused Absolute Happiness – Freedom Being ItSelf.

The only difference now is the personal experience of seeing that all of this referred to an assumed person named ***** and that person upon looking cannot be located (the man behind the mask is not there).

Exactly!

All that I can account for is that which all this coming and going is taking place in and that is ordinary, everyday awareness (nothing fancy there). The heavens did not open up, no lights or mystical auras, just seeing what is my actual situation. So, there is still pain of various kinds, it just isn't happening to anyone that I can find. This body sometimes suffers and sometimes feels good and sometimes has no feeling in particular.

At the risk that this is "preaching to the choir" – a few points perhaps need a bit of clarification and examination: The body does not suffer. ONLY a mind – the subtle, inchoate idea of someone, can suffer.

As I turn to this ordinary and common awareness and away from the content it contains I get a clear sense of peace and a feeling that this is it, this is what I remember and what I have always sought. It is that which I have had glimpses of big and small. And that is what I have always been - beyond the identification of myself as a thought, idea, object or body.

In this expression, there is still a subtle sense of an "I" here – a subtle separateness - that "turns away from content" – an "I" that "gets a clear sense," – an "I" that "feels this is it."

THIS – the Absolute Eternal Stateless State – is NOT a feeling and cannot be known or experienced. Yet - IT IS. THAT cannot be grasped in the intellect - the mind.

These pointers where initially very clear and I resonated with them, but having the verifiable first hand experience of their truth was not part of the immediate resonance.

I repeat – This – The Absolute – is NOT an experience! It is attributeless and formless. That is unimaginable, inconceivable, and non-perceivable.

I am this awareness, this presence, I am not the changing content of awareness, and the two are not separate.

STOP HERE.

I am not an idea or an emotion, I am not some part of this body, and I am not anything I can point to and say, "See, that's me."

Now – the final tweak: Who Says So? RIGHT NOW: Ask who sees? Who is "seeing that there is No Person?" Who is the knower, the knowing? Who Am I that is talking and thinking and typing? WHO turns to ordinary awareness? Just a few final tweaks – if needed. The words that triggered all this in your message were these: The body sometimes suffers. ALL suffering is mental ONLY. What body? Where is any body - or any pain or suffering – outside of subtle deeply held thought-stories?

Thank you for your continued patience and support.

No worries. It's absolutely a pleasure.

81. Why Do You Rave About Tony?

A seeker asks, I see you are quite fond of Tony Parsons. Why is that?

That's easy.

I love Tony because Tony tells the truth - so to speak - he points with words and love to the Love that is beyond words and which is appearing AS the words - and the entire manifestation.

A deeper response might be:

Why do you rave about Tony?

Because I rave about Tony.

And one more?

Why do I rave about Tony?

Why NOT?

82. Reiki - A Pointer To Oneness

An old dear friend writes: *Howdy - Love the new website, at least its new to me. If you don't remember you helped me realize oneness two years back. I was working at University of Baltimore. Since then I have brought the Oneness into my Reiki classes and have incorporated it into my life ... I am Life simply.*

Well said. That – Life Living ItSelf – IS all that is. Once That is seen there is effortless living – whether teaching Reiki or watching television or selling used cars or performing heart surgery. No one doing – all simply happening.

I have been writing poetry and got a friend to publish for me. cool eh. Its gonna be called "Selling Nails On the Beach" Concept being that it does not matter what you do its all One, so you could sell nails on the beach. Don't know if folks will get it, but when they do they will re-member. Haha...

Yep. Selling water by the lake, selling nails on the beach, being a soldier, being a thief, being a saint – it's all the same Consciousness at play, with nobody home doing any of it...

I have found that Reiki is a great tool to help others experience oneness. Think of how the symbols are drawn into the nothingness that surrounds us. How we touch nothing etc....

The pointer of the word Reiki itself, – Rei Ki – Universal Intelligence-Energy - when made clear, can open a seeing through of the transparency of the ego-self and unconceal the Being-Self. However it is a good "plan" to always remind students or recipients of healings that the <u>experience</u> of oneness is <u>NOT Oneness</u>.

And that Consciousness – Reiki – is the ONLY healer or teacher, and the appearance of two – a healer and a recipient – is an illusion. Just to keep it straight.

All experiences pass. Oneness is Always On – Presence, Awareness – just That – regardless of any and all experiences! Making this clear was essential for the Self- Knowing, or "Understanding," to be complete and end the search here.

I am also now working at a Hospice company bringing Reiki to them and doing marketing.

To sit at the illusion of death's door on a daily basis leaves you no place to be but One. Best part of all these changes is that I did nothing. Just lived as Life and all this cool stuff unfolded. Aaaahhh letting go is the way.

Letting go happens. Trying to let go NEVER works – it is still someone letting go. Who is that someone? Through the inquiry into the nature of a "me" and the seeing of it as false that "me" becomes what it always was – a nonexistent fake.

Once through the gateless gate it is clear that this "me" did – and does – nothing. But before that happens the dreamed character still believes herself or himself as a real separate subject in a world of objects called "not-me" – and so the tools and pointers arise, as happened for you two years ago.

"You" are doing great work, and that is wonderful! Keep going. Sharing this Natural Aliveness is a great expression of true empathy and compassion.

Great to hear from you. Stay in touch as the Love moves you to.

83. 'Perfect Peace' Wiped Out The "Me"

A reader of the e-book "Perfect Peace" (available at www.awake-now.org) writes,

Thanks very much for your e-book. It certainly cleared up a lot of doubts, in fact it wiped me out - all there is left is clarity - Just this clear space in which everything appears. I can't say what it is or who it is - I only know that it is.

I would love to come and see you in person but you are in the USA and I am in the UK. It's too far away..... But, in a way, there is no distance between us really, is there? The Presence/Awareness that you are is the presence/awareness that I am.

No difference, no separation - except in thoughts. And those thoughts come and go in this Presence/Awareness. Thanks again.

Welcome back to Being- The Home You Never Left.

84. Presencing-Beingness is Always 'ON'

Q: *There is something about your presentation that seems to stop the internal dialectic process. It just quits working briefly.*

The stopping of ANY thought process, even an "elegant" one like "dialectic," is actually not the Natural State that is being pointed out. ALL thought are just patterns of energy and not the least bit separated in any real sense from Being Itself.

In any stopping of thoughts OR the NOT stopping of thoughts, there is what always is - Presence-Awareness. BEING. It just goes unnoticed. Early on the Sage may offer a pointer (or a Koan) that may momentarily halt the mental churning, and then point out that "you don't fall apart when the mind is silent" - because what you are as livingness itself does NOT require a thinker or any thought at all.

I like to ask, who is thinking? The mind delivers - automatically - the statement "I am." Okay, if that is true you should be able to stop any suffering or painful thoughts at will. If you think you can stop thinking then stop for e few weeks! Try that one and what is noticed is by the time we try to alter or stop a thought, IT HAS ALREADY HAPPENED! We are, quite simply, "late to the party."

Thinking happens, then we say - as a mental construct - a conceptual overlay - "I think." But it is simply that thoughts arise, including the "I" thought, and NO thought, "positive or negative," has ANY power to do or not do anything. Once you see this, ALL thoughts, feelings, emotions are naturally allowed to arise and subside in the Beingness that you are. Like storms puffy clouds appear and disappear in the Empty Sky, which embraces all that arises with it without resistance.

And nothing is wrong any more.

Simply stated there is are brief moments of.... well.... just being. The illusion tends to be predominate but even on the intellectual end of the scale I'm no longer entirely absorbed by it.

Taking a look right now, are you ever NOT Being?

THAT - Presence-Awareness - must be here first, for ANY experiencing to arise - thought or no-thought. It's all arising presently. Pain arises in That Being that you are. Pleasure arises in That Being That you Are. All that is - noticing, not noticing, feeling great, felling crappy - all arises in That Being. If there were no being there could be NO experience - none whatsoever.

Can you STOP Being? Thoughts can stop for that instant you point to - but does Being ever EVER stop?

<u>No.</u>

That, Timeless Being, is always on - even in deep sleep. This can be easily seen when you observe that in deep sleep - though there is no one present and aware - Being beats the heat, breathes through the lungs, cells grow and change and die - all without a "person" to make life and living happen.

The person is clearly false - see that and there are no more worries about thought or non-thought. Everything IS That Being - arising as Presence-Awareness AND all the CONTENT OF That Awareness.

That is what you are.

All that is seen, known, felt, read, heard IS That. Being appears as Being AND Not-Being. Awareness Presencing AND the Absence Of Awareness Presencing (as in deep sleep.)

That's the grand paradox.

So there is absolutely nothing to get and no one to get it... As in ever-present fact, you ARE it.

Stay in touch! It's great to hear from you.

85. What Is It That I Don't Know That I Don't Know?

A visitor poses a question: *Having been to seminars where the proposition is that in the weekend they will reveal, "what I don't know that I don't know," looking at this question "Who Am I" seems to be similar. Isn't it pretty much the same thing?*

No. When the proposition is to seek out "what you don't know that you don't know," there is still a "SOMEONE" there who wants to now discover what that someone doesn't know that he or she doesn't know. That you that wants to know ANYTHING - the "someone" - IS the problem.

Why? Because it is a false idea of a separate "me" that wants new or better knowing - a fresh collection of knowledge for an ego to show off. Why do you think the joking (sort of!) translation of "PhD" is Piled Higher and Deeper!?

A big fat IQ can be a huge obstruction. In my case, the brighter my "140 IQ" got the more I suffered. Until I finally saw "IQ" as my "Ignorance - Quantumly."

Knowledge – mental comprehensions of concepts referring to other concepts – is the booby prize. All knowledge enhances ignorance – in an ultimate sense – because what goes unexamined is the so-called "owner" of all that stuff and nonsense. What need to be looked into is, "Who wants to know?" That can reveal that ALL that we know is "specious balderdash!"

That obviousness of the fact that you exist, you are doubtlessly BEING is all that is needed for the immediate and permanent ending of suffering. Who thinks otherwise? Who thinks? WHO?

Something thinks. Call that something IT. IT thinks, we then take IT'S thinking of this one word on letter concept "I" to be what we are. IT is YOU. IT is IT. You are IT. So IT thinks - and we believe that stuff IS us.

There is NO actual separation whatsoever. The IDEA of separation IS the false belief that must be looked into.

You are this: "I Am - Being." That is undeniable. What thinks I am other than that? ASK IT that thinks "you" up, "Who Are You?" Go for that. Forget knowledge. Rather, ask Who wants to know?

As Leo Hartong notes in "Self to Self" (p.73) –
Just keep it simple. Non-dual... Not Two... One!
Whatever 'you' think, it is IT thinking AS you.
Whatever 'you' do, it is IT doing it AS you.

86. The Self Was Never Lost

Once upon a time there was a boy lost. There was panic and fear. The sheriff was called and a search party formed. After a few hours passed, while the sheriff's posse sought the boy all over, the boy emerged from the attic. He had been happily playing with his old toys up there all day.

Nobody had thought to look there.

The announcement came across the police radio: "Call off the search. The one we were looking for was never lost."

87. No Thing Happened

Q: Hello All- Some writings from the inquiry today:

Who am I?

-Who is it that's asking?

I'm Me. But I wasn't always "me." Before that "I" was born I was simply alive. I am alive. My given name is X, but that's just the name they gave me. Who I am is neither X nor not K. I say I'm me. You know... ME! I'm the guy my whole life has happened to. No, I'm the guy my whole life has happened with. No, I'm the thing that has happened with my life. No, I'm the guy who has happened along with my life.

These memories belong to someone or something! They lead me to believe that I have remained the same while life has gone on around me. Memories have persistently located themselves!

I am the person who had these experiences...but, in fact, I don't own them, I remember them. The experiences happened and I was there.

-Who was there?

I was.

-Who is that?

Me!

-Who are you? Who experiences anything? You think your life happened to you!

That's what it seems like.

-Did it?

Right now it looks like "me" and my life happened together.

-That is correct.

They happened together...I suppose the next question is are they separate – "me" and "my life"

-Are they?

They both appear in my awareness. In that respect they are the same.

-Who is aware?

I am.

-Who are you? Who has life "happened to"? Who "remembers" things? Who "has" awareness?

I guess it's impossible to "have" awareness. And yet it seems like the awareness is mine.

-Yes it does!

But it can't actually "be" mine. I'd say the right answer is not that I <u>have</u> awareness but that I <u>am</u> awareness.

-Is that so?

I don't know.

-Who doesn't know?

It just doesn't seem like I'm awareness. I've been told I'm "me" for as long as I can remember – that I'm a separate entity that things happen to. And yet, no-"thing" has happened to me. No-"thing" has ever happened "to" me. No-"thing" has happened with me. No-"thing" and me happened together.

No-"things" happen...

with me

near me

around me

inside me

but no "thing" happens to me ever.

The awareness of no-thing and me happens at the same time.

The awareness of no-thing and me happens.

No-thing has ever happened?

-What is a thing?

A thing is an object.

No-object ever "happened".

Therefore, No subject apart from that no-object ever happened.

I am no "thing" and no "thing" happens.

That's all for today.

Peace.

A: That's a good bit of chewed up spit out mind-noise! Well done.

Here a bit more to chew on...

Who Are You?
(No Answer.)

Who Are You?
(No Answer.)

Who Are You?
(No Answer.)

Who Are You?
(No Answer.)

Who Are You?
(No Answer.)

Who Are You?
(No Answer.)

Who Are You?
(No Answer.)
Who Are You?
(No Answer.)
Who Are You?
(No Answer.)

Q: Awesome!

88. Investigate The False And See It AS False

Q: *You say, you did the investigation 24/7 at one point; that strikes a chord, something yearns for that. To go deep.*

Go for it! What do you have to lose except that very '"you" that causes all the suffering?

Also do you think meeting a "teacher" in the flesh can assist in a way reading etc may not?

Yes, definitely. Unless it doesn't. Then - definitely NOT.

That seems to be arising in me to, as someone who has never really got involved in teachers and practices, although teachers are scarce here in Eire. Maybe I'll drop out to LA or England and clear up this mess before the body checks out:)

I would encourage you to phone and meet with those who are no longer 'persons' if you can. Meanwhile stay with the looking: Who? Who Am I? And please do stay in touch! Much Love to you.

Follow-up - Q: *Thanks for the reply, Charlie, how you do this (the replies) gives some clearness into how things are seen here.*

Glad to hear it. That is the whole pointless point.

Yet there was suffering with 'me' today,' I' turned to stone with fear. Common occurrence, it drains me and it's strange, this mind keeps looking for an out!

Just keep looking at every possible moment of Now - WHO is this mind? WHO wants an out? Who is this that arises as a voice in my head claiming it is a "real me?"

Turning to stone with fear, as horrid an experience as that can be (and I have also been there on a number of occasions) is still ONLY something that comes and goes in what you actually are – pure Presencing Awareness.

First, You ARE. Then anything arises in that – and everything is That.

You know, it thinks, "let this be done with."

That is a very good sign, in a way. Now just take up a solid and earnest commitment to finish the suffering and irrational fears once and for good. You might want to get a cheap calling card and give me a ring. I am generally available from 10 AM until 6 PM Pacific Time

It is my privilege to do whatever it takes to help eliminate suffering - so why not go for it? What have you got to lose? Only your small self – leaving the Eternal Self that you are.

Take up these pointers in earnest right now:

1. What you Are is the I Am that I Am. Nothing else.

2. Who thinks otherwise? Find out: Ask that one, "Who Are 'You?' Who Am I?"

I hesitate to write such things, Charlie, feeding a story that's already just an image remembered. I will keep in touch.

It takes real courage to "out" your ego-self in this way. It is moving and inspiring! You are quite correct in calling the story a story. Just ask, WHO is the storyteller? Ask yourself until there is no more 'yourself' to ask or not ask! "WHO AM I?"

89. Not Knowing Is The Death Of The False

Q: *Hi Charlie - your writings are of great help for me.*

A: I am happy to hear that!

My interest about spirituality started about 12 years ago. I was in spiritual group for about 10 years. I was not happy in this group and I left. After some time I have found these teachings I must say that the non-dual pointers are very direct, simple and liberating.

Yes. Taking up the two basic pointers with unswerving commitment just WORKS - maybe not always - but often enough to make it worth the shot for the ending of your suffering:

1. I Am, and that I Am is a simple and indisputable fact

2 I Am NOT anything other than That. If I think I still am separate, asking, "WHO thinks that" often works to burn the false belief away. Ask, "Who Am I?" THAT is a question that counts. Or, take up The Work of Byron Katie. That is also awesome stuff.

After short time of inquiry, the understanding of the simple truth that I am awareness is clear, and it is great relief for me.

Yes. Now watch as the ego-mind pops right back up like a jack-in-the-box and claims, "I know I Am That, Presence-Awareness, ... B U T" ...! That is why the inquiry must continue until there is no one left to ask any questions whatsoever.

But this dream character sometimes believes ...

That But is the actually false ego protesting against being "killed" by the inquiry. That is all. And that ego is actually non-existent – it is not solid or real. Yet all that "I – me – ego" IS is a thought arising IN presence-Awareness, like a cloud in the empty sky. It is only a thought believed in as "what I really am."

WHO believes? Ask that believer-thought: "Who are you? What are you really?"

See that IT IS ONLY A THOUGHT.

But this dream character sometimes believes that this entity and the world are real, and this false belief is a cause for arising of fear, jealousy suffering... In the moment when the fear is arising I forget about this simple fact that I am not this fear, and the suffering is reaction of this misunderstanding.

So, at the end of forgetting ASK who forgot? Who needs to remember? RIGHT NOW, look at this one! What does all forgetting arise within? BEING. You ARE. Being is always ON. Forgetting is an occurring within that same Awareness. If you are not being then where could forgetting happen?

This teaching is not about remembering ANYTHING.

Thank you. It is my pleasure. Thanks for a great, heart felt, and sincere question.

Follow-up Q: *Charlie thank you for your beautiful and clear response. It is true that false ego protesting against his death. He wants to control the thoughts. This entity who wants to take control is another thought. He wants to know everything, and is afraid of not knowing. Not knowing is the death of the false, and what is left? Nothing.*

A: Well said. This clear seeing of what is false, along with the undeniable seeing that the pure Awareness, "I Am" before the thought I am arises, is in your True-Nature, is all that is needed.

Welcome Back to Timeless Being - the Home you never really left.

90. A Note On Discussions Of Teachers & Teachings

In an ultimate sense all meanderings on websites about the authenticity or inauthenticity of various teacher, teachings or whatever, including "Charlie's," is a distraction.

The story of this and that concept being better than or purer than this or that other concept is a great way for the seeker to keep herself or himself from recognizing the simplicity of Self-Knowing Awareness - the Natural Stateless State

But ONLY so to speak. Because actually NOTHING obscures that Awareness of Being.

Does someone say it DOES? Who says so? Who thinks so?

There is no teacher or teaching "out there." There is NOTHING apart from what we are – Being. We are that and only that.

Challenge any and all such assumptions. Who thinks there are others - and a me separated from others?

91. New Age Babble Will Not Erase A Suffering 'Me'

Q1. J. wrote: *Love your web site and all the helpful pointers. Having spent a lot of time going to Tony Parsons Meetings and generally got to the point that I've been that many times that the same jokes and message are being repeated it has become so frustrating -- spoke to him recently about this and the only advice he could offer me was it not being heard. I spoke to him about self inquiry and he just said as Tony does who's going to practice self inquiry. I love Tony but I think I was better off before I heard about this subject matter, now there's just a feeling of absolute frustration as there is nothing to be done by no one. There is a sound grasp intellectually as to what being said but I know feel stuck. Hope you can help.*

Q2: Then S. wrote to him: *Hi John, Where you are at, is exactly perfect, is where you need to be. It might not feel like it, but it is. This confusion and frustration is all normal on the spiritual path. We all have gone through it. Most sages have gone through it too. You will see when it is time to see, and not before then, no matter how hard you try or how many books you read or how many teachers you see. And you will struggle if you should read this or that book or see this or that teacher. This same frustration, struggle, seeking, conflict, will go on, will continue, until one day it just stops. What you can do is just try to accept this. Acceptance of it sort of reduces some of this suffering. Don't be so hard on yourself. You are doing perfect, exactly what you need to be doing. Just more acceptance and love for yourself is all that is needed. And if you cannot do it, accept that.*

A: As long as there remains a belief in a me that suffers, is frustrated, there IS something that must in fact be done, sooner or later - The investigation! NOT some sappy love yourself accept what is affirmation! It's just more of the same old psychobabble that never leads to anything more than suffering in the end.

You say, "one day it just stops." That's another load of crap. When is this someday one day? Where does now begin? When will Here be someday? It stops when the you is taken on and thoroughly investigated by the simple pointer, the Great Question: "Who Am I?"

Do you think your knowledge is superior to the Pure Seeing of Ramana Maharshi and Nisargadatta Maharaj!?

The questioning is accessible to anyone who suffers; right here an right now (NO other "time" exists!) WHO suffers? WHO can "TRY" to do or not do? WHO needs to "love himself!?" Who is that "himself" that who needs to love? Looking within your mind From the Great Question, "WHO AM I?" will end the seeking, and the seeker. But without that then all that can be created in the dualistic false mind-ego is a concept – the concept ONLY – of acceptance of what is happening.

It's all crap. There is no relief from the underlying root cause of the suffering in mental acceptance.

Without the investigation into "who accepts?" or "does NOT? Accept!?" the frustration will continue forever.

That idea of a "me accepting - or not" is just more of the endless mind-games and ultimately false. It can keep the seeker stuck in seeking.

I Am Speaking To I Am. False concepts will simply propagate suffering. Cut that out.

Stay with the basics:

1. What you are is Presence Awareness Here and Now.

2. What you are NOT is ANYTHING other than That.

If there are thoughts that "you" are ANYTHING other than That, ask WHO thinks so? WHO AM I?"

Do not listen to those still seeking but trying to "teach!"

I love you both. Now, just stop and look in the Pure Not-Knowing before leaping up and responding from hearsay and concepts of New Age babble like that!

92. Why The Apologies To Tony and Wayne?

Follow-up from S: *Hi Charlie,* thanks *for replying so quickly to my first post with a couple of questions. I appreciate this forum and your taking the time to share so freely.*

It's a privilege to be used by Aliveness HerSelf this way ...

I read the previous posts and got caught up. If you are willing to share, who was the public apology to Tony? And why did you feel the need to do that, and also to Wayne Liquorman? Are you just clearing the air?

As written the question does not make sense. Did you mean, "<u>Why</u> were the apologies made"?

The apologies, like the original rudeness that provoked the eventual apologies, simply arose from Oneness. It simply happened. Part of the Dream Life. It seemed apologies were appropriate in that dance of life.

Nothing is or ever was wrong with any of it. "I" did NOT "feel a need to do that." It simply was an arising thought expressed in words on a website and in e-mail. Just that.

There is nothing particularly significant about it!

Yet out it came. Perhaps some who are still "stuck" in believing that others are wrong and they are right – or vice-versa - will see something about their own unwillingness to, as you say, "clear the air."

Regret may arise. Regret is NOT guilt. Regret about an action that happened through an organism can arise – ANYTHING can arise. What is totally GONE is any sense that anything that happens - "then" or "now" - should be in any way different. The overlay of the entity, the thought-construct "me" that DID or does something "wrong" and thereby suffers from guilt, is totally erased (so to say) when the investigation into WHO says they do or do not do anything is complete.

I recommend a little book by Ramesh Balsekar if you want to get more on this topic: "*Sin And Guilt – Monstrosities Of Mind.*"

I noticed you also seem to put Charlie down. Calling him dumb, worthless, a piece of meat, or whatever phrases you used. That kind of surprised me. Why would you put Charlie down? Charlie doesn't exist, the ego is an illusion, is not real?

Actually, that is a misinterpretation: I did not "call Charlie dumb or worthless." As I recall the wording, I pointed to the BODY as "a bag of piss and shit called Charlie."

But that saying is just a pointer.

Don't take anything pointing words as cast in stone! Use them to Just LOOK - These are pointers from Nowhere to Nothing. NOT to be taken literally.

Some appearances are quite stuck in the identity "I am the body." The pointer can break into that false concept - pointing to the object labeled Charlie as a bag of excrement may stimulate a looking at that identity by the reader.

Regarding ego being illusion, YES, standing as no thing, outside of all creation. NO, standing in and as mind that is still ignorant.

That paradox MUST be embraced - in my view.

Your teachers were [several are named - with whom I had shared dialogue and Satsang.] Right? Was [one is named] your final teacher?

The question is moot.

Ultimately there is no teacher, interim or final. All is a dream.

Right now, right here, there is the always and only Infinite Awareness. Arising as content of That is the dream-story.

Seeing the dream AS a dream and asking, "Who is dreaming that I exist separate from all that is?" and you have actually done all that is needed by a "doer."

Thanks for sharing whatever you feel moved to about the above. And once again, thanks for this forum and your sharing freely with us.

Three responses.

One, you're very welcome.

Two: It all just happens.

Three: Let go of explanations and stories and look right now:

Are you suffering?

Ask questions that will erase that suffering.

As the Zen Poet said, *"die before you die than do what you like. It's all good.*

93. Doesn't Self-Inquiry Reinforce Separateness?

Q: *it seems to me that this investigation or self-inquiring you insist on is a dualistic practice. A few quite well known nonduality teachers stress that any effort to self-inquire will keep the 'penny from dropping' because a practice strengthens the sense of being a separate individual. What do you say to this statement? I am asking because this business of there being no-one just doesn't fit with the experience I have of living, paying bills, taking care of my husband who is quite ill, etc.*

The idea that Self-Inquiry or the Investigation to reveal the unreal is somehow wrong or of no value is just a misunderstanding of what is being pointed out.

This questioning of who it is that thinks ANY thought is an effortless, natural looking within the thinking-feeling mechanisms to see what their source is, in much the same way a curious child might take a clock apart to see what makes it tick. It is an affectionate perusal of what the source of thought is, and what it is made of. As in the book title, "*What makes Sammy run?*"

What's pointed out is that inquiry is a natural questioning, a happening, that often arises when all other methods, dogmas, spiritual 'trips,' retreats and all else have failed.

Or it can simply arise despite there being NO interest in "spiritual" matters whatever. It is a functioning of the totality of All That Is, that brings inquiry and the "sacred quest" of the core of looking, "Who am I?" ... From itSelf.

This arises naturally out of the loving being that in essence is what you are. Loving to be, when there is suffering, "Self loving itSelf" brings about inquiry and natural non-conceptual seeing appears.

That fact that you are asking this question points to your dissatisfaction with "easy answers" and "pat sayings" like "all there is, is nothing, there is no you." While that may POINT to what is actually so in "Noumenality" it does little good to one seemingly stuck in identification, as a body-mind in "Phenomenality" ... in other words, as an individual trying to uncover the Real for herself or himself.

Knowledge of absolute truth (not there really in one!) is of little use to someone trapped in a sewer of negative thought and emotion

To simplify: <u>What you always already are is Presence-Awareness,</u> Consciousness, Beingness, whichever word-pointer you like. That is non-conceptual, prior to any thought or feeling or objective-subjective duality. IT IS. That is ALL.

<u>What you are NOT is anything other than That</u>. If there is still a belief that there is a real and separate "I" ... a "me" in a world outside "me" ... then the investigation needs to arise. Bring it forth from the background of what you are, as pure pre-conceptual pre-perceptual Awareness Herself, and ASK.

The Christ said, "Ask and you shall receive." Ask WHAT? The inquiry: "Who Am I?"

Does the I thought see or is there just seeing through an organism's eyes? The thought I is ONLY a one-letter word - and actually cannot do *anything*. Seeing this, the false self-ego crumbles into dust and is seen as never having actually existed at all.

Then you receive what?

True seeing of what you are as the eternally peaceful Freedom Itself.

In a manner of speaking: the final Seeing – Knowing - <u>is</u> in fact that there is no one to own this seeing or freedom. But only after the investigation is complete.

Finally, all that remains is what Always IS, The Natural State of Absolute egoless Freedom.

Go for it. What have you got to lose, except your suffering?

94. Fascinated By Imagination

Q: I feel my predicament at the moment is best described by your phrase "fascination with imagination."

Who is it that is fascinated with imagination?

Who is it that feels? Who is fascinated? Find out. Investigate. You know beyond doubt that you are ... you cannot say, "I am not." You must BE to experience, feel, and know. Who is that Being? Look within. Look without the mind - just look for your I Am and see where it is, what is it made of; does it even really exist apart from the thought-story?

All you are fooled by is a mistake in identity. You take yourself to BE this imaginary small creature with a name and a form (body-mind.) There must be the earnest desire to be free from suffering. This core longing for what is Real will propel you to the Home you never left. You are the Guru.

I mentioned before, do the homework. There is no way around that. The investigation into what is false must happen, as well as the seeing of what is real. What is false? The imaginary person with its foibles and failings, its stories and feelings. What is real? Presence-Awareness, the simple ordinary undeniable knowing, I Am, I Exist.

Staying with the deep sense of I Amness, inquire, Who Am I? You know that you are. Now look, what is that "I AM" that I AM? Is it really a separate entity? If so let me locate that! Where is it? The investigation will show you that the person you persist in believing in is actually ABSENT! Then your True Nature will shine forth unimpeded by false beliefs and concepts.

I feel my attachment with ego is too strong to be just watched dispassionately.

Who is saying so? Isn't that sentence simply more thoughts arising in the presence-awareness that you are - your simple Beingness? You sentence yourself to prison in thoughts! Look for the author of these sentences and you find it is a phantom! Totally UN Real.

So again, WHO feels or says they feel this? A writer, Richard Bach, once noted, "Argue for your limitations, and sure enough, they're YOURS."

Why not investigate along the lines we have discussed rather than keeping on steadfastly and stubbornly arguing for your limitations? Who is arguing? Find that one!

Therefore "complete surrender to the present moment" and acceptance of whatever life brings forth appears very difficult.

It is not difficult; it is IMPOSSIBLE. For the mind. The thinker says "this appears very difficult" - but LOOK: WHO is the thinker?

My sense of you is that you really need to buckle down and get real and serious with the pointers. What you are is undeniable, and at the same time unimaginable. What you are not needs to be thoroughly looked into ... do the investigation. The pointers are there to be used for looking, NOT intellectual understanding. In this non-duality, intellectual understanding is the booby prize! What is needed is for you to take on this Self-discovery for real and in earnest.

The good thing that you said is, "It appears." YES! It appears, as the earth appears flat and the sky appears blue. We know the neither is TRUE but simply APPEARANCE. Keep that distinction in the awareness.

I wonder if you have a piece of advice for me?

See how the above pointers do. I encourage you to take on the investigation as though your very life depends on the completion of it! It is time to get real. No more ivory tower philosophy; let's get down to it and dig deep enough to find the diamond in the "Heart," your own presence-awareness ... right here, right now.

Because whether you "realize" it at the moment or not, You Are That – Being-Awareness, Loving to simply BE. Full stop!

95. The Habit Of Identification

Fred writes, as you suggest in your book, I've been asking 'myself', "Who am I?" and "Who is asking this question?" Even though it is" wrong," the feeling is that this body and thoughts are who I am is still around. Even though, logically I cannot be thoughts or a body because I am aware of those things and I cannot be whatever I am aware of. Intellectually, I know that I am not the body or mind, because I am aware of those things, but still this feeling of identification with a body-mind persists. But "I" will continue to investigate. :-)

Sounds good, keep looking for an entity called me-myself-I and see that it is ONLY an idea appearing in Presence. The habit of identification *can* be seen through; stay with it.

Don't forget the other side of the non-duality coin: What you ARE is non-conceptual, presence-awareness - your own simple being-knowingness. You cannot deny that you exist. You are the awareness in which all there is, arises. Without that awareness, your own "I-Am-ness" not a single thing can be. That Thou Art.

96. What is the "I" that says, "I see?"

Frank writes, I can "see" the "story of me " taking place within me all the time. But at the same time I also feel the past conditioning of mind continues to give momentum to this "I" story and does not allow it to disappear or to fall apart.

A: Just notice that there is still an "I" that "sees the story of me" - investigate, who or what IS that "I" that says, "I see?" Seeing is happening. Seeing trees, seeing a "me-story", seeing cars, seeing marks on a screen forming words and concepts which mind interprets. There is NO "I" in Seeing. The I thought comes later, a nanosecond after the appearance of whatever is arising. "You" are NOT needed for life to be lived through that body-mind organism!

Seeing your true nature as presence-awareness is one side of this non-dual coin. The other is seeing that the "I" or "me" is FALSE. This can only happen through looking in the space of your own non-dual awareness and seeing that this vaunted "I" is only a thought appearing in the empty sky-like awareness that you are. Then the story is seen AS just a story with no power to disturb that pure awareness. What power does a thought have? None. It is the unfinished investigation into whether or not thoughts are real that keeps the mind fixated on the phantom of the opera, the totally false self-center, "Me, myself and I" ... !

Just see the false AS false, and then the energy of belief no longer goes into that story. Then you realize in your own space that nothing can trouble you except your own imagination.

You had mentioned in one of your messages to me that I should do the homework first in order to know the truth. Could you kindly elaborate what homework needs to be done?

Just this gentle persistent looking to see: What is True is Presence - Awareness. What is false is this idea of there being any separate entity whatsoever. The thought "I Am" is NOT the true I Am of Being-Awareness. Seeing this takes just a willingness to look without the mind; the answer is

NOT in the mind. Look within yourself right now: Is there a separate entity? Where is it? What is it made of?

Looking in this way you may realize that this ego-entity is utterly absent. There never has been an entity! Don't stop till you see beyond doubt that this "entity" is a chimera, a phantom, like a dream character, that never was, as is seen on waking from the sleep dream.

Consider these pointers, look into the space, and see what you see- and keep me posted!

97. All that is, just IS, AS it is

Ray writes, I'm getting ready to read chapter two of your e-book, Perfect Peace. I've read the intro and chapter one, but late now for me and chapter two looks too interesting to start and not finish. Great book so far :-) Will finish it tomorrow most likely

Great to hear! I look forward to your comments when you are done with it (or when it is done with you :-))

Can I call you? Or schedule a time to call you? Do you work, or are you retired?

I *am* retired, and all I do currently is this, sharing with others what worked to end the suffering here. You can certainly call (1-714-708-2311.) If you get the machine leave a message and I will e-mail you available times I can be reached.

Been feeling lately that everything is what it is, neither good nor bad.

That is a powerful insight. However a word of caution ... the brute fact that all that is, just IS, AS it is, is NOT a particular feeling. It is simply what's so, before the mind/emotions take over and co-opt That into a sense-feeling for a separate "me."
Nevertheless, that seeing is a great sign!

Only imagination makes it good or bad.

Exactly! As Nisargadatta said, the ONLY thing that can trouble you is your own imagination. It's good to ask here, WHOSE imagination? Do "I" author that thought story? Who am I? Whose thoughts are they? Mine? Who is the "me" referred to by the thought "me?"
The always already response of the mind? "I Am." Then in looking at that thought "I Am" and effortlessly rejecting all appendages TO that

thought, the Source of the THOUGHT "I Am" reveals its Self to its Self ... in a manner of speaking (look where the concept points, NOT at the concept itself!)

Thinking can be a debilitating disease...I just about got an ulcer worrying about the future the other day.... what if I don't pass this math test? What if I don't pass this math class...OMG....

And there you have it: The disease of the mind. Applying the same inquiry, into the "one who thinks" - who IS that!? - then it can be seen that all these thoughts simply show up ... uninvited. And for whom do they show up? "Me." Okay, who is that "me?" Is it real? Or simply another thought arising unbidden!?

Turning the focus back to the "I Am" - represented in the mind by the thought "I Am" - and refusing the additional subjective add-ons - I *am a student, I have "my" math test, I am a person, I am not good enough, I am small and limited, I am afraid* - cuts the cord on the suffering. It's worth some work! Then the Pure Subject shines brightly (as it always already does anyhow) and WOW the seeing happens, by no person, Aha! I AM That Light. I am NOT the object called "me" - and never was.

And that's it. Therein is the clear and present Seeing that there is no "me" and never was. And nothing is "wrong" any more. If a thought of "wrongness" arises, when the "me-myself-I" is seen to ALSO merely be a thought, the idea of "something wrong" has nothing to attach to and the illusory fixation (that never actually was) "ends," as the energy of belief can no longer attach to that which is now seen to be unreal. Then the thought just dissipates like a cloud in the bright light of the ever-present empty sky. And that Light is Home - the Home you never really left.

The game of hide and seek that Self has played with its Self is over and done. Allee Allee In Free!

Here is a quote from "I Am That" that may resonate for you given what you are sharing currently:

Give up all questions except one: 'Who Am I?' After all, the only fact you can be sure of is that you ARE. The 'I Am' is certain. The 'I am this' is not. (p. 70)

The inquiry leaves you squarely in the lap of the undeniable "I AM" that you are - the space-like presence-awareness represented in the mind by the thought " I Am." Then abiding AS that I Am-ness is effortless and sublime.

> "The Raw Crispness of Now" - "Look to the root, before thought arises. What is the essence of that? That is not apart from this, but is what supports and contains it.'
>
> – Burt Jurgens, writing in his book
> *Beyond Description"*

As Burt knows full well, this Now is actually yet another concept, and in actuality there is NO Now.

"Now" presupposes some "time" - past, or future - OTHER than Now. Impossible - as all there is, is Not Now.

As the sage Seng T'san noted, the great way is timeless and formless:

> "The great way is beyond language. In it there is NO yesterday, NO tomorrow, NO today."

Timeless Being.

Absolute Presence-Awareness, arising as Consciousness and its content, manifests as all that is - Consciousness-Totality arising as the impossibly immense appearance IN that Absolute.

Sounds like two things - but only to "a mind." Reality is, simply, Not Two. It's Being. Just That.

> *The moment you know your real being, you are afraid of nothing. Death gives freedom and power. To be free in the world, you must die to the world. Then the universe is your own, it becomes your body, an expression and a tool. The happiness of being absolutely free is beyond description.*
>
> –Sri Nisargadatta Maharaj

98. It's All So Simple

A visitor here writes a few days later, *Hi Charlie - I'll be down to visit again soon ... the reality really seems to be sinking in that effortless presence/awareness has NEVER been absent. IT is what I am. NO MATTER WHAT arises.*

This is really good news!

And that is IT - the search is totally done in this Perfect Instant before "time." Insights arise from nowhere and seeing happens. Then there are no more "insights" needed, and no one to need them!

Then fresh insights may arise as this "good news" is shared with phantoms that still believe there is a "Me-myself-I-and-mine." Naturally expressed without agenda or any attachment to an outcome. (Who would an outcome be for and when, as Timeless Being is all there is!?)

Not much to say...

Yep. That is kind of how it occurs for some appearances that see the dream as arising in what is Real ... and are firmly established AS That. Then again some talk a lot about nothing. Neither is right or wrong, as you are aware ... just the natural expressing of Oneness to Oneness. Comparatively from what I have read, it seems that Ramana said little, Nisargadatta said a lot. Same No Thing Silence sounding.

There was one thing another "teacher" said that seemed to hit home and I think he was quoting Ramana about ending the search and that was 'if you can't stop the search find out who can't stop the search and that'll stop it.' (Kinda like what you said about Ram Dass when you said' WHO'S not done?'

That was actually not Ram Dass, but anther teacher, who blew a circuit or two when he pointed that toward this Charlie thing! I could almost smell Fried Mind.

Oh, there was one other thing that seemed to help (referring to enlightenment: What is illuminating or making possible the thought ' I have lost it '?

That is a great pointer to help sink the "mind" into inquiry. Well done!

See you soon. Meanwhile enjoy the now.

99. Bodhi Svaha

A visitor here writes, *Something just clicked for me... Say a body has a "dream," a house on the hill, for example. Then after some "time" has passed that same body builds that dream house and moves into it.*

That body would be tempted to say, "I made my dream house happen"...except for one thing, who dreamed it in the first place? The initial thought belonged to no-one, and as such, even if the "goal" was "achieved" it pulls the rug out from under "I made my dream come true".

The dream belonged to no-one and appeared in presence awareness effortlessly. The mind grabbed it and said "MINE!"...and so people think they "make" their dreams happen...or fulfill their goals. But who is having those dreams? And aren't things just happening? Cause and effect ---> dreams to fruition ---> soup to nuts --> All just ideas in the mind.... just ideas passing through.

Lovely! Welcome Home to That you never left ... Presence-Awareness, the Unborn Cognizing Emptiness.

As the Zen Master Bankei noted, "Everything gets resolved in the Unborn."

What bubbled up a nanosecond ago Here is - everything and nothing *both* DISSOLVE in the Unknown. Not Two. Not One either.

Have a cup of tea?

Peace.

Yes. Just that and nothing else!

100. Stay With The Basics And ASK "Who Am I?"

Raymond wrote, *I like and agree with what you say. It is helpful and reinforcing. Your posts are on the long side and I wondered if you could be more concise for those of us (myself) with selective short attention spans, who still want to read what you have to say.*

Okay....

1: Look right now, do you exist? Awareness, Being, is Always ON.

2: Look right now, Who are you?

Toss all answers out! Ask "Who Am I" until you drop.

If lots of words come they come. If not they don't. Who cares? I don't care a damn for opinions - not even mine. As to agreeing, who cares if a false entity agrees or disagrees? I am mostly only interested in hearing about any suffering or doubts that remain for the "seeker."

How is the Self-Investigation going for you? Realize that any answer is crap. Go back to the question until there is NO "you" to ask "Who Am I" any more.

Follow-up:

Thanks Charlie.... For your reply. And thanks for keeping it simple for we, the simple minded, who already are full up with a wide variety of pointers. I am doing fine and starting to take more seriously your (and others) advice to be persistent. I also have love for you and your joy is my joy.

Great, Raymond!

That simple thought, "Who Am I," can, as Ramana Maharshi said, burn out all but the ever-present Self- Shining Pure Awareness.

You remember the depth of suffering here for the 'Charlie' thing? It's gone.

Wiped out by that Self of all.

It's a natural giving all thinking, feeling, knowing, experiencing, perceiving - ALL that arises - over to that, often just works.

WHO AM I? Ask until 'you' drop :-)
Or take up The Work of Byron Katie.
Much Love to you!

101. What A Paradox!

BC follows up: *Was thinking of the paradox, how I cannot be anything that I perceive, but at the same time, since reality cannot be sliced and diced, I must be everything.*

As cool as the insight seems, and it is a fine one, taking that answer as 'Real' will leave you incomplete. ANY answer and four bucks gets you a fancy extra Grande coffee thing at Buckys! But NOT Self-Knowledge!

Perhaps it is only a paradox because of the dubious "I" entity. :-)

The "I entity is NOT dubious. IT DOES NOT EXIST. All there is is a thought, "I" - arising presently - in the undeniable Beingness-Awareness that you ARE.

All insights are crap until there is the seeing that no one exists to have any insight. Paradoxically (since you use the word!) there are insights that show the false as false ... just don't get attached to any of these marvelous wise concepts! They are all ultimately false ... as the quest of Self-examination shows in the end.

I'll keep asking, "Who Am I?"

That works! Keep going until there is absolutely no "person" left to ask the question. Toss everything into the furnace of that query.

When there is bliss, WHOSE Bliss? (Mine. Who is saying 'mine? I am. WHO AM I?) This is What Works. When there is pure witnessing, WHO witnesses? When there is pleasure whose pleasure? Pain? WHOSE?

"Who Am I?"

No answers.

Just the question.

Burn baby burn!

102. After The Questioning

G. Writes, The great question has shown that all that can be said about "me" is an idea, ideas are without form or substance. My life has been a story, the story continues but is seen for what it is. There is only this ordinary, simple perception of just this. I am this shining awareness, it has never come, it will never go.

Beautifully shared.
Clearly the search is over!
Welcome to Being - the home you never left.

103. Burn Away The False Cause Of Suffering

Q: I think I am coming to a resolution of my illness. From my own experimentation and research I'm pretty sure I have what is described as "Melancholic Depression," brought on by chronic stress.

Ultimately I found that it was the question, "Who Am I?" - and varieties of that such as Byron Katie's Work - that finally released all the stress and strain that was at the core of my depressions and melancholy, despair and frustration, and all my other mental illnesses.

When that hit home, and it was seen that the "me" that was ill and suffering was nothing more than a concept with NO actual reality or solidness, that game was over.

Self-Inquiry is an ancient path shown by the Sages.

Take it up in earnest and the suffering WILL disappear. There has been NO medication needed here since early July (with my Doctor's blessings of course.) There will come a time when there is no more suffering IF you take on this question in earnest!

I think I'm ripe hopefully something soon. If not then I'm in no hurry. I feel I still have some growing up to do, there is always work to be done.

Asking the question "Who Am I" and/or doing The Work is the fire that burns away the false cause of suffering - the belief in a separate person who has this or that ailment or condition. Bring it to bear on all thoughts that "I" do this or that. WHO does it all? - "I do! The mind answers. Put the question to that! "WHO is this I that claims 'I do?' WHO!?" Who or what IS this I-sense that believes in its own limitations and problems and free will to change What Is?!?

Ask. "Who Am I" that thinks believes knows identifies is depressed is sad is unripe OR ripe? Give all of that thought-story over to the quest for Truth: "Who Thinks? Who Knows? Who?"

Don't stop with any medications though. Not yet. Just include this tool of Self-Knowledge along with competent professional help for the organism!

Please do stay in touch. The end of your suffering is right in the palm of your hand. Take it up, put the question "Who Am I?" to work.

Endless Peace amidst all pain and illness is available right now. Because THAT is what you truly ARE. In That there can be great pain. But NO suffering.

104. 'Who Believes This?' Is My New "Koan!"

BC writes, *Asking myself (whoever is asking) the question honestly 'who am I?' I look and see an empty open awareness; there certainly isn't a bronze statue of ego sitting on a shelf inside me that can be grasped. The empty awareness is nominally full with whatever of is manifesting but the manifesting does not seem real.*

Who looks? Put that one back into the fire: "WHO IS THIS that looks and sees?"

That Emptiness, Awareness, IS what you truly ARE. That cannot be expressed, seen, or known! That is the uncaused a priori Absolute - that can only be represented. And the representation is NOT the actual!

The pointer of this "Teaching" is that there IS no such thing as "an ego." It's a thought, or a subtle sense even before thought, of that which sees. The fullness of all that is, and the emptiness of no thing - space-like Awareness - is NOT TWO (Ad-Vaita.) The end of the end as the inquiry hits home is Vedanta - the end of all 'truth,' the end of the (false) persona-driven language game. Maya.

RIGHT NOW Have a fresh look ... Who sees empty open awareness? That is the last to go ... the much-vaunted (in 'spiritual' circles) "witness" of all. Who witnesses the witness? What is THAT eternal non-conceptual Being that IS the knower AND the known?

Leaving nothing to remain through asking "Who Am I?" Until there is literally no one left to ask – this is the pointer – keep the quest up: WHO is seeing whatever is seen? Even when what is seen is nothing, looking continues ... who knows, who sees!?

Is there anything I am missing in what I am seeing?

Missing for whom? Actually it's not that anything is missing. It's that there is still something present. What is present? A "me" that wants to know "Am I doing it right?" Who is THAT?

"Sailor" Bob's question 'does the 'I' see?' is a good pointer to undercutting the belief in a self-reference point, do you any know any other good ones?

Even THAT excellent pointer needs to be stuck into the furnace! Who asks THAT question? WHO? Ask incessantly: ANY thought, any concept, has to GO. All of that is a story told by a "someone." Who is that? "Who Am I?" Be ruthless with the questioning. 24/7. Rather than "seeking" more, better and different concepts, get at the root of all the concepts with the inquiry: "Who wants more? Who wants different? Who Am I?" This thought alone burns out other thoughts and is itself burnt out in the end.

I will continue on with the investigation,

Excellent. NOW, right now right here, ask yourself, "Who continues? Who is it that asks Who Am I? WHO?"

Thanks again, Charlie.

It is a privilege to share this Freedom.

PS: 'who is it that believes this crap' is going to be my new Koan.

Wonderful!

105. Continuing To Identify As A Body-Mind

Q: Is 'fire' within to know the truth a prerequisite for liberation?

The fire is brought forth by your own inner Self arising as a suffering "person." That fire is Self-Inquiry!

Asking the question "Who Am I" <u>is</u> the fire. Bring it to bear on all thoughts that "I" do this or that. WHO does it all? ("I do, the mind answers.) WHO is this I that believes in its own limitations and volition!? Ask. "Who Am I" that thinks believes knows identifies! Give all of that over to "Who Thinks Who Knows Who?"

While I intellectuality understand everything you say I continue to identify myself with the body - mind apparatus. I wonder what prevents me to detach myself from the mind - body and know myself as aware presence.

Who understands? The intellect? That is a thought. Put ALL thoughts into the question: Who Am I? Who thinks all the thoughts - including the thought "I?"

"Whose intellect? Whose thoughts? WHO is the thinker?"

Intense desire for Liberation is a no nonsense commitment to get this question going 24/7 as much as is practical!

Who waits for a taxi or a tram?

Who looks at a menu?

Who orders lunch?

Who is the boss and who is the underling?

Taxi and tram, boss and lunch, these are ALL THOUGHTS. WHO is the thinker? WHO?

Give up ALL your intellectual understanding. <u>Start from NOT-Knowing</u>! Asking Who Am I does the trick. That thought, "Who Am I," burns away all other thoughts and is in the end burned out – leaving Self-Realization.

Thank you so much for writing this. For most "seekers" this is the last bastion of the ego – the refusal to ask the question that destroys the ego - so to speak; actually it does not even exist; it's only a thought believed to be solid!

But that can only be seen as real through the questioning, Who Am I?

Or not.

Ask "Who Am I" until "you" drop.

Or not.

106. Who Answers The 'Unanswerable Question?'

I am still asking, Who Am I, when I can remember.

Sounds good, keep at it with 110% commitment. Be relentless! Paradise beckons!

How am "I"? For the most part, living is effortless, grounded in the Endless Uncaused Joy of Being. And if and when it is not that wayless way - I have inquiry to end any and all moments of mis-identification and suffering - on the spot!

Inquiry unconceals the ever-present Timeless Being – and THAT is a Loving Open Presence.

That is what I am. Loving To Be.

That is also what YOU are.

When I ask "Who am I" the answer/feeling seems to be, "this mind and body, dummy" so I accompany that with "neti neti".... as in "not this body, not this mind or these thoughts" as I can't be what I am aware of, otherwise I wouldn't be aware of it.

You will quite likely find more power in not answering at all - not even neti neti. ANY answer is ultimately crap, even (especially!) "enlightened" ones. Go back to the question, let all that arises BE and ask, "Who thinks this?" Who answers the unanswerable question? WHO? Who Am I? Discard ALL but that One Thought. Be ruthless and loving – loving yourself, root out the false.

107. Who am I? Who are you? Don't Know!

G wrote, on a public Internet board, the more I ask the question "Who am I? the more it becomes painfully obvious that everything I can know about "myself" is a thought and refers to nothing else except another thought. Everything I can know about anything that is not my immediate experience of my awareness is a thought or fantasy.

It has dawned on me that I really don't have any idea of who I am apart from a thought, and that what is left is this immediate experience of life. In taking Charlie's advice and being relentless with this question, I have also seen that the question gets into this feed back loop of thought and ideas.

The question never arrives anywhere so to speak; it shows anything I can answer with is a thought about someone, but never the someone. There is just this awareness or consciousness. It is a relief, but kinda scary that I don't know who I am and even scarier that I never did.

Who am I? Who are you? Don't Know (as the Zen master said).

Great sharing of your actual direct experiencing. Well DONE G!

108. The Little Person Inside Insisting 'I'm ME'

Q: *I sit here and see that I am presence awareness and that's all there is, but the presence still seems most of the time to be coming from a me viewpoint, as if my head was a light bulb and there is a little person inside insisting, "I'm me!"*

That is all story. Why persist in telling a false story? Turn back to that Light. THAT is what you are.

I make only one suggestion. Once the clear seeing is Presencing, that this Being, Presence Awareness, IS what you are, all else needs to placed into the Furnace of committed and earnest Investigation. The inquiry, Who Am I, works. Use it.

You may want to read "From I Am To I Am, With Love," for more details on this non-practice practice, looking deeper and deeper.

I know and can understand the world is not real; I am still, out of having nothing better to do apparently, chasing addictive practices like food

The world IS real so long as YOU are taken to be real. Who Are You?

We take the world to be real so long as ignorance prevails. "Knowing" that the world is unreal is <u>crap</u>. It's a concept held by a mind – the thought I, appended by I am Me, I am a person etc - that as yet has not put to the inquiry and found to be false. Until that happens, all your knowing of "enlightened concepts" is more ignorance - fancy ignorance.

When I get the insight into this stuff in flashes I realize the problem is discursive Mind and trying to solve problems with it, like a monkey on your back, the monkey jumps off for a bit and then climbs back on.

More story. Quit telling that story.

Look for the storyteller. Who is THAT? Who thinks? Who says? Who reads right now? A "me?" I say with all Love and Respect for who you are, stop feeding yourself Bullshit. Look for real. WHO AM I? Is the question that counts. And finally it melts into "Who Asks This? And poof. Gone Forever in seeing that the "me" was never real at all.

I listen to a teacher or read some profound stuff in a book and may feel calm and serene for a while but then the identification comes back.

Totally False. The identification does NOT come and go - that is a story arising presently. WHO tells that story? There is no identification apart from a false belief in a discrete, separated "I." And that "I" or "me" is nothing but a thought. Stop putting your trust in a thought, which IS powerless. The thought "I" has no substance whatsoever! Serenity, fierce anger, happiness, peace, chaos - all these arise in the non-conceptual Presence-Awareness. That, perfect peace, remains untouched.

But THIS IS NOT AN EXPERIENCE FOR A PERSON! Experiences come and go and nothing that comes and goes can be real. What is real? What you actually ARE in Deep Sleep.

What is needed here NOW is to find out, who, what is it that thinks IT is separated from that Awareness?

All the lovely experiences after hearing Bob or whomever are just as much crap as are the addictions to food etc.

I am not seeing through the me problem.

YOU NEVER WILL.

Call off that search in the mind, stop! Quit trying to figure it out! You never will! STOP NOW and ASK - Who Am I that thinks and believes this load of crap?

Who Am I? ASK! And stay in touch, my friend. The abyss beckons. Asking Who Am I is the last thing the ego wants, so just do it!

109. Investigation Critical For Ending Suffering

A Friend Writes, This is a letter to Charlie and to all apparent others who have ended up on his site just as I had myself less than a year ago. Having read book after book, listening to CDs over and over, going to satsangs and all that spiritual stuff, I needed to speak with someone because what I was hearing was making sense but not really resonating for reasons I now know. I was reluctant to call one of these apparent enlightened teachers, as it was intimidating to me. Until I rang Charlie...I wish to share my appreciation and love for Charlie because in meeting him in this dream of separation, he has, with sincerity and absolute honesty pointed out to me what is real and what is literal imagination (not real) on many, many occasions. You may get very confused, frustrated, whatever in trying to figure this stuff out in the mind as I had. To the apparent others that are seeking and/or wish to express anything, this is an invitation to call Charlie as he will compassionately share and point to you the way home; by the way, YOUR'E ALREADY WHAT YOU SEEK!

Investigation (moment by moment by moment seeing) into who you REALLY are and who you think you are may be critical in order to truly see what is being pointed out here as it was for 'me' and Charlie will show you the way.

Just a bit of a side note:

I urge to those who have questions to call Charlie. There's no need to read any more books. Call him, share with him, as he will point you home. Also, if you feel the love, appreciation and gratitude for what he unconditionally offers as I do, I suggest donating whatever you can to just give him a bit of thanks in return. HE DESERVES IT! He won't ask for it, so I ask for him.

I absolutely love you C, and THANKS YOUR FOR POINTING OUT HOME!

Thank you so much for your heart, your commitment, and your generosity in sharing this. Welcome Home.

Follow-up Question: *Gary asks the writer, "I'm sure you knew (intellectually) what is real and what is unreal from your seeking "career," as I do from mine.*

Can you therefore describe how talking to Charlie made the difference (to you) between mere conceptual understanding and the LIVING reality of "not two-ness" or whatever your term for "it" is.

Writer To Gary: Last December I had absolutely reached a point where I was just fed up reading [a famous teacher's] books, listening to [another famous teacher's] CD after CD, going to intensives, and all that stuff, I was still feeling frustrated, confused and miserable with glimpses and pockets of peace and happiness.

I wanted to figure out how to get what they seemed to have. I always knew that my mind was the cause of my insecurity, my unhappiness, my anger, my fear, my impatience, my uneasiness and even my temporary experiences of happiness and fulfillment. I just didn't know how to stop it! I thought those guys were enlightened and I wanted to learn and get what they had.

PEACE and HAPPINESS was being sold and I wanted to figure out how I could get this stuff because I couldn't take the suffering anymore. I thought if I could learn to hold my attention in the present moment all the time, I'd be like them, enlightened. The more I seemed to understand what was being spoken of, intellectually, the closer to enlightenment I thought I was getting. I also thought I was getting really good at holding my attention in the present moment and eventually all of my suffering would just fall away with more practice. I was like a dog chasing my own tail.

Charlie's link happened to show up on the Google site while I was searching out some stuff on one of the other guys. At the time, Charlie's site was in blog format and he seemed a hell of a lot more accessible than these others, as well as a lot less intimidating to talk to than one of the "enlightened" teachers. So I called him.

In speaking with Charlie, he has been a guide, so to speak. He is not a teacher, though. He is just a wonderful friend sharing what had been so compassionately and patiently shown to him by various teachers he mentions on his site. And from what I hear - from Charlie himself! - He was sometimes a tremendous a pain in the ass!

In my own case, he's patiently shown me over numerous conversations how to do the investigation. This is about getting to the root cause of suffering and Charlie has been the guide to show me how to uncover my false beliefs and get to the "root" - and also pointed out that what I seeking to become is what I already always AM.

He does this unconditionally and compassionately and for this I am so grateful. Now, here, moment by moment, it is seen that "I" am not a believed, real, central character or reference point to which things are happening to, rather what I really am is that which all is happening IN, the ever-fresh, ever-present, CONSCIOUS-AWARENESS, just that. Ultimately, there's no Charlie, there's no me, no you, no teacher, no one except for the ONE. Therein lies Real Peace.

The non-duality teachings can be some confusing stuff, and Charlie has been there to compassionately nudge me out of the confusion and point in the right direction, so to speak. The mind CANNOT figure ANY of this out. Give up or 'die' trying! A thought is NEVER the actual, and Intellectual knowledge is NOT IT.

The mind may try and try to figure this out until maybe it falls under investigation. How? Asking it, "Who am I"? That is what worked for me.

What is the thought "I AM" referring to? See for yourself. If you don't know what I'm talking about, call Charlie. Words cannot express this stuff without being paradoxical and can lead to a lot of confusion.

Much love here,

PS:

In short: Intellectual understanding without investigation is not home!

Follow-up from Gary: *Thanks for your heartfelt and sincere response. And thanks to Charlie too, for the work he is doing on behalf of suffering seekers, who, (like myself), are confident that there are no more merely intellectual realms to explore and that now ONLY the living, non-conceptual reality of Oneness or Not Two-ness, will satisfy and fulfill (no one!)*

110. "I Woke Up At Home As A New Self"

A weekend retreat we offered here in Southern California participant writes in: *Thanks for your meeting this weekend. It was an awesome experience! Just seeing you and being at your place was a big event.*

I woke up this evening at home and felt a new Self arising. It was a mind blower, a new seeing.

Bang ON!

Thank you! I love how you are real and straight to the point. Just you, a Phantom in a body.

That's it.

It's a privilege to be used by Livingness this way - and a pleasure and privilege to know you. So thank *you* for coming all the way from Arizona!

Your own innate seeing is simply recognizing (RE - Cognizing) it's own true nature - YOU are the Guru!

With love from nobody to nobody ...

Right Back Atcha, From I Am to I Am ...

111. The Essence Of Freedom

Sum Ergo Sum

An e-mail correspondent who freed himself so to say - from his ignorance and suffering using the simple pointers that were first offered in the book, "*From I Am To I Am, With Love*," recently wrote to Charlie.

He graciously gave his permission to make his insights and freedom in Being public, for the benefit of those still searching and suffering.

The simple tools for release from psychological suffering are available, for all who desire True Peace and Ultimate Understanding. Those who take up these tools and use them are finding that all suffering is ending, and life is lived in a state of Loving To Be.

E-mail follow-up is recommended until all questions and doubts are dissolved and the search is over.

Write if you like - to non.duality@yahoo.com -

Charlie will answer as time and other commitments permit. There is no charge for e-mail dialogues.

"I Think Therefore I Am:" *Totally* FALSE

"I Am Therefore I Am:" *Almost* TRUE

However, in the Final Seeing,

Neither the thought nor the thinker is "true."

Q: *When does the nagging doubt finally stop?? I have read everything: Sailor Bob, Tony Parsons, John Greven, John Wheeler, Nathan Gill, Joan Tollifson, Leo Hartong.... I have met Sailor Bob, Nathan Gill, and Tony Parsons.*

I have corresponded with many of them. BUT...I have nothing more than a good intellectual understanding of Oneness, Advaita and that same old feeling of not KNOWING it. When oh when does the doubting stop and the knowing start??

NEVER. OR, JUST NOW. There IS No Time - No Someday. You Are That Awareness, Right Now. Call off the search and BE what you are. Full Stop.

However, since you've apparently been at this for a while, in all likelihood nothing that can be said to you – the above or any other pointers about the nature of What Is - will make any impact. You have heard it all, read it all, know all their pointers. Now there is the lament that all this knowing does not erase doubts.

So I have only one core question for you to ask yourself (in a few various ways) - who are you that knows all the 'intellectual knowledge' AND who knows that you are missing the pure knowing? (Which is crap anyway: There must be knowing itself for there to be the knowing of 'something missing called knowing!)

Who knows that you doubt? Who wants the doubting to stop? Who!? You say, "I have met, I have corresponded -" WHO is this I you so staunchly claim to be YOU?

WHO owns all that knowledge? WHO owns 'Intellectual understanding!?'

Who types and asks this question? (Who responds to it?) Who wants an answer; who believes any answer will erase doubts, whose doubts are they, 'mine'? WHO is this me that says these are mine? Who? WHO? Who thinks that there is something to get? Who wants happiness, peace, knowing, resolution, realization, liberation?

ALL knowledge is ignorance. Wisdom starts from SEEING: I Exist. Period. I AM. That is the only true statement you can make. All else is ignorance, hearsay, book learning. Useless as a cloud in the empty sky. And just as volitionless.

Other than that ONE UNDENIABLE FACT that you ARE, ALIVENESS IS, all else is <u>mystery</u>. Be with the natural state of knowing, I AM - Nothing else. Be THAT, not knowing ANYTHING else. Stay only with the always Presencing prior-to-thought NON-conceptual I-Am-Ness - Being-Presencing-Livingness - that you are. Reject all else as NOT-you. Even the THOUGHT 'I Am' is NOT You. That thought is only a re-presentation of what You are, in the intellect. The Intellect is NOT You.

I'll paraphrase a quote from Ramana Maharshi I found helpful, as I was going through pretty much the same spaces you find yourself in.

"The thought 'who am I' will destroy all other thoughts, and in the end will itself be destroyed, like a the stick used to stir the burning fire is burned away itself. Then there arises Self-Realization." Use that stick, the

question, *Who Am I?* Stir the fire that burns the ego-mind, the question-ER doubt-ER, right OUT. Snuff! You ARE. Nothing else is real.

Let me know how that looking at what or who you are unfolds the clear seeing for you. Dig deep; unconceal the Source of the belief that the thought "I" is a separate "entity."

Find out for yourself that this "me-myself-I-mine" is nothing more than thoughts arising here and now. For WHOM do all thoughts and feelings arise?

ASK! *'WHO AM I?'* That is your question for Now. BEING IS UNDENIABLE. THAT THOU ART. NOTHING ELSE - FULL STOP. Who thinks otherwise? Seek out that Source. *WHO AM I* is the question that can dissolve it all.

<u>Follow-up One</u>

Reply, "*Well, the answer to just about every "who?" question in your email that was shouted at the screen as I read each questions is: I DO !!!"*

Look at this one: "*There is a principle which is a bar against all information, which is proof against all arguments and which cannot fail to keep a man in everlasting ignorance - that principle is contempt prior to investigation."* - Herbert Spencer

You say the answer is "I DO." WHO SAYS SO? Who answers? I told you NO answer is worth crap. So why do you keep believing in "your answer!?" Investigate. Watch the reaction and go back to the questions.

Who says that this is the only answer? Who thinks that thought?

Looping back to "I DO" will quite likely make you more nuts than I was (that would be going some!)

You asked me, "*Where or what is "deep" in this that I am?"*

That is the question you want to be asking Your Self.

But NO Answer is "IT."

I can tell you, when you ask me, "Where or what is "deep" in this that I am?" that IT is NOWHERE. (NOW HERE.) THAT is the Absolute Absence of any separation. The closest metaphor in our human dream-story is - DEEP SLEEP.

But that answer and four bucks will get you a fancy cup of cappuccino. That's all.

The answer is crap. The question will ultimately destroy the apparent confusions and seeming obstacles to the always-So Space-Like Awareness – however, it seems we cannot escape the homework. Set at it with love for yourself. The kingdom is in the palm of your hand. All that is need now is to get after the falseness with the looking, using the tools of Self-Examination.

You say, *"Here there is just clear present awareness, right now, but that is not Liberation because there is still the sense of being a separate person here. There is still separation, or at least that is how it feels."*

1. There is NO SUCH THING as Liberation. That is a conceptual "holy grail" held onto for dear life by the seeker. That last thing that seeker wants is to find out he does NOT actually exist apart from a THOUGHT arising in Awareness itSelf!

2. So long as there is a sense of separation, you need to get after that with the question: WHO feels senses believes "I AM Separate?"

A one-sided teaching says, you are that and since there is nothing and no one, there is nothing to be done about suffering. This is half-baked, from my perspective.

The authentic Teachings tell you that as long as there is belief in a separate suffering person, that person MUST LOOK for itself, so to speak. That one must investigate. And find out what is real.

This seemingly prepares the seeker for the final blow that ends all seeking. But in fact the whole notions of cause and effect are illusion. This is seen - when there is no longer a seeker!

Meanwhile, ALL thoughts must be put to this investigation. WHO THINKS?

The first Pointer, I Am Presence-Awareness, often isn't enough. It wasn't for me.

I assert that the second pointer must be taken up with commitment and unswerving dedication for the final dropping of that totally false, suffering "me" to be seen as the fake that it is. In this dropping that phantom "me" to be seen to be nothing substantial whatsoever; it is thought-form ONLY, appearing to be real as a separate person.

My sense of it is all that's needed is for you to STOP telling these stories of "me" and look for the Source of that me-idea.

Then and only then (actually NOW) will you find that there never was or could be a separate "you" or anything else, apart from the Awareness Itself.

Where is there any you in deep sleep? Yet Awareness Itself beats the heart and breathes air in and out, digests food, all the rest of it. "You" are redundant, not required in any way for Life to Live Itself.

Look with these pointers. And do keep me posted - write as needed. Or call. (+1 714 708 2311.)

<u>Follow-up Two:</u>

I appreciate the no bullshit responses. This is a tough nut to crack.

With all Love and Respect:
There is no nut to crack! Who tells <u>that</u> story!?

Let me do as you suggest and come back to you.

NOW you're talkin'!

Many many thanks...

It's a privilege and a real pleasure.

<u>Follow-up three:</u>

Q. *"I have been working with the "WHO?" questions as you suggested"*

C: Excellent!

Q: "First result is that it removes all tendencies to try to understand or work things out intellectually, because it kind of short-circuits those thoughts."

C: Exactly. Great news. Now you see directly in your own experiencing of This – the enormous Transcendental Power of this simple Self-Investigation. The question Who Am I arises from, is brought into creation from, OUTSIDE of creation. By You - the Real You, not the ego-thought of a separate "you."

Q: "This is a good result because that has been a habit in the past – to try to understand. It is now clear that understanding will not help. There is no intellectual answer that can achieve anything."

C: Yes - you are well into it now. Keep it up.

Q: "Second result is that each time a WHO question is asked, there is a kind of stop, and there is just present awareness, a kind of empty looking. It's a kinda of curious looking, interested but disinterested. There is seeing and hearing etc. very clear, very present, and nothing much else. Then usually thinking starts again and then asking "WHO?" again."

C: Now you see that what you are is that Perfect Silence – the "stop" reveals what was already always there - YOUR REAL SELF-NATURE – AS THAT SILENCE.

Q: "So asking the "WHO?" questions seems to clear everything away, leaving just a knowing aware presence that just is quietly aware of its own knowing presence. Nothing fancy, just a quiet looking.
In fact that quiet knowing looking is there as things get done. It seems to dispassionately watch what the body is doing. Like making the tea or taking a leak - and in that, everything is very clear and alive and bright."

C: Spot ON. That Clear And Present Brightness-Aliveness IS what you are. And now you know That.

But Only Always Now.

There is no yesterday no tomorrow no today in That.

Q: "The thought arises: 'well this doesn't feel blissful or special like others have written about' - but then that is just a thought or words on a page in a book. None of that is what this is, here, now and that's the only thing which is real here, that knows itself to be."

C: This is a terrific bit of insight. The idea of something (some thing) blissful or special is the delusion of the false Guru who claims to have something you don't have. Now you see that it's all crap. GOOD.

Q: "So I can only stay with that knowing presence and see what arises. I pay no attention or time on the content of any thought, but just return to this present awareness."

C: Good job of sharing the seeing of the Actuality and exposing of the false. That is IT - just as you so clearly and beautifully articulated it. Very well done.

Follow-up four: NOW It Is Done

Both the futility and the temptation to pay attention to the mind to understand all this has become clear. A metaphor arose about this:

A long-term seeker is like someone who has walked around the world wearing a big coat that he has got so used to wearing. The seeker finally arrives at House of Awakening and at the door they say "you have to take your coat of if you want to get in" and he says "oh but I can't do that, I never go anywhere without my coat and what if its cold in there??"

And the reply is "but you don't need your coat in there, its nice and cozy warm, you'll be fine without your coat and anyway the door isn't big enough for you to fit through with that big heavy coat. You can just leave it out here" and he says, "You know I think I'll go and find another place where I can keep my coat on inside"!!!!!

Only by asking the "Who?" questions and resting in the silent looking that that reveals has that resistance to drop the coat (mind) become clear.

Its like the other problem with asking all the why questions and wanting an explanation of non-duality instead of just asking the "Who?" Questions and seeing the answer. Just give it a try and see!!

Another metaphor (see to be a lot of those coming up here!!): Someone wants to try skiing down a slope. Their friend who knows how to ski says "yeah no problem, we just put these boots and skis on and you face down the slope and let the skis just gently run down" and the guy says "yet but what are the skis made of? And why are they red skis? And how deep is the snow? And what's it like once you get going? And are all mountains like this?" Instead of just putting the skis on and giving it a try and then he would know and all his questions become kind of irrelevant and just delay the pure enjoyment of actually skiing and none of the questions can give any idea of what that's like until you try it.

So Charlie that's what the "Who?" Questions have revealed here.

Absolutely Dynamite!

Your expression is SPOT ON! You may want to share with those "others" in your life who express an interest in what happened that allows you to know the True Nature of what is - so clearly! It's beautiful!

These metaphors are really nicely done. Clear and resonating - Loving Being - Aliveness full blat! - Obviously there is a True Seeing of That - Here and Now. It is just great to hear this. I would like to include these (with credit to you if you like) in my upcoming book "Loving To Be." Is that okay?

Dear Charlie, of course, no problem - the metaphors don't belong to any one!!!

So Be It.

112. That Non-Personal Self Of All

How did we miss it? I Am - and You Are - Already That

A friend writes, *Swimming in the sea of this "hereness", "nowness", "aliveness", "awareness", "consciousness". And down to the essence of it all, which is all there is!!! Anything else is concept and not IT.*

I found out that these teaching pointers that are offered by nonduality sites and teachers are just descriptions of what you and I ARE, and what you are seeking, you ALREADY ARE. You are, in essence, by seeking, chasing your tail – like I did. And the belief that by figuring the teachings out (like the mind has been trained to do) will lead to final enlightenment, IS FALSE. It's just another one of the many false beliefs in a "you" – a "person" who can "learn" and be enlightenment.

That story kept me going around in endless tail-chasing circles - until it was exposed/pointed out by my best freakin' friend Charlie - who in essence is no one, who is oneness, which is who you are in essence too!!!

And In That One Instant of Now...

The search officially ended and the belief in me that could ever figure this out ultimately just - dropped!

I found out that this is about SEEING what is real/not real, through moment by moment by moment by moment by moment investigating. It can be seen right here, right now.

Always accessible because you're already IT! You've always been IT.

How I missed it I'll never understand.

My sharing - like the sharing on Charlie's site and in his books - is just descriptive – pointers, pointing to what you are (as I was) seeking - which is total freedom from all the suffering about "me" and "my life".

The mind is a machine, in essence, and it is conditioned to do what it does, and there's no YOU responsible for thinking these thoughts that arise like bubbles in the space.

Now - It is my absolute complete final understanding – that there's no me and no you that is responsible for anger, sadness, bad thoughts, evil thoughts, etc. Thoughts, as you can see for yourself right now, just arise and subside on their own, in awareness, and there is absolutely no "person" inside doing that thinking - or anything else!

See this for yourself!!! See thoughts arise like clouds in awareness. You have NO control over any of it. It's a machine at work on its own, functioning as it does. It's conditioning.

I wanted to Control It

I wanted so much to control it, to understand it, to stop thinking thoughts that cause suffering and that seem to make my life, my story and my existence sheer hell. It can be seen right now that you are what is being pointed to. I saw it finally. You can too. Then you will wonder – like I did – how you missed the obvious presence of Being for so long.

I am sharing this to point out nothing to no one.

All these words are just energy playing, to communicate this one simple thing: That you are already done! Drop the story of how your life may change after you may get enlightened like all these apparent others. I once held many expectations of how my life will be after I "figure all of this shit out and get enlightened."

It seemed – ONLY seemed! – That the more I listened to, and read, the pointers offered by all of these apparent 'other' teachers, the closer I was moving along in the process towards the end all, coin dropping moment of getting over all of my shit, just like they have!!!!

But once I saw that ALL expectations are bullshit, that they're just imagined, future stories of a 'me' getting enlightened, to see all there is is this sea of consciousness, always here, always now and you and I are swimming in it.

I want to shout from the rooftops -YOU ARE IT ALREADY, HERE NOW!!!!!.

Me too. The search is over, as it's seen that there's no "person" in the machine.

The last bondage – a last belief - was that "I'm not yet enlightened because." Because there is still anger, frustration, regret, sadness, pain that arises.

So the mind says this means that "something is wrong and I've veered off path." That belief was a major source of keeping the "me" believed to be real. Then, also, within my imagined story - What that belief also says - is I AM enlightened!! Both claims are just bullshit!

I will never be either enlightened or not enlightened. The whole damn matrix is false!!

In actuality, seen in each fresh moment, EVERYTHING arises in this aware, conscious, presence on its own and there's no one inside this machine doing ANYTHING!

THIS Is Liberation.

All there is, all there EVER is, is this, here, now, presence. Close your eyes. That presence is what is being talked about. YOU CAN'T GRASP THIS AS AN EXPERIENCE, but it is there, always because you ARE IT.

IT is the sea of consciousness. You are in the ocean - and you ARE the ocean. It is what gives everything life, and everything appears in this sea of consciousness. YOU ARE THAT NOW, JUST THAT. Everything is an appearance in this sea, EVERYTHING; with no independent existence, ability or volition. It's oneness, happening NOW. NOW. NOW. NOW. Analyzing these teachings, pointers, words - that was a source of frustration for me - and another form of suffering. Don't go there.

It is also possible, when you understand you are already what is being pointed to, then you may see that YOU ARE THE POINTERS!!!!!!! It is nothing you will ever imagine!!!! You are in the sea, just another wave with no independent existence. It's all a show.

All there is is THIS. Aliveness.

If there's confusion, you may want to give Charlie a ring. He's been there for me since I met him. Again, don't try to figure this out on your own.

Beautifully and passionately expressed, my friend.

113. Stuck In The Belief That I'm Separate ...

"Q: I'm stuck in the body, apart from everything 'out there'. Do I know it's true absolutely? No, but the subtle belief that I am separate is still there

You assert, "I'm stuck:"

Is it true?

Can you absolutely know it's true?

If the mind keeps telling you YES, ask another question: Hey mind! How do you know it's true? What is your evidence? Notice that all the evidence you can offer to make that assertion "true" is more thoughts, stories, perceptions, and experiences. Body sensations are words - speech, in subtle form.

Perceptions – what is seen and heard – are thoughts in gross form. "The mind" is all of this world-appearance – the world and you as a "me"-thought – and "your" body - are ALL thought-forms.

All this is arising in Empty Space - which is a metaphor for You- as Awareness-Consciousness.

Like the sun and planets and galaxies appear in the empty sky, All That Is - manifestation- Is an appearing - in the emptiness of space – pure awareness-consciousness. The Dance.

Right now - take your attention off the content of the space in which all that is happening – and refocus on that Space.

Notice what you notice. Now ask that mind again – can you absolutely know that this thought (that "I am stuck?") IS TRUE?

All answers are ONLY another thought – a yes, or a no, is just a thought!

Can you truly know that ANY thought is true? It may be seen now that the only thing the mind can think that points toward the Reality is - I Don't Know!

So: Let's go with NO – since that is closer to Reality.

The mind is thought and thought can only know more thoughts. Mind cannot know Space – Emptiness – Timeless Being. Mind is appearing within that!

How can Oneness know itself? Nothing exists outside space to know space.

And how do you react when you believe the thought "I am stuck?" I'll reduce it to one word:

UPSET.

SO: Who would you be without that thought?

See it now. Without thought is nothing. No Thing. THAT is what is Real. Just That.

Stop there. If the crap comes up in mind again – ask that mind – who are you?

It appears (ONLY appears) that core beliefs must be dealt with. Self-Investigation andles that stuff. And makes the prison a helluva lot more comfortable - before "Liberation." (Not that the re is any such!)

As the pure "Who Am I" inquiry is taken up again and bliss arises - and goes until not even bliss is lefet - until nothing is left - inquiry may well continue.

As Ramana Maharshi put it: *"The thought 'who am I?' will destroy all other thoughts, and like the stick used for stirring the burning pyre, it will itself in the end get destroyed. Then, there will arise Self-realization."*

Was he right? Who knows? Once Liberation has happened - or at least solid Awakening - who cares?

There's no one to know or care.

Now: Self is defined by Ramana as Existence - Consciousness- Bliss. And:" When you know the Self, the 'I' 'You' 'He' and 'She' disappear. They merge together in pure Consciousness."

So if you like to "do something" - Then sit with the question: Who Am I?

Rest in Peace.

Follow-up:

Yeah, man. WHENEVER there's a sense of being separate/me, that's the here, now cue to ask...it's almost automatic here; going STRAIGHT and directly to the root. It seems very common to take ownership of this stuff after SEEING the real/false and insights occur, and to then unknowingly believe that "I am now enlightened".

This is when the inquiry stopped for me. I thought I was done!!! We know what happens then...! That sneaky, back door belief! Now it's an alarm clock to inquire.

I knew you'd be there whenever I needed. And it's obvious the exchange in dialogue and willingness to do whatever it took to get the bleep out of a shitty existence were part of the apparent process of uncovering THE bullshit belief.

That's a big ten-four, bubba.

114. Where's The Bliss?

Q: "The recognition (or was it a thought) occurred yesterday that "me" is an idea - Yes, a persistent one, but an idea like every other. Just an idea, a reference point, a habit. The sky didn't fall apart and I haven't been plunged into bliss - and yet...something appears to have shifted, moved, etc."

Charlie: Yes. Beautiful! This identity - "me" - IS ONLY AN IDEA - a thought - yet it persists – and eventually brings pain or suffering - when it's held deeply as a fixation that this idea IS what I am. That's been happening from around the age of three. When that "I" is born at that age, then all our suffering and pain branches out from that root idea.

All suffering, pain, identification - and an entire universe of the living dream (or nightmare!) of "an individual, bound-up person" arises from that birth of "me." All the vast matrix of identifications arise from that - so when that is seen to be ONLY an idea in consciousness itself, that signals the onset of Self Realization. In my view now, all appearances - the universe itself - is a pattern of thought - that has been cast into a seemingly solid matrix - and once that core begins to be examined it begins to crumble like a solid looking cloud begins to crumble when the breeze arises (in the same space as the cloud - interestingly!) and the whole matrix ultimately collapses - leaving nothing-but-the-Self.

Which was already always the only Reality.

Then if any pain, suffering, fixation on a "personal entity" or identifications of "me and mine" - "I and other" - continue to plague the person - there are many methods for dealing with that so that it is no longer troublesome. Asking Who Am I? until there is no one left to ask is a time-honored method.

And when that doesn't seem to quite finish the job, we can take up a most powerful and effective contemporary expression of Inquiry - The Work of Byron Katie.

For me, Katie's Work is right up there with Ramana Maharshi's questioning - it is that Inquiry which finally destroys all traces of identity.

My proposition is this: I AM - and You ARE - in Truth - YES - Eternal Timeless BLISS.

The ancient sages of India called this Eternal Stateless State "Sat-Chit-Ananda." Translation: Existence-Consciousness-Bliss. Or, Isness-Awareness-Ecstasy.

Why settle for Sat and Chit without Ananda? I am observing that way too many are expressing that this so called "knowing" or "understanding" that "I Am That" - "That" being Existence - and the absence of belief in a "me" - is the "final truth" - and the "ultimate Self-Realization."

I respectfully challenge that notion. Why exchange the Diamond of Bliss for the dust of some paltry "knowingness?"

So: take up Inquiry whenever there is seemingly no bliss: And The Work is Simplicity in Self Expression, easy as breathing!

In essence: Ask four questions, and turn it around:

1- Is it true?

2- Can you absolutely know that it's true?

3- How do you react when you believe that thought?

4- Who would you be without the thought?

Then - Turn it around.

Here is the way that inquiry might unfold - you state, "I haven't been plunged into bliss."

I am looking into this - real time - right now: Because there is this same thought from time to time - "where's the bliss?"

I can easily see this thought as "my" thought. In fact it might be that there IS only One Mind thinking ALL of us into a false "existence."

We are "being thought up" by "It" - this One-Mind. Try that one on! Anyway, the inquiry is happening right now here - this way:

"I haven't been plunged into bliss."

First, let's see what one dictionary (Microsoft Bookshelf 2000) defines Bliss as:

"Extreme happiness; ecstasy. The ecstasy of salvation; spiritual joy."

Let's use that one. I LOVE that one! So, on to the Inquiry...

"I haven't been plunged into bliss."

1- Is it true?

<Wait -look inside>

Yes. It's true. Here is my evidence: I am not experiencing any bliss or ecstatic joy or uncaused happiness like some teachers claim is the "natural state." Plus, I worry about money sometimes. And I feel angry sometimes - like yesterday, when a guy in a van almost ran into me as I was walking around it in a parking lot - he didn't see me. I yell out in anger, at the top of my rather loud voice - "You stupid *^#!*&*&()!!!! " - in a fit of rage! I was just SCARED - and lashed out in verbal violence. That's being at war with What Is.

So then I feel guilty when he sheepishly apologizes - "I am SO sorry." First a say, angrily, "you should be!" Then to my surprise, and his, I say "Thank you!" He smiled and drove off – it was like he knew it was all just the play of the Divine! And wasn't taking anything person. What a great mirror.

> *[Sidebar: Thanks for what? In retrospect - I knew that incident was prompting me back into inquiry. At first I'm sorry I blew my cool and ranted at him. Then a few moments later I took up the questioning and it all disappeared! Understand though – all that stuff is appearing in what is Real – Awareness itSelf. This anecdote is just a way of pointing out that anything can arise and be diffused, in Totality.]*

So yes, it IS true. There is my proof. Because these authentic sages have pointed out that this Self-Realization IS permanent and unshakable bliss and that anger is not able to arise when that is finally realized.

The final answer is YES.

But Wait - There's More!

Moving on to the next question now -

2- Can I absolutely know that it' true?

<Close the eyes - listen inside - no rush - take a few minutes to meditate on this>

<A few minutes later>

When I meditate on that question - finally after pondering that - I disappear - as the "I" is "plunged into Bliss!"

(Just keep an awareness that I am describing something utterly indescribable. So don't BELIEVE this.)

But - wow. The "I" dissolves into Bliss.

There it is - the always so - ecstatic happiness! FOR NO ONE. NOT for "me!"

As the thought arises of a "me" that experiences this bliss, at once that too burns away in the fire of this Question.

So what is the clear and present seeing - "Can I absolutely know that it's true?"

An unequivocal NO.

<u>3- How does this body-mind mechanism – the organism - react when that idea is believed to be true?</u>

<u>Meditate – eyes closed</u>

To be specific: "MIND:" Frustration arises. A new thought, "why settle for understanding when there is no bliss? I want THAT."

And some anger attaches to that thought. "BODY:" Tension arises, starting deep in the gut. A feeling of emptiness also starts and both that sense of emptiness and the tension spreads into the chest - and the mind labels that FEAR - feral, threatening, a sense of deep insecurity, vulnerability, and along with it sadness wells up, pressure arises in the forehead, pressure behind the eyes, the thought I want to cry and sob and I can't I can't I can't I cant help it I am powerless - heart rate going up now - tension mounting - breath shallow, short - OH! It HURTS to be me -

And relaxing now - remembering all this is coming up only because a thought is being BELIEVED! Now - there is waiting for a few moments - and then, moving on: Who would I be without the thought? But first, A pointer -

the word "without:" What is it referring to? The absence of a thing. And so I ask now:

<u>4- Who would I be without the thought? (Or, who am I - sitting right here right now - without that thought or belief?)</u>

<Taking some time - meditating on this question>

< A few moments later>

Here is a description (a description is of course NOT the Stateless State being described) of what is - Here Now - As this final question is Returning The Real to The Real -

Endless Peace. Absolute indestructible JOY. Complete unalloyed - BLISS.

Home.

This "bliss" is NOT an experience for a person!

It is what IS.

The mind simply cannot ever grasp or know that bliss - that bliss-consciousness-presence is what the mind appears *within*. And ultimately - even that *mind* is an aspect bliss.

When there is no one present - that Bliss of Presence - IS. It Just IS. And when there is "someone" present - that Bliss of Presence - IS. It Just IS.

I Am That Bliss.

So Are You.

The incredible beauty of The Work is that it is always available whenever there is any trace of "Not-Bliss!" Thank the Is that Katie appeared in this life!

<u>Now, the "turn around:"</u>

I AM plunged into Bliss.

Is this idea as true or truer? For me now it is true-er.

Bliss is what I am. Totally as true – remembering that no concept is true – nor any experience of bliss. BLISS IS WHAT WE ARE!

And next, there's what Katie calls Number Six:

I am willing to experience <u>not</u> being plunged into Bliss.

I look forward to being plunged out of Bliss into anger, rage, or frustration.

Radical. Why this pointer?

All experience of NOT bliss can be a "dharma bell:" A wake-up call to put any anger or upset or ANY "not-ecstasy" into this Inquiry.

The Work is after Truth. The Truth - arising as Inquiry - IS setting us Free. Let it! If this moves you - do inquiry until there is no absence of bliss or presence of a person to be in pain or suffer - or even to be relatively happy.

Integrity – wholeness – shines through the mind as these inquiry questions. It's Self returning Self to Self.

That's my take on this. The invitation is to take what you get from this and if it resonates, go into The Work with a commitment to never settle again for anything less than that Eternal Bliss of Freedom - Sat-Chit-Ananda - FULL Self-Realization. But only Now.

My deepest thanks to you for being in touch. Please do keep me posted.

From Bliss to Bliss - With Great Love,

I Am.

Response:

You're awesome. Thanks for this. Just perfect.

YOU are awesome. Thanks for responding!

> *When your heart is immersed*
> *In this blissful love*
> *You can easily endure*
> *Any bitter face around*
>
> - Rumi

115. Seeking & Psychological Suffering Have Ended

Q: I'm so happy to make contact with you, as I've seen your name floating around the same nonduality circles that I've been into the last few years. I've especially enjoyed your reviews on Amazon, which have helped guide me in my reading on the subject. I had checked out your website once a couple of years ago, and from the tone of your writing, and some of the things you said, I really felt a kindred spirit there. So I both was and wasn't surprised to see you emerging with the book, "From I Am to I Am with Love," which I purchased through Burt Jurgens' site. I really love Burt and Gilbert Schultz' work, so I knew if Burt was publishing your book, it would be a winner.

I have now completed the Part One, and I must say that I am not disappointed. You seem to take all the best pointers to This-sing (as Wei Wu Wei would say), and present them in the most clear and effective manner I have yet seen.

I was particularly impacted by John Wheeler, whom I spoke to on the phone about a year and a half ago after reading his first book, and who succeeded in clearing up a lot of doubts and misconceptions for me. Since then, the Understanding has been settling in quite nicely with me, with new insights opening up almost daily. And so it is with great joy that I imbibe such vital, clear and powerful non dual expressions such as yours, Gilbert's, and Burt's, pounding away at what's left here of the conceptual coffin. The pointers have definitely hit their mark, and the seeking and psychological suffering have ended.

GREAT news!

I am greatly looking forward to hearing your CDs, a little of which I got a taste of through Burt's first "Non dual Expressions" CD. Again, like your said about yourself, some of my "best" seeing happens while I'm driving, and listening to spoken message really helps me look ever more deeply into the Infinite. I know your work will be just the remedy for many confused seekers, and I look forward to your future offerings, and maybe getting a chance to talk to you on the phone sometime, if possible.

Call any time. I love talking about nothing and sharing Inquiry with my Human Family!

Keep up the great work with your writing, CDs, and website. No immediate burning questions at the moment, but I cherish the invitation to explore with you any questions that may arise as thing unfold. I will be keeping in touch with you, and giving you some more feedback as I read/listen more to your work. I hope this finds all going well on your end. Peace and happiness all ways.

Thanks for your heartfelt expressions - I really am happy to hear it's all going well for you. There's not much left to talk about - just that being the ocean, the ocean can never ultimately know it is the ocean :-) Much love to you, dear friend.

Thanks, Charlie, for that last bit of wisdom. It doesn't get any clearer than that. Hope you are well. Love from one wave to another.

My pleasure!

116. The Deep Yearning For Truth

Questioner: For me, there is no seeking nor is there non seeking. It's VERY weird to describe. I am still suffering and yet the desire to seek a way out of this suffering has ebbed. All there is is a deep YEARNING for release and FREEDOM from this petty, petty self.

I am a prisoner who gets intellectually that this WHOLE thing is self imposed, and yet.... the condition called "suffering" by me still lingers and hovers loomingly about just waiting to pounce!

The ENTIRE issue is the sense of being a separate self, obviously. ALL the great teachings and living realizers give us the same message: THERE IS NO SEPARATION. ALL is ONE!! (Even Dr. Bronner's soap tells us that, haha). And yet the living from the perspective of a separate self continues. It's a real BITCH, but I guess that's the Koan we all (or at least me all) have to solve.

Charlie: Try the inquiry.
You say, "I am a prisoner."
Is that true?
Can you know absolutely that it's true?
How do you react when you believe that thought?
Who would you be without that thought?

Questioner: "Is that true?"
As long as I'm not free it's true.
"Can you know absolutely that it's true?"
No. All knowing is relative to something else. Nothing can be known absolutely.
"How do you react when you believe that thought?"
Everything is relative. Relative and subjective, therefore anything and everything is true, relative to something else.
"Who would you be without that thought?"
The same person I am now.

Charlie: Okay, good - Beautiful - I love that you began this inquiry. If the simple loving "Who Am I?" questioning has not yet erased the sufferer - you may want to go deeper into this.

I just spent the day with Byron Katie (Saturday 11 November 2006) - I wish you could have seen the freeing up from lifelong pain that happened for everyone who worked the four questions and the turnaround! It looked miraculous. And yet SO simple and easy to do - once we just try it in depth.

Katie - actually The Work of Self-Inquiry that came to and through her to us - is the real deal - I can verify that there is no person in there - it's just Oneness speaking to Oneness. She is a living Sage in the vein of Ramana Maharshi, to me. You can download the worksheets to facilitate freeing yourself from yourself so to speak :-) Go to www.thework.org. Roam around. Feel Katie's Love for you - her Love for all humanity. It's unmistakable, palatable.

All you have to lose is your suffering! All you have to gain is Absolute Freedom. I invite you with great love and respect to give it a good effort - really have a go with it.

Yes, as strict Nondualists say, in Reality beyond this dream, there is no one to do or not do this. AND - so long as there is a belief in a person who is suffering, why not use any and all possibilities for freeing ourselves from that - as rapidly as possible? Telling the same story over and over gets us nothing but suffering. Been there! No joy there!

I have done The Work. In great depth. I would not recommend it had I not experienced its beauty and power first hand.

It is nonduality at its very practical best - from the perspective here. Hey? <u>Two nonduality teacher friends turned me on to Katie.</u>

They love her - and The Work. Me too. Because it works.

It's not that is the new "right path." NO. It just WORKS. It's brilliantly effective! That is all I care about. It is freeing countless wonderful divine expressions - people - from their pain and suffering. Me included.

My dear friend - Regardless of what you do or don't do, I love that you are here, and I love that you are being. As you are and are not.

Here is a brief example of The Work - I did this one recently:

(I used a remembered incident from the past to demonstrate:)

I wrote on my sheet, *I still occasionally feel deep down that I am a again a "me" - a person - and that I am still separate from all else that is - despite all my understanding and clarity.*

And I'm frustrated and sometimes still blow my top and get pissed off at people who criticize my writings. Then I feel like a fake and I don't want to admit that to myself - let alone readers on my web site.

From that rant, I picked out the MOST stressful thought - which happens to be the CORE thought from which all else branches out - to put into the fire of The Work.

I don't recommend anything I haven't tested!

I've devoted the next chapter to this for the clearest seeing of how Inquiry works to end even the most significant OR the most insignificant suffering - right now - but ONLY right now.

117. The Work

"I am separate:" Is that true?

"I am a separate person - an individual."

Is it true?

<pause - looking>

Yes, for me right now.

Can I absolutely know that it's true? <long pause, eyes closed, looking long and deep - no rush - Listening>

.... and then it arises, direct seeing, not a concept, not hearsay- No, not absolutely. I cannot know absolutely that I am separate.

How do I react when I believe that thought?

I feel shaky - afraid, insecure. Depressed. Frustrated. Hopeless. My gut is nauseous - there is tension in my legs, spreading to my chest and head - and my heart starts to beat faster - I get short of breath - I hurt. I feel scared and sad and feeling sorry for myself.

Then I want to fix that - to eat or get coffee or some sort of drugs to mask the pain.

Who would I be without that story?

Who would I be if I wasn't believing that thought? <pause long long look within eyes closed>

Umm I don't know - uuhhmmm freedom. not knowing - no controller - just empty Being Loving myself and life as it is. Just - Loving Being - Being Life.

Turnaround: I am not separate.

Whole different reaction - like - NO reaction to that thought. Space - Loving being.

There is a lot more to it. A superficial pass - which I tried over a year ago - won't work.

Like anything else in the dream world we believe is real, it takes an earnest commitment.

The lovely Paradox. There is NO you to self-inquire - AND! So long as suffering is there, investigation can and will end that suffering.

It works for me.

Final note – ask yourself, dear friend:

Do I want to be right - or free?

118. A Perfect Storm

In response to some text that appeared on my web site – an open and honest expression – a self-appointed "teacher" e-mailed me and, among otter interesting things, yelled in CAPS "I AM FREE – I AM AWAKE!" And then wrote some very rude, vulgar, nasty words. I reacted – a "me" got caught up and took it on as an attack on the entity – wow. It – the false entity - can come back in at any time, it would seem.

After all the dust settled – after doing a bit of easy inquiry on the happenings - I looked at that teacher not as "separated and outside" of "me" - but rather AS "me (Self)" - in yet another wild and woolly, vulgar and loud, costume.

Yet - confrontation is not empathic compassion at least, not to my sensibilities and to most of the seekers I have met. Although I admit it can happen – through any teacher, any time - and when it does – it's perfect. Because, confrontation can reveal pockets of unseen ignorance.

But, to me now, ANYONE who goes about CLAIMING LOUDLY "I AM AWAKE, I AM FREE" is clearly NOT awake and free. Because the implication in that ranting is, I AM AWAKE AND FREE - AND YOU ARE NOT. Totally false! <u>We are all already always free and awake.</u> This is a perfect example of an ego claiming it is a sage.

Awakeness and Absolute Freedom are NOT a personal attainment. This person was a perfect example of what the ancients pointed out, "He who knows, doesn't say – he who says, doesn't know."

There are so-called teachers of nonduality that are quite confrontational in style. That one in particular has been raising quite a ruckus from time to time. For some that one's caustic sharpness which I paraphrase as "You're fulla crap and your teachers are too - they are wrong my Guru is right but I love you!" seems to somehow - strangely! - actually *work*. One author of several excellent books and CDs, whom I respect and appreciate, acknowledges that particular teacher as one of the sources of his own "Final Understanding." It DOES seem that this "nasty" stuff <u>can</u> be valuable – perhaps in this way:

If I see that "other one" as myself - and catch my reactions through inquiry – instead of blurting out what is "on my mind" - *then it all dissolves.*

Leaving – Bliss.

There IS no "other" - you are

always meeting your Self.

- Eckhart Tolle

Not that any expression that doesn't "resonate" for us needs to be endorsed or put up with - not at ALL! However, IF I am willing to drop the zeal for "being right making him wrong" - which I see is all just impersonal, automatic reactive mind stuff - I CAN see that any "person out there" is a reflection of my own projected consciousness - and THAT - the projections of mind - is all just a universal, impersonal, mind story. No fight, no blame.

My perspective RIGHT NOW is: *We don't invent this thought stuff. IT invents US* - moment by silent moment - so to say. IT thinks and we believe we ARE these thoughts - "the thinker" - and that they are MY thoughts. And "I" am "RIGHT" and "he" is "WRONG."

That's the mind – and that *is* suffering.

THAT'S what has the mind attack any "other" for something he or she says or does - just as THAT has thought-up "individuals" fly perfectly good airplanes, filled with perfectly innocent people, into tall buildings that were also filled with perfectly innocent people. Just THAT - the IT thinker we take to be US. Then, IT'S WAR - The I of Bin Laden or Saddam Hussein – versus - the "I" of Mr. Bush!

And "we" are just along for the nightmare ride.

But our sons and daughters and husbands and wives get killed off in airplanes and tall buildings - and in Iraq. It's all so - unnecessary - and avoidable - just all mind-projections. This begins to click in when I recall - right now - two pointers from "A Course In Miracles." I paraphrase - "It's ALL projection!! There is NO 'other'." And, *"Nothing Real can be threatened. Nothing unreal exists. Therein lies the Peace of God."*

In my view now, what really brings it all back to Home is - you guessed it - inquiry!

I found out - the hard way, after alienating a few sincere yet argumentative ones who came to see me before this hit home - that VERY few seekers really do resonate with the kinds of confrontation that some express. So we do both really know confrontation rarely works - for you and me - and, I assert, from my own experience - for most seekers. That said, some are so thin-skinned that most anything said – even in a mood of jest or teasing playfully – can be interpreted as a threat.

This is where compassionate Inquiry comes in.

True Inquiry is *much* more palatable than ANY out and out "off-with-their-heads" style confrontation! Katie's Work - which I've mentioned a few times because I LOVE it - is a great boon to those still stuck in ANY story - even any variation of "enlightenment" stories - "This Is All A Dream" or "I Am That!" - or "I Got It" - or "This Is IT!" - it's all more story!

If the job isn't finished after seeing a Bob or a Tony or any other "Teacher of Nonduality," then Katie's tools of inquiry can be immensely valuable in getting ALL the last bits dismantled.

"The Work" is utterly NON-confrontational and very deeply empathic and compassionate - right from Katie's Heart - and her own direct experience. I've met her twice – most recently in December 2006 - and worked The Work with her. She IS absolute clarity *and* Heart - and that's the real deal.

For me - it's just this: If we are still believing any story - even an "enlightened" story - let's dismantle it.

Anyway, in the long run, sharing works better preaching or confronting - that's what I've found out - the hard way! Asking questions rather than preaching, and sharing my own experience - and suggesting ways of looking at who thinks or tells a story - that's what seems to resonate for people who arrive here. Not screaming invective!

In any event - many, even so-called "teachers" who are in fact NOT really "done," cannot seem to see their own remaining blindness.

That's unfortunate - yet - it is what it is.

Is it wrong? We might well say yes.

But is that true? Or just another story?

If I think "he's wrong" and I express that - then, *I* need to look:

When I say, "He's negative and confronting," implied in that is, "He should NOT be negative and confronting."

Is that true? Can I know absolutely that it's true? No. How do I react when I believe that thought? My pulse rate goes up, I feel tightness and tension in my body, an energy comes rushing up out of nowhere, and is labeled anger, and thoughts go with that - "He's such an asshole, can't he see the harm he's doing?" - And then, I ask, "Who would I be without these thoughts?" - and it's Dead Bang Gone - it all just GONE - all of it. What remains is the Is that I Am - perfect Peace, dead CALM.

That is who I am - unless thought is believed and attached to as "my" thoughts. Bingo.

He's nasty. Is it true? Can I know absolutely it is true? NO. I react - energy labeled anger!

Then there's Katie's turn-around. *I* should not be negative and confronting. "I'm such an asshole!" "I" should be different than I am. This lets me see that ALL thoughts of that teacher, or any "other, out there," are projections of my own unexamined mind-stuff - unseen back stories still running me but so subtle they are not noticed until taken apart in inquiry.

So - "I am nasty." Is it true? NO. It's ALL stories! Dismantled here and now - by inquiry! Turning that around – it's my uninvestigated thought – not who I am – that can be negative and confronting. That does it – the seeing is always clear when these impulses of energy arising as thoughts are seen to be unreal.

119. A Perfect Storm Subsides

A Friend Writes, Dear Charlie, I felt compelled to write - I've been following with some interest your recent "process" regarding reactions you apparently had to some teachers words to you - and now your current inquiry into the whole affair, using, for example. Byron Katie's method in the most recent sharing on your site to question the ultimate truthfulness (and usefulness) of those mental stories/judgments. I guess I just felt moved to say that I really honor what I feel is a beautiful and deeply honest process and unfolding.

Apropos this, you said something that really struck a deep chord, and that is that "integrity thrives in these questions..." I absolutely love that... and I simply want to acknowledge how moved I am by your willingness to continue to inquire, again and again and again if necessary.

Very beautifully said. I love your Heart and your embracing of it all. Many, many thanks! I have now discarded all the posts and have returned the site to clear expression - no distractions. That said, I am not sorry it appeared – and stimulated this loving response from you. I continue to use Inquiry - The Work, and the simple query, "Who?" - to uncover any remaining ignorance. Thanks again. Warm Regards!

Part Six

Who Is There To Inquire?

120. Ask You

Ask who? Who is asking who?

This is the paradox of the seeking - when the seeker dissolves in the Pure Love Of Being - the whole story of "someone" who can do Self Inquiry - or any practice - falls apart. The entire matrix - the glue that holds all our stories together - simply collapses in a heap of laughter and tears.
But If There Is Still A Believed-in "Me"
Ask It – Who Are You?
Who Am I?
Take no answer as real.
Lovingly investigate ALL answers –
Respectfully challenge ALL <u>believed</u> thoughts.
Are they real?
Is any thought true? Or simply a thought?
What is a thought? Subtle words. Languaging – letters forming ad referencing to ... what? me? "I?"
Who is this me? Who AM I?
Awareness IS.
I Am/You are That.
"I Am Awareness" -
That thought - is it true?
No.
Can I know absolutely that the thought I am Awareness is true?
No.
How do I react when I believe that thought?
Arrogant. Like I know and you don't.
And I feel unconnected to you.
Who am I when I do NOT believe that thought?
Simple Presence - Awareness - That in which the thought forms and is seen here in the awareness and then dissipates – just like a cloud in a clear sky forms – changes – stays awhile- and is dispelled softly by a breeze
Awareness is the Sky.
Thought is the cloud.
Inquiry is the breeze.

Softly dismantling to false beliefs
leaving only the already always Reality - Sky-Like -Awareness.
Turning the Pointless Point
YOU are that Awareness.
That IS
untouchable
True-Nature.
You.

121. Paradigm-Ing

A Paradigm Shift to No-Paradigm?

These are all concepts and NOT to be taken as "Truths." All this that follows is the ponderings of space-like seeing – Awareness ... just that. Nothing special or significant.

Now: What If . . .

Once upon a time, Descartes arrived with an invocation, "I think therefore I am" was a kind of declaration, that created a new Matrix, a paradigm, for "human understanding."

Oh. So that's what I Am ... a thinker. (Poor Rodin bought into it. And look at his sculpture of "the thinker:" Bent over, clearly not very happy!)

Freud and Psychology created another kind of paradigm, a context in which (ultimately seen as false) persons could "understand themselves and their lives." I feel, therefore I am. And the Id (ego) is the thinker-feeler, with which there is definitely something wrong, and we must invent fixes! And so it happened that a rather large "body of knowledge" was born, psychology, psychiatry etc ... all to FIX a "person" who was flawed in some way and was therefore suffering.

None of that addresses the "core issue" of the actual absence of an "entity" that can "think" or "feel" or "suffer."

My old pal of 28+ years, Jack Rosenberg, (aka Werner Erhard, of est fame,) once said, about the catch-phrase "thinking outside the box," that the only "box" that interested him was "the box that ALL the boxes come in."

What is THAT?

Nothing. No Thing.

Space-like awareness.

Victor Hugo once said, "There is nothing so powerful as an idea whose time has come." Perhaps the idea of non-ideas - a paradigm of No Thing, is a non-idea of a space-less timeless BEING as the real essential knowingness, by which life can, rather than being "understood," be LIVED fully and completely with no suffering, is an idea whose time has come.

In other words - Living AS Love.

The proliferation of really excellent books, Videos, CDs and web sites devoted to dogma-free Advaita "nonduality" - and other pointers from the unreal to the Real - is a pretty good indicator, perhaps?

So is this appearance in the "Dream of the One-Self" a new Paradigm-less Paradigm coming forth from Self?

In this dream of life, as "I" see it from nowhere, aliveness arrives and transforms itself out of nowhere. Anything is possible.

In my viewless view, it is an exciting "time" to be alive ... and fully alive, as no thing. And everything. Wow. Neat dream.

Loving to be!

Wakey Wakey

The small man
Builds cages
For everyone
He
Knows
While the sage,
Who has to duck his head
When the moon is low,
Keeps dropping keys all
night long
For the
Beautiful
Rowdy
Prisoners.

- Hafiz

122. Now There Is Morning

    gray sky skying

            trees treeing

    love living

                alive

    a cereal bowl is full

           a juice glass empties into a mouth

    happiness arises

    all is well

    nothing is wrong

    a book is writing

    itself

    a computer freezes up

           now there is raging angry shouting

    all is well

           nothing is wrong

    now there is hunger

           great pain

                a back feels broken

    a foot is swelling

    there is hunger

    sadness arises

           tears bubble up

    but stop before

    raining on a sad face

all is well

nothing is wrong

is it joy or sorrow

    who knows?

knowing is

    useless

not-knowing

    all is well

    nothing is wrong.

123. "Advaita-Speak"

A common occurrence amongst seekers that are still someone who thinks "I am done" is "Advaita-Speak." Having been caught up in that delusion myself for about four years, I can usually recognize it when I see it. I may or may not respond to someone here or on e-mail who is interested in non-duality with a pointer that "there is seeing" or "no one sees" - but that is like the needle a doctor uses to inject some anti-virus in the organism. After use it is discarded in the "sharps" box.

When Bob Adamson spoke about my book, "From I Am to I Am, with Love," he used the phrase "I think," with absolutely no belief that he is separate from all that is, or that he is an "I" that thinks! He speaks like any normal person, "enlightened" or not! (Thank God.)

He said, "I certainly endorse this book. I think the book is very good."

So what? The Advaita Police would jump on this.

He uses the I-word. So - he's a fraud.

That's just another egoic story.

Those who try to always "speak correctly" demonstrate either an essential ignorance, or perhaps arrogance "spiritual ego."

Been there done that. I was a true-believer, mostly in "est" - the Werner Erhard Zen-like seminar popular in the seventies and eighties. est was a helluva wake-up call - and I stuck around there, and at the successor to est called Landmark Education, for 27 years. "Trying to get IT." I was a typical 'est-hole' - playing trainer to the hilt. Not pretty! Yet it clearly had to happen - 'cuz it did.

Anyway - let the pointers work - and then discard them. Self-Knowing Presence Awareness requires NO fancy language, and often it's off-putting to those who are not "ripe." ALL expressions are in duality; that is the limitation of language.

In normal everyday conversation with other people, I use personal pronouns just as everyone else does.

There is absolutely NO value in adopting a new jargony way of talking in the world. Once the dream is seen as a dream, there is no need for posturing. It's just a pretentious way speaking that is an egoic thinker-mind "trying to look wise" or play "guru."

I see it clearly only because I know it SO well - like I said, been there done that, no joy in mudville.

Hey, I just sit at the computer in my bedroom (I love my bedroom!) - in my underwear, under a window with an awesome view - and type a bunch of stuff like this, only because I ain't got a real job at the moment.

Who knows, maybe a better offer will come along. Then this yakkety-yak will very likely die a natural death. Or only happen at meetings here. (Don't worry - I shower and put on clothes for meetings with others!)

These days I use personal pronouns with impunity. Once you know beyond any vestige of doubt or question that the I is a phantom, then it matters not in the least what words get said ... or how they are said.

If you are infected with the virus of Advaita-Speak, fuggedaboudit. Just be yourself as you are. When the "Understanding" is solid, no fancy adjustments in speaking are needed. Or wanted, usually!

I had a lot more friends before I tried to do Advaita-Speak on them. Those who are resonating with a heart felt desire to be free - and sincerely seeking authentic Self-Realization - will doubtless find the authentic non-duality teachings. They'll will be led by that One Self to find their way to the perfect teacher or book or website - or whatever else is next for them.

I don't play guru. It is a no win game that can only be played by a fake who thinks he is enlightened.

I ain't a guru.

In Reality I am no thing.

In the dream of life and living ... I am a friend.

124. Residue

After nothing happens to no one (so to say) the appearance of "residual" habits of thought that have been embedded in the brain cells by years of repetition can still arise. Once the Non-Conceptual Understandings ... the so pointers ... have been imbibed fully, these pointers can immediately arise on the heels of the repetitive thought-pattern and cut them adrift at the root ... because the root of a habitual depends for its (illusory) existence on the core "I" thought. When root is severed its branches must (eventually, in the appearance of "space-time," wither and die.

Keep the presence of the pointer that even all these so-called habits are nothing substantial in and of themselves ... just the pure Absolute Presence-Awareness arising as energy-intelligence, patterning into sounds forming letters into thought-feeling-words ... concepts ... referred to more concepts and all branching out from the dead root.

As the energy of false belief in a false believer (the "I") is no longer fed to these thought forms, they just fade away into the Cognizing Emptiness. They just die - as any unfed "thing" dies.

No energy no life. Have you noticed? Unfed bodies die eventually. All "things" come only to pass ... not to stay. All that stays is no thing / every thing.

The Absolute alone (all one) IS. That arises AS Aliveness, which manifests as all there is, including the ideas of separation and completeness, endarkenment and enlightenment ... everything.

Unicity. That alone IS. This cannot be known ... it is no more possible for any "one" (which requires the existence of the concept "other") to know That, than it is for the eye to see itself or the ear to hear itself, as all there is, IS That.

Liberation is not seeing not knowing not two. One Is. That is Life - Being Love.

YOU are THAT - YOU are the light - the Life - the ALL.

125. What Is Love?

What is love?
   Who knows what love is ... really is?
Maybe all the things I think love is, are not love
   Maybe love is nothing ... no thing.
space - no thing - lets every thing be as it is ... and is not
So maybe love is un-knowable ... yet as real as the breath of living
   And as precious as a lover's kiss and as real as ... ?

What is love?
   You.

126. What is the Mind?

Some say, "The mind is time."

Some say, "The mind is a collection of presently arising thoughts, memories, imaginary futures.

Some say, "The mind is a linear arrangement of successive moments of now."

Some say, "There is NO mind."

I say, the mind is both real and unreal, existent and non-existent. And neither real nor unreal, existent nor non-existent.

But I'd rather say - *mind is a four-letter word.*

Like shit. Or love. Or them. Or four. Or word. or time.

But who is saying all this? Thinking all this?

Find that one. She does not exist. He never did exist.

Is there any sayer-thinker or is there just thinking-saying?

Thinking is happening - when it is. No one is doing it. Thinking says, "I am thinking." It's a thought arising presently. No one really owns it.

Is any concept about mind true? Or are ALL these squiggles and spaces arising presently in the space that IS just nothing more that an appearance?

Is the so-called mind a real thing? Apart from wakefulness, the beingness that IS, awareness itself, is there any "mind?"

Find it. If you can.

What is mind? Nothing. No Thing. Everything. Every Thing.

Appearance.

Hard and soft spoken persons - myriad places, things, actions, non-action, sleep - wake - dream, all simply nothing at all in Reality.

What is Realty?

THIS. YOU. ALL.

127. What is worry?

The Greek word that is translated "worry" or "to take thought of" is a word which means to divide, to pull in different directions, or to tear apart. When a person is in a state of worry or anxiety, they are no longer focused because they are pulled in different directions and are being torn apart through this dividing pull.

The second thing that you need to know about worry is that it is always about the future. No one worries about the past. You may regret the past, you may feel sorry about the past and you may worry about the consequences of the past but you don't ever worry about the past. You never worry about the present. You may have fear, apprehension, guilt or conviction of sin in the present, but you don't worry about the present. Worry is always future tense. We always worry about something that has not happened. Therefore, worry always deals with some imagined fantasy of events, circumstances, interactions or reactions. But worry always takes place on the level of fantasy because, if it has not happened, it's not real.

According to a Microsoft dictionary:

Worry: The Old English ancestor, wyrgan, meant "to strangle." Its Middle English descendant, worien, kept this sense and developed the new sense "to grasp by the throat with the teeth and lacerate" or "to kill or injure by biting and shaking."

Pretty nasty stuff, isn't it? Points nicely to the suffering that ensues as a product of the core belief that there IS a "me" to worry.

Who is this "ME?" Find out!

A paraphrase – which one of you can grow a single inch taller by taking thought?

Who thinks?

128. I Live In Language

An "I" lives only in language.

If there were not language - where could there be any I? Or you? Or us? Or world?

Not a thing exists outside of language.

Language is the water I swim in. without language - what is there? What is here?

No thing exists outside of language.

Don't believe it. Look.

I am. That's words - language.

I. That is a one-letter word. Language.

Where is a universe without language?

I am in language.

Is that true?

Can I know that to be true absolutely?

No.

Who am I without that thought - belief - story?

No one - before language.

Loving being non-language.

No more words.

No more me.

Yike!

    Who got scared of his own absence?

Whoever that was - he told a sad sad story

    And disappeared in a cloud of You - O Beloved

129. "Brain" or "Mind?" Too Many Thinkers

I have been pondering (in Advaita speak pondering is happening,) and I notice - there is for many seekers a confusion between the concepts of the brain and the mind. I remember that early on I had this question. After the initial awakening this became a ponderation for me ... and I became interested in making some sort of (notional) distinction.

While brain and mind are only linguistic terms, concepts, and in fact not two, and in fact there is no mind (it's just another thought) there is a potential for confusion - from my own experience I can verify this.

I won't get into the pointer that in Reality there is no brain either! This text is more for an intellect that is confused - and so this text may serve as a tool for the subsequent inquiry: Who am I?

First, what is the brain? In my view the brain is like hardware, formed from the DNA of the egg and the sperm. How much of the subsequent behavior is out of that? Perhaps that is a mystery.

The Microsoft dictionary offers this much: Brain: The portion of the vertebrate central nervous system that is enclosed within the cranium, continuous with the spinal cord, and composed of gray matter and white matter. It is the primary center for the regulation and control of bodily activities, receiving and interpreting sensory impulses, and transmitting information to the muscles and body organs. It is also the seat of consciousness, thought, memory, and emotion.

This points to assertions that the brain is a receiver of thought-impulses as stimuli. In other words, hardware. And if there is a receiver, there must be a sender, so to say. What is the sender? Perhaps as non-duality points to, the sender is Consciousness, pulsating and forming into bursts of energy perceived LATER by that brain ... including the idea that there is a "person" in the brain that takes credit or blame (I did it!)

Then in my model, the mind is the software. Conditioning. After the organism is conceived and begins to form, at some point, I suggest, when that fetus reaches a certain (who knows what) level of development it begins to be conditioned by it's environment (crack addicts give birth to addicted babies.)

As I see it, the brain is like a huge hard disk. It searches its memory banks, like searching a zillion-gigabyte disk drive. Sometimes it seems you can even hear it whirring as you try to recall something you need to know (where did I leave my car keys?)

Respected non-duality teachers, particularly Ramesh Balsekar and Stephen Wolinsky, assert that the mind and brain are distinct, in that the brain, being like a receiver, recognizes the arising of a thought ONLY AFTER the thought has arisen as a throb of energy in Awareness.

And if a thought gives rise to action, that action has already begun. They quote studies that say the thought shows up as a non-conceived cognitive arising, and a split-nanosecond before the brain RE-cognizes that thought -and of course in the one who still believes he or she is a "person" that pattern of letters-words is then seen as being conceived by "me" as MY thought.

Many years ago, a teacher that I had the good fortune to meet and study with, Chilean Philosopher Dr. Fernando Flores, often said, as a pointer to this notion - I paraphrase - "what you call 'yourself' arrives LATE to the party." Brain-cognized thought does not precede action. It is the other way around.

What prompted all this pondenation? I notice here sometimes, actually quite often now, that (for example) I have already started to get up - the body is already on its way to the fridge - and then a nano second later the thought arises, I am thirsty, think I'll have some veggie juice.

Action has already happened BEFORE the brain recognizes the thought-impulse!

I recall from my racing days, that there was no thinking before action! (Racing at 170 MPH is a good way to see this but it can be awfully expensive, and a bit hard on the body sometimes when wheels fly off and it all goes bang! against the wall.)

Anyway, all this prattling is a lot of fun!

What do you make of all this? Yes, it IS an appearance. But the seeker does not know that. Anything that can provide a service, especially to those whose intellect can be a major obstacle, I am totally in favor of.

130. What is the real authentic me myself and I?

Who is asking all these questions?

When "I" talk about "my" life it seems very real - and then there is a vulnerability and insecurity - what will become of "me?"

I am scared of living and scared of dying ONLY when there is a belief in a "real me" called Charlie or Ishan or whatever name is tacked onto this body at any moment.

When there is clarity and seeing hearing experiencing living there ain't any person here - that feels - no, IS - much more real than my story filled with touching moving shared experienced - experiencing already past and JUST NOW now now do nothing more that perpetuate this idea of a separate me STOP.

Now - warm body sensations clicking keys blaring TV cop show buzzing chewing on a thumb god eating god if ya know what I mean sounds I don't know what who am I? What's happening NOW? I Don't know.

All I can say or know is what happened a nano-moment AGO past passed on. What is happening NOW??

Too Late ... !

That Not Knowing ...   IS

T h i s

131. The Big Bang is NOW And Not Now.

The idea of a "big Bang" that happened "sometime a loooooong time ago" is the simply a thought-story appearing NOW.

Notice a belief in such a "thing" as "time?"

Who believes this!

Right NOW the BIG BANG! Is.... apparently.... happening.

In THIS, the Eternal Instant before all concepts of Time, Space, Separation and a "me" with free will to choose, believe, and remember - and all that jazz simply IS.

Living Silence. Fullness In Emptiness.

BANG! You and Universe appear!

POOF! You and Universe disappear!

IT is all happening so fast IT goes unnoticed.

BANG! You ARE The Big Bang!

Just before a time called now.

The dream is not

The real is not

The living is not

The one is not

The two is not

The not is not

    That is all.

The Big Bang is NOW And Not Now.

132. Being Not-Knowing

Ultimately
Being the ocean, the ocean can never know
or understand that it is the ocean

Understanding or knowing Being is not BEING.

Being Is Inescapable. And Indescribable.
That - Being - Is All That Is.
Everything.
Nothing.

All Our Seeking to Know and understand This
Is The Folly Of A Dreamed Character
Trying to wake her/himself from a Dream.

when there is no one
'this is seen'

he or she who says 'i know,' knows not.
do you say or believe, 'i am an individual?'
do you say or believe, 'i am love itself?'
do you say or believe, 'i am bound,
trapped in a human form?'
do you say or believe, 'i am free?'

all these knowings are false.
do you say, believe, think, know - "I Am That?"
is there absolutely clear understanding - "That I Am?"
do you know - as 'charliehayes' knew - "i am all there is?"

"I Am Oneness?"
all these knowings are false beliefs.
if you or i believe you or i
are 'one with everything'

who believes that?

if you or i believe that and think that now
you or i are enlightened,
then look out, dear One.
in all likelihood, you and i are in for a great fall
into despair.

it happened here - just a moment ago in time
yet never happened at all in Timeless Being.

that was all a story - a tale told by an idiot
signifying nothing.

THIS - all that IS - Consciousness - the Absolute
simply can NOT be known.
the knowing - experiencing - being in-the-moment
"everything is ME!?"
is NOT the nondual inexpressible One.
the One-Bliss-Being cannot know itself.

THIS can only be pointed at - so to say with useless words - as
NOT KNOWING.
all anticipations of outcome are mind.
all seeking for Oneness is mind.
THIS - Oneness - is unknowable.

THIS is all that is.

paradox: even that looking and anticipating
is THIS.
the story is both it - and NOT it.
THIS is Oneness - storying.

Not Knowing.
Being is Not Knowing -

nor is
Being NOT not-knowing.
impossible to see or know
THIS IS ALL.

who writes this?
not knowing.
just that.
IT ate 'me' alive
and spit that out
into nowhere

If you meet a Buddha on the road

Love Her.

133. Not Being Not-Knowing

Q: Dear Charlie, as with many others, I have followed the developments on your site concerning your participation in The Work of Byron Katie. I have read her website, listened to the audios and taken a look at the worksheets. A number of different reactions/thoughts have arisen here, caused only by past conditioning etc. no doubt. But there is no criticism of Byron Katie herself intended. Firstly, the "Who am I?" question has been so direct and so effective that anything else seems far too heavy and involved, almost noisy by comparison.

"Who Am I?" Yes. That's IS the bottom line of inquiry! And ultimately the bottom line to "The Work."

So -If that one simple query works – that's great. I know it worked for you – as it did for me. My interest in sharing my experience of The Work is twofold:

One, if ever "the me comes back in to claim its own absence" – as it happens here and can happen there - from time to time – and suffering ensues - and the simplicity of the question "Who Am I" doesn't work to dispel that self-centered thought-feeling story - THEN– these four questions and the turnaround can set it all straight in seconds. It needn't take a lot of time – for me the whole thing is nearly transparent – a thought of a self-center arises – immediately the questions arise – and poof. OR the space-like awareness of a naturally arising Who? Arises and that brings about the poof.

Secondly, there is also some concern that if not used skillfully, the Four Questions and the Turnaround could just become another wonderful playgroup for the ego even perhaps providing some form of self-justification.

It could take a great deal of thought etc. to answer those questions and just get lost in the story, compared to the clarity of just being pointed to the Seeing, a la Sailor Bob.

You have taken a look at the worksheets. But have you used them to take this story apart at the roots?

I'm taking this on – since in a profound sense – your thoughts ARE "my" thoughts – consider the possibility that there is only One Mind of humanity and that Mind happens to have six billion or so brains to have thoughts in. Anyway, here we go:

"People could get lost in a story."

1) Is it true?

2) Can you absolutely know it's true? (YES OR NO. Be still. Let the heart answer – here - the Heart always says NO to this one. I cannot know any thought to be "true." All thoughts are just words – that the mind assigns the quality "true" or "not true" to. The real "knowing is "I Don't Know." Dwell THERE!)

3) How do you react when you believe the thought? (For example, 'thoughts of concern arise' – and I assert with confidence that 'concerns' are suffering - subtle egoic judgments – comparing this to that – Katie to Bob – ad infinitum!)

4) Who would you be without the thought? (This is the end of the game for ALL thinking of concern, right-wrong, better worse etc. – and it takes - at most - a few seconds!)

Turnarounds:

"'I' could get lost in a story." (Didn't you just "get lost in THIS story?"

There is nobody "out there."

Or "people could get free of their story." We don't know - and it's arrogant to believe we know what is right for anyone's path!

Or, "My thinking could be free of this story." Bingo.

NOW - take it down to the core: There are people "out there" apart from me. IS IT TRUE?

In my view - anything is possible in this manifestation. Bob does not have "The Answer" – nor does Tony or Katie. All any teaching can do is point us to look for ourselves. And it's crystal clear to me that many "Advaita-people" analyze The Work – instead of just USING it! No wonder there are all these stories about it and judgments that one method is better than another method etc.

I have observed that some teachers that I have worked with in the past have subtly judged me when I share - in a friendly and loving way - that The Work has been helpful in erasing last vestiges of suffering that arise here.

1. The Work defuses all upsets it occurs like this - if at all.

For example - "I am disappointed in Teacher X because he judged and invalidates what is happening to end confusion if and when it arises. He should not judge other teachers and teachings."

Distilling it – X should not judge others.

1) Is it true? "Yes – every spiritual person knows – "judge not lest you be judged."

2) Can I absolutely know it's true? NO.

3) How do I react when I believe the thought? I get an empty feeling in my gut – feels like I have been sucker punched – below the belt. My breath gets short and shallow and my heart rate goes up. I feel a flush in the face – and pressure in the head. I have thoughts about wanting to either fight him and argue – or hang up on him – run away. Fight or flight.

4) Who would I be without the thought? (Perfect stillness is unconcealed immediately!)

Turnarounds:

1) X should judge me. Is that as true or truer?

Sure. He does judge. That's what IS! And when I argue against what is I suffer.

2) I judge X. Yes – I judge him for judging me!

It's always back to me.

3) My thinking judges X. Yes – ONLY thinking. Who would I be without the thought-story of judgment? Who Am I – without a story?

Now let me play back what arises in thinking here as this is getting written: Who is saying all this? Who is commenting and who is commenting on the comments? Who are you? Who am I? WHO CARES what anyone else is "doing?" WHO is the do-er of all this – Self Inquiry, or The Work - asking 4 questions and the turnaround - or the one big question – Who Am I – and who is "pointing to the Seeing?"

WHO?

All this stuff just arises – then we say – this is what "I think, I feel, I wonder" – or "There is some concern" – who is concerned? Is that doer really GONE? For good? Being "advaitically correct" is a new spiritual disease that in my observation – of thinking appearing here and elsewhere – can subtly reintroduce or reinforce false ideation of separateness.

Is Katie – and her "seekers" - not YOU? Is anyone not YOU? Not me? Is Charlie not YOU? Who is concerned? Who is bound? Who is free?

Thirdly, having seen it happen many times over, there is concern when any one person/teacher gets put up on a stage and treated as somehow special or gifted. Her website and testimonials make her look and sound like a movie star!! This seems to be so far from the pure simple truth of Presence-Awareness and Seeing itself. Again, there is always the risk that the highly praised teacher is just again a prized object of worship out "there", who "has" something "I" don't - all just more distraction from pure Seeing. This has nothing to do with Byron Katie, but is what is being projected onto her by seekers.

"Being an object of worship – projection by her seekers – all more distraction" - who is saying all this? Who would YOU be without that story?

What makes us think we know ANYTHING?

Who cares what "others" do or don't do? Who Am I? Who are YOU? "This seems to be so far from the simple truth ..." who says so? Is it true? Who makes it either right OR wrong? Who?

I am NOT saying either you or myself or anyone else! - is either wrong OR right. I am inviting you – and myself - to look and see if WHATEVER is being said – positive or negative – is true – and who makes it true or false? It's all in the mind – and ultimately Ramesh Balsekar's pointer is wonderful for all this bubbling up babble (both "yours and "mine") – WHO CARES!?

It appears to me that we either are being and expressing love for what is – ALL of what is – or subtly judging some part of what is that is making a reaction happen in the mind. Let's not stay half-baked about this.

I have one favorite position now – for any discussion, or point of view:

I DON'T KNOW.

Having said that, I found the piece you posted where she describes her experience of waking up to be more powerful than anything else. That is exactly the spot where the "Who am I?" question leads to and she has described it perhaps better than any I have read before. Reading that piece (peace) is almost enough by itself. (Note – that piece is on www.awake-now.org/thework.html.

For you that is enough. For you asking Who Am I is enough. But "you" are one insignificant member of a family of over six billion. As is "me."

As a sage once pointed out – with but one trivial exception, this world family is comprised of others. Not that that's true - in Reality! It's a pointer to the possibility of compassion for the family members who are stuck in the story and for whom Katie's Work is an awesome tool for ending suffering!

Is that true? I don't know!

So, thanks again for being the catalyst for all this sharing and exchanges. The people who post on your site are really helpful. I just wanted to pass on the reactions here to all the enthusiasm for The Work. Love, (xxxxx)

You're completely welcome – and I really LOVE that you expressed all this here. I take it all as something The Universe wants me to hear and consider. All Love to you too – all ways. And – other than the simple undeniable fact that I love me and I love You – about all this or anything else – I Don't Know.

Who cares? Or not? Who? Dwelling in Not Knowing – herein is Peace.

I LOVE what you wrote and I love that you care about the suffering of "others" - that comes through clearly in your expression. Stay in touch!

Follow-up

Yes, thanks for the response - there is no reason or purpose or benefit to any of what's written and WHO really cares? It all just arises and passes in the breeze. It is what it is!!!

In the end, like your "DON'T KNOW", I prefer silence, where no thought is needed, and no thought gets expressed to be either right or wrong. In pure, clear Present-Awareness that is all there is, and all THIS too, then nothing more needs to be said. If there appear "others" who don't or can't see It, then perhaps a pointer or a nudge can be offered, but otherwise just SILENT DON'T KNOW!!!

134. Life It-Self

lifing
        undoing it Self just Now
doing it Self back up
        Just Here
Before and after are

gone

now
is gone

life undid it Self
and OutDid
It Self

when?

playing
the
endless
beginningless

game of
0ne
being
two

135. Coda To The Riff

What's Next?

Once upon a time there was a Zen Student, sitting quietly in the courtyard eating his luncheon meal of rice and vegetables. As he was dipping his chopsticks into the bowl for the last morsel, suddenly there came the chirp! of a bird in the tree above his bench. And ... bang! IT happened.

There was no more "person." That had been erased, and what remained was nothing - and everything. Not One Not Two.

The Master happened to be passing at the moment and noticed, "nothing had happened to no one." With a smile he sat next to the (former) student, and said, "So. It has Happened, my son." "Yes, Nothing Happened. I am not separate, I never was. What a marvelous joke it all is!"

Both spent a few moments laughing. Then the student asked, "Well, that is it. But Master, what comes next?" Looking down, the Master noticed that the fellow's rice bowl was empty.

The Master asked, "You have finished your lunch?"

"Yes." The student said, patting his tummy.

Softly, the Master said, "Wash your bowl."

~~~

Blessed am I; in freedom am I.
I am the infinite in my soul;
I can find no beginning, no end.
All is my Self

- Sri Dattatreya, in The Avadhut Gita

136. R.I.P. ... Listening To Love

What IS what is often called the "Original Sin? An idea - just a thought - *"I'm ME - and Separated from You & The World.."*

We "know" - I'm Me.

Really? Is that True? Lets find out -

There is a subtle conviction in virtually every human being on the planet - an unexamined "knowing" that *"I'm separate from you - and the whole world."*

Is It True?

(Possibly the surface answer – the superficial answer – is yes. Look deeper.)

Can I ABSOLUTELY KNOW that It's True?

(Where are you looking?)
(What is your evidence?)
(Isn't all that evidence JUST A STORY?)
(What is your "reference point?"
IS there a reference point – outside of thought?)
(Consider: All knowing is Ignorance....)
(Let the question Reveal the Truth to you.
Don't rush to judgment - as is our habit.)
Can I absolutely know that it (*this thought*) IS TRUE?
(Be silent. Let The Truth emerge and Show Its Self to you.)
How do I react - when I believe that thought to be true?
That is to say -
When "I" believe that the "I" thought ITSELF is a True Thing?
A Real Subject "inside me" - apart from a world of objects "outside me?"

(Notice feelings of aching in chest, an empty feeling in gut, fear or anger arising, a sense of unhappiness or self-hatred - or a feeling of hopelessness - and just BE with these feelings, stories - whatever comes up - let the little "me" thought fall into the inner abyss - that gut-feeling of emptiness -)

(Now we dismantle is - leaving the Freedom that you Are In Truth)

Who would I be - <u>without</u> that thought?

(Ponder the question. Let the question sink down deep – to the bottom of that empty pit inside – and let it toss "you" INTO that pit. When "you" are GONE - That Is Freedom!)

(What makes you think you are you?)

Some say -

Just do it (whatever IT is at the moment that "they" want "you" to "do")

What makes them-me-you-us think we-I-me- you *have a choice to do or not to do anything? or not*?

What makes us think? Ponder This Question

Anyway - I Love You -and there is not a thing you can do to prevent that!

When I didn't know Self I sought Love.
When The Self is Known I AM Love
That Ain't Personal

You can seemingly - in the dream-story - lose the awareness of love. But you can NOT lose love itself - because Love Is What You Are.

Finally - In This Love That You ARE - There is NO suffering, No seeker, No truth, NO goal, NO path, No gate, No thing, and finally NO "No thing."

Natural non-conceptual Seeing is that This, all that is Here and Now, is the beloved, holding, and being held. No subject-object is, in This. This is the Eternal Subject. All so-called "objects are That, in the costume of "other-than-that."

All the world is ITS stage. IT is all the players, and the audience, and the stage, and Space the stage appears within, and the Spaceless Space that appears as the pure Awareness, in which arises - "I Am."

That I Am is not a thought. It is the Aliveness of Natural Beingness. Just That, Nothing Else. Then even THAT goes.

That expression is a pointless pointer to the Real - "our" essence before a conceptual me arrives to (seemingly not actually! co-opt That into something "it" thinks that "it" can own.

When the owner is seen to be totally false, the phantom of the opera of "its" life, the whole paradigm of "me and other" simply crumbles, so to speak.

The final seeing is simple. No one sees!

The "paradigm" never was or will be, and it never is. In this seeing, knowing before a knower or an object of knowing are "thought up" by a false thinker, there is NO past NO future NO present.

All there is, is This - as it is. Full Stop. Now can anyone understand this? WHO. The "understanding (mind-comprehension) is the booby prize. Lot's of so-called "non-duality teachers" are making quite a nice chunk of change for themselves selling the booby prize. So what? Who really cares? Only a "me" that resists what is. Bombs and Roses, "inauthentic and authentic" are all the same Essence. No worries.

That is That. Know it or not, see it or not, this solid absolute silent stillness is (metaphorically) endless beginningless Reality, untouchable by any thought construct or (false) belief in separation.

That is invincible. That is indestructible.

That alone (ALL-ONE) is REAL.

notes

The End: The Last Of Me. This As-It-Is Really IS IT

This Is It.

Near the end of the writing of *"Life After Death"*

One Moonlit Morning

I heard Tony Parsons say

"If you are sitting here saying '*Bleep* This'

That '*Bleep* This' is IT".

I disappear - and then laugh

for a very loooong time

The phone rings.

It's Tony- calling from England

Loving Laughing Being

and we laughed and we laughed and we laughed and we laughed and we laughed and we laughed and we laughed and we laughed and we laughed and we laughed and we laughed and we laughed and we laughed and we laughed

A Few Books & Websites To Ponder

"As It Is - The Open Secret of Spiritual Awakening" - Tony Parsons

"All There Is" - Tony Parsons

"Invitation To Awaken" - Tony Parsons - (www.theopensecret.com)

"Loving What Is" - Byron Katie

"Self Realization" - Byron Katie - (www.thework.com)

"Beyond Description" - Burt Jurgens - (www.beyonddescription.net)

"Oneness" - John Greven - (www.onenessjustthat.com)

"Right Here Right Now" - John Wheeler (www.thenaturalstate.com)

Website of Annette Nibley - (www.whatneverchanges.com)

"Posthumous Pieces" - Wei Wu Wei

"Already Awake" - Nathan Gill

"Being - The Bottom Line" - Nathan Gill - (www.nathangill.com)

"Awake In The Heartland" - Joan Tollifson - (www.joantollifson.com)

"What's Wrong With Right Now?" - "Sailor" Bob Adamson

"I Hope You Die Soon" - Richard Sylvester

"THIS Is Unimaginable And Unavoidable" - Guy Smith

"Perfect Brilliant Stillness" - David Carse

"The Myth Of Enlightenment" - Karl Renz

"No Way" - by Ram Tzu (Pen name of Wayne Liquorman)

"The Tao Te Ching" - Lao Tzu - Translation by Gia Fu Feng & Jane English

Contact - "One on One"

There is an Energy of Aliveness in direct sharing that can arise when there is voice communication. One on one sharing can seem to facilitate the Energy of Love awakening to Itself - in the apparent "dialogue."

Call USA +1 714 708 2311 to explore the possibilities.

who am i?

Am I enlightened? No. Am I unenlightened? No. Am I a bound soul? No. Am I free? No. <u>*None of that* is either true - *or* false.</u>

I am nothing special at all. I just ... AM.

I have never not been that *I Am*.

Neither have you.

One I Am - many Voices - All together in the Eternal.

Now. That is all there is. That is Home.

notes

Keep It Simple, Seeker!

THE BOTTOM LINE IS JUST THIS:

1. Awareness is present; PRESENCING- that's what you ARE.

2. The separate "person" is a myth; that's what you're NOT.

What You ARE Is NON-conceptual I AM-Ness, Presence Awareness, Being, always fresh, self-knowing and self-shining, One-without-A-Second, Intelligence-Energy-Cognizing-Emptiness... Timeless BEING. Just That.

Starting from this, ask what thinks or believes otherwise?
Who or what is that one?

Inquire!

Simple form: Who Am I?

Being committed to freedom, investigate the identity with that question. Who Am I? Don't stop until there is no one to either *do* or *not do* this.

> *"The thought 'who am I?' will destroy all other thoughts, and like the stick used for stirring the burning pyre, it will itself in the end get destroyed. Then, there will arise Self-realization."*
>
> Sri Ramana Maharshi

You can also use The Work - four questions and a the turnaround - as taught by Byron Katie (Chapter 114 page 256.)

1- Is it true?

2- Can you absolutely know that it's true?

3- How do you react when you believe that thought?

4- Who would you be without the thought?

Then - Turn it around.

notes

the mind Is a puppet

a six-billion-face puppet

who is the puppeteer?

There Is Nothing That Is Not IT.

Have a cookie?

who am i?

thank You for loving to be

- charlie

To You

Tonight as I was finishing up the book
the book died in my arms
i died in Your arms
a singular knowing
enveloped and devoured
everything - once and forever:

when I reappeared as "me"
this me was none other than Thee

all that is and reappeared as all that IS

and all that me-ing and be-ing?

It Is All YOU

MeBeingMeBeingMeBeingYouBeingYouYouBeingYouBeingMe

just YOU

www.awake-now.org

+1 714 708-2311

non.duality@yahoo.com

www.ingramcontent.com/pod-product-compliance
Lightning Source LLC
Chambersburg PA
CBHW070722160426
43192CB00009B/1281